ADVERTISING WORKS 14

Proving the effectiveness of marketing communications

ADVERTISING WORKS 14

Proving the effectiveness of marketing communications

Cases from the IPA Effectiveness Awards 2005
Limited to agencies with incomes up to £20m

Edited and introduced by

Les Binet

Convenor of Judges

World Advertising
Research Center

IPA

First published 2006 by the World Advertising Research Center
Farm Road, Henley-on-Thames, Oxfordshire RG9 1EJ, United Kingdom
Telephone: 01491 411000
Fax: 01491 418600
E-mail: enquiries@warc.com

A CIP catalogue record for this book is available from the British Library

ISBN 1 84116 183 7

DVD of the 2005 IPA Effectiveness Awards winners produced by Xtreme Information.
Typeset by Godiva Publishing Services Ltd, Coventry
Printed and bound in Great Britain
by Biddles Ltd, King's Lynn

Contents

SECTION 3: BRONZE WINNERS

CONTENTS

Foreword by Thinkbox

In today's climate of increasing accountability, we should applaud the IPA's decision to move their prestigious Effectiveness Awards to an annual event. The more public evidence we have of the influence of advertising on business success the better.

When Thinkbox was approached by the IPA to be a sponsor of the Effectiveness Awards, our interest was natural. As the marketing body for Commercial Television, we champion the role of television at the heart of successful marketing campaigns. And each time Advertising Works is published, we find more captivating success stories in which television has starred in a leading role.

In celebrating the successful winners this year, we're encouraged to read about the range of tasks that television has fulfilled in delivering return on marketing investment.

The perception that you should only consider television if you've got a seriously big marketing budget is challenged, amongst others, by the University of Dundee, Roundup Weedkiller and the Oral Cancer Awareness project.

The pre-eminent ability of television as the springboard to enduring brand fame is well demonstrated by Bakers Complete, while Travelocity shows us a compelling picture of how to achieve a more rapid journey to fame.

There is also a demonstration of the potency of leveraging a programme sponsorship throughout the communication mix and into the retail environment. You can read about this in the story of First Choice's partnership with *I'm A Celebrity, Get Me Out Of Here!*

Congratulations to all the winners – both for the business success they have managed and for sharing their stories with a wider audience.

Justin Sampson
Chairman, Thinkbox

Foreword by The U TV Group

This is the first year that The UTV Group has sponsored the IPA Effectiveness Awards and we are very proud to be a title sponsor in its inaugural year as a national competition for small- to medium-sized agencies with incomes up to £20m.

It is also the first time the Awards have been held in Northern Ireland so we are delighted to welcome the IPA Awards to Belfast where our group headquarters are based.

When we were approached by the IPA to become a sponsor it was a natural partnership as The UTV Group incorporates television, radio and new media, offering IPA members targeted advertising solutions for their clients on a local, regional and national level.

Not surprisingly perhaps, this book of winners represents a diverse range of communication issues. From the Inland Revenue's Self Assessment, Oral Cancer, ScottishPower, Silentnight and Blood Donation to Tizer, Travelocity and Bakers Complete. Each one of them showing their creative hand and demonstrating how the effective use of marketing was able to deliver a real return on investment.

Looking at the data collectively, most of the shortlisted cases used more than just one media channel. What more proof is there that effective targeting and integrated media campaigns can make marketing and advertising budgets go further. This is very much the ethos of The UTV Group, so we are glad of this vital reminder to business of how a broad range of media builds brands.

We congratulate the authors, agencies and clients involved in the winning case histories, for the inspiration that their imaginative thinking provides.

Long may it continue.

John McCann
Chief Executive, The UTV Group

IPA Effectiveness Awards 2005

Communication is a kind of magic. Using only sign, symbols and sounds, we can influence other people's thoughts, feelings and actions, and so change the world. Organisations that harness that magic can achieve great things – whether they are trying to change the habits of a nation, or merely trying to sell things.

However, in today's hard-headed world, magic itself is not enough. That's why, in 1980, the IPA launched their Effectiveness Awards – to reveal some of the science behind that magic. The aims of the competition are simple: to prove that marketing communications really do work, to show how they work, and to measure their effects in hard financial terms.

Over the years, the competition has evolved. For example, early entries focussed on short-term advertising effects, whereas nowadays the measurement of longer and broader effects is common. The Awards used to be advertising-centric, but today the competition is open to all forms of marketing communications. This book marks another step forward. In 2005, the IPA launched a new national effectiveness competition for small-to-medium sized agencies. Limited to agencies with incomes up to £20m, this will run in alternate years to the original biennial awards scheme, which is open to any agency, worldwide.

The aim is to widen the effectiveness franchise, and the first year's results look promising. Forty-eight papers were submitted, many from agencies with no previous experience of the IPA Awards.

However, broadening the franchise does not mean 'dumbing down'. These papers have all been scrutinised twice over – first by a panel of industry experts, then by a jury of senior clients, led by Lord Heseltine – to ensure that effectiveness has been proved beyond reasonable doubt in every case.

The result is a fascinating collection of cases that proves that, even with a modest budget, communications can work magic. Small is beautiful, they say. This book shows that it can be profitable too.

Why papers fail

In any competition, there will be losers as well as winners. Less than half of this year's entries succeeded in convincing the judges, and the ratio has been similar every year since 1980. This reflects the difficulty of the evaluation task.

Measuring the effects of marketing communications is inherently hard. For most channels, there is no direct link between stimulus and response. Nor can one always see the effect 'by eye', because consumer behaviour is influenced by a multitude of other factors besides communication, many of which have bigger effects in the short term. Disentangling the effects of communication under real market-place conditions can be like trying to find a needle in a haystack.

Good evaluation is possible, of course – the cases in this book are proof of that. And there is much we can learn from these winning papers about how communications work and how to measure their effects. But there is also something to be learned from the papers that didn't win. If we can identify the barriers to good evaluation, then perhaps we can improve things.

One reason why papers fail is a lack of a statement of clear objectives. It is hard to know whether a campaign has been successful or not if we don't know exactly what it was intended to achieve. When clients brief their agencies, they should set clear goals. Not only does this make evaluation easier, it also makes it more likely that the campaign will be effective. Where possible, quantitative targets should be set, with timings.[1]

Another reason why evaluation is so difficult is that it is often an after-thought. Ideally, evaluation should be built into every campaign, right from the beginning. Thinking about evaluation early on allows you to build tests and controls into your media plan, and gives time to put the relevant research in place *before* the campaign breaks. Regular evaluation of this kind then builds up a body of data and learning that should make writing a case history relatively easy. In reality, evaluation is all too often a one-off exercise done to win an award, some time after the event. It is much harder to gather the necessary data and evidence under these circumstances.[2]

A third and very obvious reason that papers fail is that they do not show a clear effect. It's not enough to show that you've got good advertising recall, or that lots of people were aware of your sponsorship. It's not enough to show that you beat the category norms for these things. You need to show how communication changed people's relationships with the brand, and how that affected their behaviour.

To do that, you usually need to present data over time, showing how your campaign improved things. This is another area where authors fall down. Often there is not enough 'pre' data to put the results in context. Yes, sales may have increased, but was that just seasonal variation? Yes, market share may have risen, but was it already rising before the campaign started? Showing a good run of historical data can help answer these questions. (Of course, a lack of pre-campaign data is often due to the fact that evaluation is an after-thought.)

Another common reason why papers are rejected is that they fail to show a behavioural effect. Changing how people think and feel is good, but you should also show how that translated into action. This is obviously true for commercial campaigns, where the ultimate aim is to increase sales revenue and profit. But even for not-for-profit clients, changing people's attitudes is rarely an end in itself. For example, one of the reasons Ardmore Advertising won a prize for their paper on fire prevention in Northern Ireland this year is that they showed that their campaign not only raised awareness of fire risks, but also led to a reduction in the number of fires.

It is of course much easier to show a behavioural effect for direct response media. But direct response cases often fall into another trap: they fail to measure the effect on sales properly. Responses that don't convert into sales are a cost, not a benefit. To demonstrate effectiveness, you need to show how responses convert

---

1. See www.ipa.co.uk for *The Client Brief*, a best-practice guide to briefing agencies.
2. See www.ipa.co.uk for *Evaluation* best practice guide.

into revenue, and to what extent that revenue is truly incremental (as opposed to cannibalised from your retail outlets, for instance).

Having shown an effect, you then need to prove that your campaign was the cause. Lack of proof is the single most common reason why papers fail. To simplify enormously, there are two broad methods of proof. The first method is to look for correlations between communications activity and results over time. For instance, if market share rises every time you run a burst of activity, then it's pretty strong evidence that your campaign is working. The second method is a test-and-control approach. For instance, you might compare areas that were exposed to your campaign against areas that were not. Or you might compare advertised products with non-advertised ones.

Sometimes papers fail because the proof they offer is flawed. The commonest mistake is the so-called 'Rosser Reeves Fallacy'. For instance, suppose you find that people who remember your ad are more favourably disposed towards your brand. Surely that proves that the ad worked? No, it does not. Research shows that people are more likely to notice ads for the brands they use. So a sample of people who recall your ad will contain an unusually high number of brand users, who will of course be pre-disposed towards the brand. This means that there is nearly always a (spurious) correlation between ad awareness and positive attitudes to the brand. Correcting for brand usage won't necessarily help either – people who recall the ad could be unusual in some other way that biases them in favour of the brand.

Similarly, there may be a spurious correlation between exposure to your ad (as opposed to recall) and likelihood to buy the product, due to the fact that the campaign is targeted at potential users. The way round this is to look for correlations between exposure to the campaign and *changes* in attitudes and behaviour.

Econometrics and other forms of mathematical modelling can be helpful, but use them carefully. Explain your results clearly, make sure that all the necessary technical details are presented to enable the specialist judges to assess the research, and above all, make sure that the research really is sound. Don't try to baffle the judges with science![3]

Showing a positive relationship between your campaign activity and your results is still not quite enough. You should also rule out alternative explanations. A lot of papers fail because of a nagging feeling that there might be some other reason for the results. Was there some change to the product at that time? Did distribution increase? Was there a promotion going on? Your proof should take account of all the other factors that might affect your results. Failing to discuss obviously important issues like price, say, will raise doubts in the judges' minds.

Finally, you should demonstrate that your campaign was financially worthwhile in some sense. This is the trickiest bit, of course. For commercial campaigns, you should attempt to show some kind of financial payback. A surprisingly common mistake here is to confuse revenue and profit. A £1m campaign that generates £2m worth of extra sales does *not* pay for itself twice over, despite what many admen think. In fact, it probably made a loss (unless the profit margin on those sales is more than 50%).

---

3. See www.ipa.co.uk for *Econometrics Explained*, a best practice guide.

What makes a great paper?

If an author can avoid the pitfalls listed above, he or she is fairly certain of winning an effectiveness award. But what makes a really great paper? Truly great papers tend to have several ingredients in common.

Firstly, and most obviously, the best papers tend to have really obvious effects. Sometimes the effect is fairly immediate: Travelocity saw market share increase by 44% in just over a year; Roundup saw an 86% increase over a similar period. Sometimes the effect is long term: the University of Dundee increased applications by 87% over a five-year period; Bakers Complete quadrupled market share over the course of a decade.

But big, clear effects are not enough. Those effects need to be firmly linked to the campaign. The paper needs to prove beyond doubt that it was communications that were responsible, and not some other factor. All the best papers tend to have really solid proof.

Proof can take many different forms. A simple method, used by the Travelocity and Tizer papers among others, is to show that key performance measures move in synch with the campaign.

Another popular approach uses some control group that was not exposed to the activity. This seems to be a particularly popular approach in the public sector: the campaigns aimed at fighting fire, car crime and oral cancer all used comparisons between advertised and non-advertised regions to make their case. Bakers Complete took the approach to an even more sophisticated level, using fine variations in regional spending to demonstrate the effect of the campaign.

The Bakers paper also used econometrics to quantify the effect, as did Tizer. Contrary to the myth, econometrics does not guarantee a prize, but good econometrics certainly enhances the credibility of a case, and enhances its chances.

As discussed earlier, many papers are rejected because the judges are left with a nagging suspicion that some other factor might be responsible. The best papers always eliminate alternative explanations. In some cases, such as Travelocity and Roundup, the elimination is so thorough that almost no other proof is needed.

Having shown clear effects and linked them firmly to the campaign, the paper must then convince the judges that the campaign was financially worthwhile. This is where many otherwise worthy papers get marked down. In cases like Bakers, Travelocity and Roundup, it is fairly clear that the extra profits involved will have more than paid for the communications. Non-profit cases are less straightforward, but there are several good examples in this book where some kind of cost benefit has been applied. The Oral Cancer campaign justified itself in terms of reduced NHS costs, for instance, and both the Hidden Treasures of Cumbria paper and the Broadband for Scotland case defined payback in terms of the stimulus to the local economy.

A paper that has clear effects, cast-iron proof and a big payback will always win a decent prize. The other magic ingredient is learning.

Clients and agencies that really understand evaluation don't just do it to win awards; they do it so they can learn. Learn what works and what does not. Learn how it all works. Learn how to do it better.

Campaigns that have routine evaluation built into them tend to impress the judges. That doesn't necessarily mean big research budgets. The West Midland Hub of Museums probably had about the tiniest budget of any of this year's submissions, and yet still managed to do some exemplary evaluation. And it doesn't mean that everything will always run smoothly, either. When Arriva evaluated their first campaign, they found it wasn't working properly. But they learned from that, and developed a second, much better campaign. That's real evaluation, and the judges approved.

Clients and agencies who are interested in practical evaluation tend to focus on how campaigns work as much as whether they work. IPA judges are interested in new learning too. After all, publication of cases is the *raison d'etre* of the Awards. This year's prize for Best New Learning went to ATS Euromaster for a paper that showed how highly localised tactical advertising could be extremely efficient in the world of retail. The papers for fire prevention, blood donation and the Inland Revenue all contained useful insights into how to get people to face subjects that they naturally want to avoid – literally death and taxes.

Learning about the roles of different media is interesting too. In the Arriva case, the need to supply detailed and highly localised information led the client to abandon advertising in favour of DM. In the Roundup case, the reverse was true: reducing the DM spend and putting more money into TV helped to take the brand to number one. First Choice holidays gives us an excellent example of how to use TV sponsorship to good effect. And Dundee University hit prospective students with a whole range of media in a co-ordinated way, thereby winning Best Integration.

The most important learning of all is about the longer and broader effects of communication. Identifying the short-term effects on sales and profit is important, but there are many other effects that are less well understood. Several of the papers in this book touch on them.

It is widely believed (though rarely proved conclusively) that one of the main ways advertising pays for itself is by supporting higher prices. The UniBond paper is a case in point. Sales volume stayed relatively static, but prices increased, pushing up revenue by 21%. Static volumes and rising revenues mean more or less pure profit. Similarly, the Rocky case showed that the brand became less dependent on price promotions, and thus more profitable.

The Rocky case touched on another 'broader' effect. Sometimes advertising can help increase distribution of a product. The Tizer case also discussed this effect, and it was the whole basis of the Broadband for Scotland case, where the campaign was intended to influence BT's distribution policy for broadband.

Another broader effect concerns economies of scale. Research done using the famous PIMS database suggests that the two most important ways that marketing increases profit margins are by supporting higher prices and by generating economies of scale. The latter effect is one reason why market share matters so much to clients, but it is rarely discussed explicitly in IPA papers, probably because agencies are less familiar with the supply side of their clients' businesses. The ScottishPower paper alludes to economies of scale when it talks about reaching a critical mass of five million customers. It would be interesting to see more detailed discussions of this kind of thing in future IPA papers.

The ScottishPower paper also alludes to another supply side-effect. A great campaign can help motivate and direct staff. First Choice holidays found the same thing – their 'Bush Tucker Trials' gave staff morale a definite boost. It would be great to see more analysis of this kind of effect, and if possible some measurement of the financial payback through increased productivity.

IPA judges are a hard-headed lot, and expect all cases to demonstrate value for money. But we are not immune to the wider social implications of our business. Some of the best papers address issues way beyond profit and loss. In this book, you will read how agencies reduced crime, supported justice, prevented deaths from fire, cancer and loss of blood, and helped to make Britain a less noisy and more cultured place.

My final tip for writing a good paper is to tell a good story. This year's prize for Best Read goes to Roundup – a ripping yarn with plenty of killing going on. Enjoy!

Les Binet
Convenor of Judges, 2005

The Judges

Chris Searle
External Affairs Director
Bacardi-Martini Ltd

Nick Smith
Marketing Director
British Gas Residential Energy

Simon Sheard
Group Marketing Director
BUPA

Helen Stevenson
Director of Group Marketing
Lloyds TSB Group plc

Acknowledgements

The IPA Value of Advertising Committee

Sven Olsen (Chairman)	FCB Europe
Phil Adams	The Leith Agency
Martin Andersen	BDH\TBWA
Les Binet	DDB Matrix
Helen Calcraft	Miles Calcraft Briginshaw Duffy Ltd
Simon Calvert	Proximity London
Jane Cunningham	Ogilvy & Mather
Neil Dawson	TBWA\London
David Golding	Rainey Kelly Campbell Roalfe/Y&R
Laurence Green	Fallon London
Sean Healy	MediaCom
Alison Hoad	Campbell Doyle Dye
Iain Jacob	Starcom MediaVest
Russ Lidstone	JWT
Sue Little	McCann Erickson Manchester Ltd
Clare Rossi	Zalpha

Many people worked hard to make the Awards a success, especially the following: Sven Olsen, Chairman of the Value of Advertising Committee; Les Binet, Convenor of Judges, and Richard Storey, Deputy Convenor of Judges.

At the IPA, the core team were Jill Bentley, Tessa Gooding, Emma Kane, Anna Foster, Richard Lambert, Carey Quarrier and Alex Rogers.

Sponsors

The success of the 2005 IPA Effectiveness Awards owes a great debt to our sponsors. The IPA would like to thank the following companies, whose support made the presentation possible, especially Thinkbox and The UTV Group, our overall sponsors, whose commitment to the competition has been so important to the industry.

IN ASSOCIATION WITH

AND

Independent News & Media (Northern Ireland)

 campaign

Prizes

JOINT GRAND PRIX
Burkitt DDB for Nestlé Purina PetCare (Bakers Complete)
Miles Calcraft Briginshaw Duffy for Travelocity.co.uk

BEST IDEA
Miles Calcraft Briginshaw Duffy for Travelocity.co.uk

BEST INTEGRATION
Frame C for University of Dundee

BEST NEW AGENCY
Miles Calcraft Briginshaw Duffy

BEST NEW CLIENT
Ardmore Advertising for Fire Authority for Northern Ireland

BEST NEW LEARNING
BDH\TBWA for ATS Euromaster

BEST READ
BLM Media for Monsanto (Roundup Weedkiller)

DEDICATION TO EFFECTIVENESS
Burkitt DDB for Nestlé Purina PetCare (Bakers Complete)

EFFECTIVENESS AGENCY OF THE YEAR
Miles Calcraft Briginshaw Duffy

GOLD AWARDS

Burkitt DDB for Nestlé Purina PetCare (Bakers Complete)

Miles Calcraft Briginshaw Duffy for Travelocity.co.uk

Miles Calcraft Briginshaw Duffy for Inland Revenue (Self Assessment)

BLM Media for Monsanto (Roundup Weedkiller)

SILVER AWARDS

The Union Advertising Agency for Scottish Enterprise (Broadband for Scotland)

Ardmore Advertising for Fire Authority for Northern Ireland

Alcazar for Cumbria Tourist Board (Hidden Treasures of Cumbria)

*AV Browne Advertising for Northern Ireland Office
(Community Safety Unit)*

*The Bridge for West of Scotland Cancer Awareness Project
(Oral Cancer Awareness)*

BDH\TBWA for A G Barr (Tizer)

Frame C for University of Dundee

BRONZE AWARDS

Cogent Elliott for Arriva plc (Arriva Buses)

BDH\TBWA for ATS Euromaster

The Bridge for Scottish National Blood Transfusion Service (Blood Donation)

Barkers (Scotland) for Scottish Executive (Children's Hearings)

Walker Media for First Choice

PWLC for Fox's Biscuits (Fox's Rocky)

*Radford Advertising Marketing for Lancashire Tourism Partnership
(Lancashire Short Breaks Campaign)*

*LyleBailie International for Environment and Heritage Service Northern Ireland
(Noise Awareness)*

The Bridge for ScottishPower

Feather Brooksbank for Silentnight (My First Bed)

BDH\TBWA for Henkel Consumer Adhesives (UniBond Sealant Range)

BJL Group for West Midlands Hub of Museums

Section 1

Gold Winners

1

Bakers Complete

Ten years of success is more than just a shaggy dog story

Principal author: Susan Poole, Burkitt DDB
Contributing author: David Bassett, DDB Matrix

EDITOR'S SUMMARY

The first of our joint Grand Prix winners is a classic long-term success story. Using a single, consistent advertising campaign over a 10-year period, Bakers has risen from obscurity to become the UK's number one brand of dry dog food.

Along the way, the campaign has delivered an estimated £58.3m in extra sales for the brand, and continues to fuel rapid growth. Not only that, it has completely changed the structure of the dog food market, by expanding the dry sector.

It is hard not to be impressed by the scale of the achievement here. Market share quadrupled, and revenue increased by a factor of 10. Even after 10 years, Bakers is still the fastest growing brand in the market.

The link to advertising is pretty conclusive too. Several other cases in this book use regional analysis to demonstrate the effects of advertising, but this one takes it to a new level, showing how fine variations in regional expenditure are reflected in the sales data. These variations are then used to quantify the effect of advertising econometrically.

With such a consistent campaign producing such huge long-term effects, we had no hesitation in awarding the prize for Dedication to Effectiveness to Bakers.

INTRODUCTION

This is the story of success with a long-term campaign, bringing together an innovative and unique product, a strong insight, a bold strategy and consistent executions. The brand's innovation and consistency has enabled it to grow from a small brand, to surpass the big players and become number one.

A 10-year campaign is a rare occurrence these days – rarer still for a brand that in this time has had three parent companies,[1] yet only one campaign. The length of the campaign is testament to client belief and strong sales response, enabling Bakers to achieve its objective of becoming the number one complete dry dog food within four years.

The story started in 1994 when Bakers appointed Court Burkitt & Co (later Burkitt DDB) following a creative pitch. At that time, the dog food market was dominated by tinned 'meat' and Bakers was one of a number of small dry dog food brands.

Dry food was seen as a niche sector, not considered attractive to dogs, and Bakers was an unheard-of player. It was argued that in order to challenge traditional behaviour and major brands, Bakers needed a significant difference in brand personality as well as product. This notion could be summed up as 'for real dogs; not show dogs'. These findings led to the idea of 'dogs choose Bakers', which was executed in a Bakers' dog-only world. This powerful campaign is still running today, 10 years on. It is proven to have provided Bakers with £19.3m incremental revenue and fuelled the brand's growth by 18%.[2]

However, not only did Bakers want to become number one, it also wanted to grow the dry dog food sector, making it a competitor to tinned dog food.

Today Bakers is the biggest and fastest-growing dry dog food in the UK;[3] in addition, it has grown the category by delivering up to 70% of its growth,[4] making it a brand and category to rival tins.

THE MARKETING PROBLEM

When Bakers appointed its new advertising agency in 1994, this small family business[5] set itself what seemed like impossible goals: to become the UK's number one dry dog food and to encourage growth in the sector. The other dry food brands were all larger: Pedigree and Winalot (both giants in 'tinned' with scale and authority), and Pascoe's and Wagg Time (smaller specialist companies). Bakers had sales of only £5m in a market of just under £150m.[6]

There were two main barriers to the business objectives that made this task particularly difficult:

1. Dry is not nice.
2. Big competition.

---

1. Edward Baker Petfoods was acquired by Ralston Purina in 1997, which was in turn acquired by Nestlé Purina PetCare in 2000.
2. Source: DDB Matrix, Econometric Model 2001–2004.
3. Bakers is still growing at 14.2% YOY (source: Nielsen Value Sales £; latest MAT, 19.03.05).
4. Bakers delivered 70% of CDDF growth 2001–2004 and an average of 30% across the whole period.
5. Edward Baker Petfoods.
6. Source: CDDF Market Value 1994; PFMA.

Barrier 1: dry is not nice

Complete dry dog food was a relatively new sector.[7] To an uninformed purchaser tinned food equals 'meat', whereas dry food is 'only biscuits'.[8] Many people felt that feeding their dog dry food was a disservice – even being cruel: 'It would be like us eating muesli for every meal'[9] and 'It's painful to watch him try and eat the dry stuff'.[10] This barrier to dry dog food had limited the size of the sector.[11] Bakers' product was different from the others available: high palatability, 'moist meaty chunks', different shapes and colourful pieces. But these could only be appreciated if the product was first purchased …

A change in perception about dry dog food was required. Bakers had the product to do it but just needed the right communication platform.

Barrier 2: big competition

In 1994, the multinational competition accounted for nearly 80% of sales. Bakers could not afford to take these companies head on. (Indeed it has often been up to six times outspent by its competitors[12] and also until 2002 had disproportionately poor distribution.)[13] So Bakers had fewer resources and also less credibility and authority.

AGENCY SOLUTION

The need to make Bakers a challenger brand

It's all about *real dogs* …

A challenger brand can exploit a weakness in the leader. What was that weakness?

In 1994 the big brands positioned themselves in an idealised dog world of pedigree breeders, show dogs and grooming.[14] This gave them technical authority, but lacked an understanding of real owners' relationships with their dogs.[15] The big brands were emotionally cold to many real dog owners.

Therefore positioning Bakers as 'the food for *real dogs*' could:

- give Bakers a motivating point of difference
- make Bakers feel more like a dog food 'for us' among many owners of everyday mutts.

'You want to see recognisable breeds, but normal dogs like the Andrex puppy … not sickly vomit-worthy Crufts ones.'[16]

---

7. CDDF contains extruded shape pieces, with 14% moisture or less. It contains all the nutrients, such as vitamins and protein, necessary for a dog's diet. It is not the same as other dry products such as mixers or dog biscuits, which are used to supplement canned food or as a treat.
8. Source: SMRC, Fresh Meat Qualitative Research, 2001.
9. Source: RDSI, Qualitative Research, 1995.
10. Source: Burkitt DDB, Semi-Moist Qualitative Research, 2002.
11. Average CDDF growth 1988–92 = 9.3%; average CDDF growth 1993–95 = 4.3% (source: PFMA).
12. Source: MMS (Pedigree vs Bakers 2003 spend).
13. Source: ACNielsen.
14. The advertising of the day featured pedigree dogs, dog shows and beautiful dogs bounding across fields.
15. Source: Consumer Segmentation, Edward Baker Petfoods.
16. Source: Burkitt DDB, Competitive Advertising Qualitative Research, 2003.

We have built on this thinking ever since. For example:

- the brand 'spokesdog' is a shaggy cross-breed
- dogs featured are normal not pampered pooches
- a range of dogs are featured – more chance of 'Ooh there's my dog!'

But what about the palatability of 'dry' dog food?

Proving to real dog owners that Bakers is actually liked by dogs

It's food that *dogs really like* ...

Dog food is one of the few markets where the purchaser isn't the end consumer. Also dogs can't directly tell the purchaser whether they liked the food or not.

Our research found that the look and sound of the product was really important to owners. The following are the key look and sound cues:

- meat inclusion ('dogs eat meat, don't they')
- moisture ('wet is like roast dinner, dry isn't')
- variety ('I don't eat the same food everyday, do I')
- human food similarities ('it looks a bit like what I eat').

So, unlike our competitors who hid the product, we ensured that presentation of the product was a priority.

- Product: ensure innovation constantly reinforces and develops these cues.
- Packaging: product prominently displayed on bag.
- Advertising: constant reinforcement by the following 'Bakers' Laws', which we've learnt and mastered over the years:
  - moist looking food ...
  - presented with 'human' courtesy (in a bowl)
  - highlight the meaty chunk
  - no dry 'tinkle' sound.

So the proposition on the creative brief was:

'Bakers is a food that real dogs, really like.'

It was at this point that the creative team made another, invaluable leap ...

The icing on the cake: the fantasy of real dogs

The ultimate 'proof' of enjoyment would be if dogs chose the food for themselves.

'I think if they showed a real dog, in real life, it would show the true extent of how much they like their food.'[17]

Therefore, we set the advertising in a dog-only world; a world where dogs choose their own food – thus highlighting the irresistibility of Bakers. The voiceover of the launch ad encapsulated this neatly:

'If dogs could choose their own food, they'd choose Bakers Complete. All those delicious, nutritious pieces and moist meaty chunks ... It's hardly surprising it's the one they all love.'

---

17. Source: Burkitt DDB, Enjoyment Qualitative Research, 2003.

A TV BRAND

Bakers launched the campaign on TV and, through its success, continues on this powerful medium (Figure 1). The brand employs a burst strategy aimed at a 'housewives with children' audience to reflect our 'normal dog owner' target.

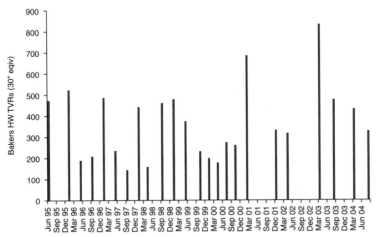

Figure 1: *Bakers TVRs 1995–2004*
Source: MMS

THE CREATIVE EXECUTION

The campaign launched with the execution 'Shopping' in which real dogs quite literally go shopping for Bakers. As the campaign developed, dogs go to increasing lengths to get the brand they desire.

There are now nine executions in the campaign (Table 1).

TABLE 1: BAKERS TV EXECUTIONS, 1995–2005

| | Bakers TVC history | |
Execution	Time length	Date
Shopping	30″/20″	1995–99
Health Farm	30″	1996
Fish	10″	1998
Pool	30″	1998
Sensitive	10″	1999
Usual Suspects	30″	2000–01
TV Dinners	30″/20″	2001–03
Wagometer	10″	2003
Heist	40″/30″/20″	2004–05

How has the brand managed to deliver such a consistent campaign across 10 years?

- Consumer and category insights were simple and true, and remain so.
- Client belief and commitment has been strong.
- Distinctive competitive positioning – no other brand has ever taken Bakers on directly.

THE CREATIVE

Examples of the TV creative are shown in Figures 2–5.

 MVO: If dogs could choose their own food …

 MVO: … they would choose Bakers Complete.

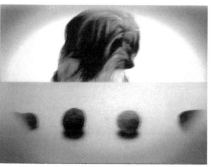 MVO: All those delicious, nutritious pieces and moist meaty chunks.

It's hardly surprising it's the one they all love.

 MVO: Bakers. Makes your dog's life complete.

Figure 2: 'Shopping', 1995

MVO: Disaster at Dogginton Hall. Some scoundrel had made off with all the Bakers Complete.

Fortunately there's no mistaking Bakers tasty pieces and moist meaty chunks.

MVO: Our hero has lined up all the usual suspects. He knows Bakers is the one they all love, but who loves it the most?

MVO: Ah-ha! Case solved.
All those delicious, nutritious pieces saved …

MVO: … well almost.

MVO: Bakers. Makes your dog's life complete.

Figure 3: *'Usual Suspects', 2000*

SFX: Daytime TV-style music
MVO: Today we're using fresh meat to make Bakers Complete.

MVO: Now first those important vitamins and minerals; a dash of fibre; iron and calcium.

MVO: And then, *voilà*, to top it all off succulent meaty chunks!

MVO: Now there you have it, new Bakers Complete. Now who's going to taste it? The chef!

MVO: New Bakers Complete, now made with fresh meat. From Purina.

Figure 4: *'TV Dinners', 2001*

SFX: Dramatic music

MVO: Bakers Complete is crammed with moist meaty chunks and crunchy kibbles.

MVO: It's so delicious dogs will do absolutely anything to get their paws on it.

MVO: Well, it is irrestible.

MVO: Bakers Complete. It's doggylicious.

Figure 5: 'Heist', 2004

RESULTS

Bakers is a brand-building success. Volume sales have grown from under 5000 tonnes to over 52,000 tonnes.[18] Value has grown dramatically from under £5m in 1994 to £50m in 2004.[19]

In 1995 the brand had sales of £5m, giving it 10% market share; it now has sales of £48m, a dominant 40% market share and is still growing +14% year on year.[20] It's the number one dry dog food brand and has grown the sector (Figure 6).

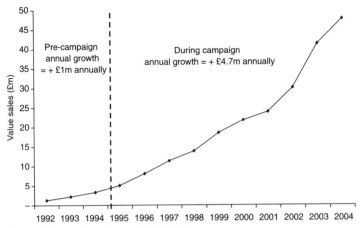

Figure 6: *Bakers value sales growth, 1992–2004*
Source: NPPC

Achieving objective 1: CDDF leadership

In 1999 Bakers leapfrogged Pedigree to become number one complete dry dog food (CDDF) (Figure 7).

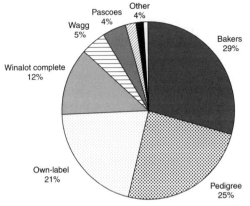

Figure 7: *Bakers achieved number one CDDF status in 1999*
Source: Nielsen, CDDF value share MAT w/e 2 January 2000

---

18. Source: Bakers Volume Sales; NPPC.
19. Source: Bakers Value Sales; NPPC/Nielsen, latest MAT, 19.03.05.
20. Source: ACNielsen, Bakers Value Sales £, latest MAT, 19.03.05.

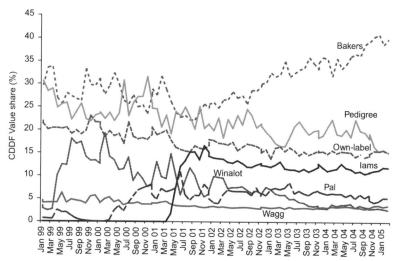

Figure 8: *Bakers continues to grow its lead in CDDF*
Source: ACNielsen, CDDF value share

This is a position Bakers has continued to grow, to a clear 25 share point lead (Figure 8).

Achieving objective 2: growing the category into a contender to tins

In the last three years alone Bakers has accounted for 70% of the CDDF category's growth. Bakers has made CDDF a category not to be overlooked (Figure 9).

Bakers is now number three dog food brand overall, behind Pedigree and Winalot – both brands that operate in all dog food categories (CDDF, tins and treats) vs Bakers single category (CDDF). Quite an achievement for a 'specialist'.

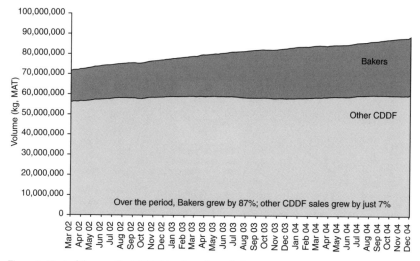

Figure 9: *Most of the growth of CDDF has been due to Bakers*
Source: ACNielsen

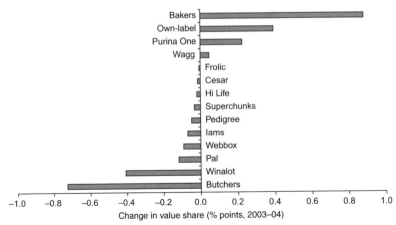

Figure 10: *Bakers is the fastest-growing CDDF 2003–04*
Source: ACNielsen

But Bakers hasn't stopped yet. It is currently the UK's fastest-growing dog food brand by far – growing sales by 14% year on year[21] and share by 0.9% year on year (Figure 10).[22]

WHAT FACTORS ARE DRIVING BAKERS' GROWTH?

Product

Bakers has a unique product, but sales pre-1995 show that without the right communication people were not willing to experiment.

Price

Bakers price has been stable across the period relative to the dry dog food market (Figure 11).

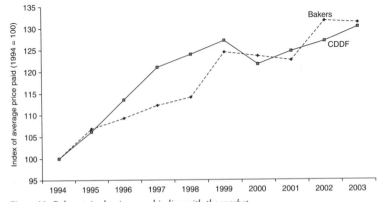

Figure 11: *Bakers price has increased in line with the market*
Source: PFMA, NPPC

---

21. Source: ACNielsen, CDDF Value Sales £ – YOY % growth, latest MAT, 19.03.05.
22. Source: ACNielsen, CDDF Value Shares, 2003 vs 2004.

Market size

Dry dog food is experiencing only marginal growth, while Bakers is experiencing exceptional growth ahead of the entire dog food market (Figure 12).

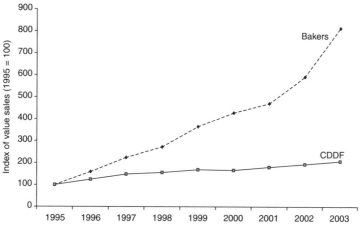

Figure 12: *Bakers has grown faster than the CDDF category*
Source: PFMA, NPPC

Competition

Success has been achieved despite the fact that Bakers has been up to six times outspent by competitors (Figure 13).

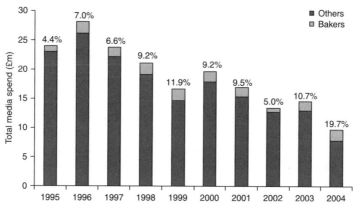

Figure 13: *Bakers' media share of voice was never above 19%*
Source: MMS

Distribution

Distribution has improved since the beginning of the campaign, but until relatively recently it was still significantly under-faced vs its growing market share.[23] It is only since ownership by Nestlé that this situation is now being reversed.

---

23. Source: ACNielsen.

15

Product improvements

Over the time covered by this paper there have been only occasional formulation tweaks and flavour introductions.

Packaging changes

The packaging has changed since 1995; it now features the brand icon 'spokesdog' from the advertising prominently on-pack. The packaging incorporates many 'food learnings' too (Figure 14).

1995	1998	2001	2004

Figure 14: *Bakers packaging, 1995–2004*

Change in consumer

Dogs themselves haven't changed, as far as we know ...

Seasonality

There is little seasonality in the dog food market. Dogs eat food all year around (though many share rather too many titbits at Christmas, like the rest of us).[24]

Advertising

There has been just one campaign since 1995. But was it the presence of advertising or this campaign that made the difference?

Bakers launched in 1992 and had run two different executions – 'Sheepdog' and 'Barkers' – prior to the current campaign. Neither of these ads was judged effective: ad awareness was zero.[25]

SO HOW WAS THE ADVERTISING WORKING?

Sales were obviously positive for Bakers, but what was driving this success story?

The advertising across this period was shown to be working strongly. Tracking results showed that:

---

24. There is a slight spike in December and a corresponding drop in January, in line with Christmas grocery shopping habits.
25. Source: SMRC Ad Awareness, 1995.

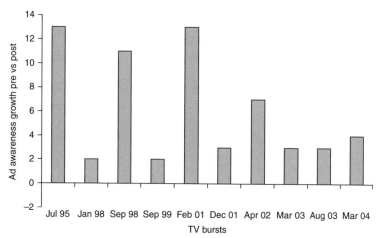

Figure 15: *TV ad awareness increased after each ad burst*
Source: Millward Brown

- the ads generated great awareness (Figure 15)
- the ads were understood and well received
- this changed attitudes about the brand.

People saw the ads

In 2004 OMD, Bakers' media agency at the time,[26] identified another impactful medium for dual viewing: cinema. This combination of TV and cinema for Bakers has been proved to deliver awareness 11% higher than TV alone.[27]

The advertising is understood

Dogs would choose Bakers:

'The dogs put food in the bowl like a chef. That's if they would serve it themselves, they really love it.'[28]

'The dog's lowered on a hoist and he drools from his mouth and the alarms go off. All dogs love it.'[29]

'Any dog will go for them [Bakers].'[30]

Bakers is a tasty food:

'Dogs will want to eat Bakers because it's delicious doggy food.'[31]

'They put vegetables in and all that stuff. It's really good and tasty.'[32]

26. On 1 April 2005, Mindshare became media agency for all Nestlé Purina PetCare brands.
27. Source: CAA Bakers Cinema Research, 2004.
28. Source: Millward Brown, 'TV Dinners', verbatim, May 2003.
29. Source: Millward Brown, 'Heist', verbatim, July 2004.
30. Source: *ibid.*
31. Source: *ibid.*
32. Source: Millward Brown, 'TV Dinners', verbatim, May 2003.

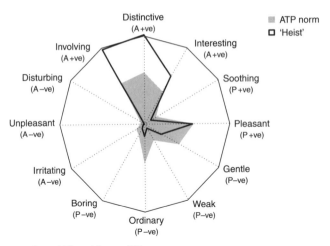

Figure 16: *'Heist' outperforms Millward Brown ATP norms*
Source: Millward Brown, October 2004

The ads are well received

Bakers ads are engaging. For example, 'Heist' scores above the Millward Brown norms on the three best ad diagnostic scores: Distinctive, Involving and Interesting (Figure 16).[33]

The ads also make people feel positive about the brand (Table 2 and Figure 17).

TABLE 2: THE ADS GENERATE WARM EMOTIONS FOR THE BAKERS
BRAND

	'Heist' %	MB UK ATP™ norm %
It made Bakers Complete seem more appealing	66	50
Made you think brand is different to others	52	37
Made you think differently about the brand	40	29
Made you more likely to use Bakers Complete	37	34
Base: Seen still	(99)	(>66 ads)

Source: Millward Brown, July 2004

ISOLATING THE EFFECT OF THE ADVERTISING

Bakers' distribution gains and price changes have been nationwide, making a regional analysis of the varying TVRs an ideal way to isolate the effect of advertising. Figure 18 demonstrates how those regions that were advertised at higher weights show faster growth.

A way to substantiate this is to isolate a region that has gone from being underweighted to upweighted, and analyse whether this prompted an increase in growth. In 2003 in Scotland we had precisely these conditions. Figure 19 shows how Scotland's growth accelerated following this increase in advertising.

---

33. Ad diagnostics weren't tracked until the latest commercial.

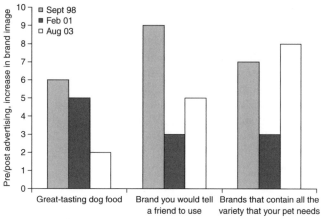

Figure 17: *Brand image scores increase following advertising*
Source: Millward Brown

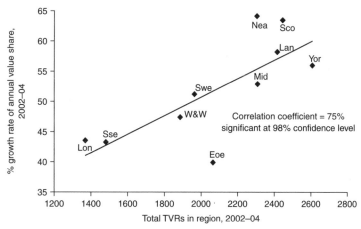

Figure 18: *Upweighted regions have grown faster*
Source: ACNielsen, BARB

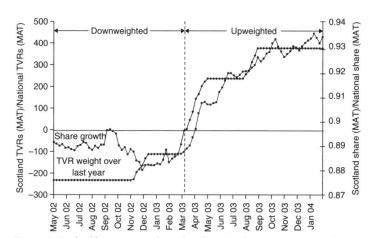

Figure 19: *Scotland began to grow faster than the national average as soon as it became upweighted*
Source: ACNielsen, BARB

CAN WE CALCULATE THE CONTRIBUTION OF ADVERTISING?

In 2004, our network partner DDB Matrix was commissioned to build an econometric model of the brand's sales. The model examines the period from March 2001 to December 2004, and incorporates all aspects affecting the brand, including advertising, pricing, promotions, distribution, competitor activity, market changes and seasonality. It was discovered that advertising has strong long-term effects in building brand success (Figure 20). Over the period studied, it was found that the advertising that ran between 2001 and 2004 directly resulted in an additional £19.3m of revenue, from £5.7m media spend. Nestlé Purina PetCare is, understandably, unwilling to disclose margin data, but it can be confirmed that the additional volume generated has been highly profitable.

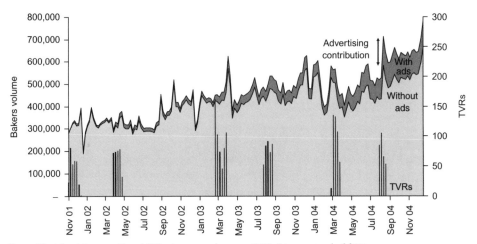

Figure 20: *Advertising contributed £19m incremental revenue 2001–04 on a spend of £5.7m*
Source: ACNielsen, BARB, MMS, DDB Matrix econometrics

PAYBACK

Using knowledge about the nature of the response to advertising gained from the econometrics, we can estimate the contribution that the entire 10-year campaign has made to the brand's success. Accordingly, it is estimated that advertising has resulted in an additional £58.3m of revenue and that 18% of the brand's current sales are directly attributable to advertising. These are conservative estimates, however, as they do not include additional sales occurring from the gains in distribution that the brand has experienced over the period, which we believe are at least partly attributable to the advertising.

CONCLUSION

This case has shown that Bakers was able to achieve both its short-term objective of becoming category number one and long-term objective of growing the category with a single advertising campaign. The campaign is now in its tenth year – a testament to client belief and strong sales response. The campaign has so far delivered an estimated £58.3m for the brand over the last 10 years. The campaign is still working and the brand growing at 14% year on year. Some shaggy dog stories run and run …

2

Travelocity

Hello world, hello sales

How Travelocity became an overnight success

Principal authors: Dominic Hall and Andy Nairn,
Miles Calcraft Briginshaw Duffy
Media agencies: Klondike, James Burgess

EDITOR'S SUMMARY

Many of the best IPA papers rightly emphasise the need to see advertising as a long-term investment. Our second joint Grand Prix winner reminds us that communications can sometimes have an almost immediate effect on growth.

Travelocity started 2004 as a little-known travel brand, overshadowed by its higher spending rivals and without any sense of differentiation. But the company saw an opportunity to create a step-change for the business, by targeting regular online travellers, or 'Aficionados'.

These regular travellers had been neglected by the competition and so Travelocity was able to corner the market by stressing its expertise and by using the ultimate travel 'Aficionado' – Alan Whicker – to convey this positioning.

After just 15 months, Travelocity had boosted brand awareness by 54%, consideration by 36%, web visits by 123%, sales by 135%, and market share by 44%. All with the most efficient advertising in the category, the lowest acquisition cost and a return on investment of £5.60 for every £1 spent.

The judges felt that this was a very thorough and convincing case that proves that communications can produce big paybacks, even in the short term.

INTRODUCTION

Many of the best IPA papers rightly emphasise the need to see advertising as a long-term investment.[1] But it's worth reminding ourselves that *sometimes* advertising's impact can be much more immediate. In certain marketplaces (typically new and dynamic), certain companies (typically ambitious and impatient for success) can find that certain advertising approaches (typically bold and unconventional) can have an almost instant effect on growth.

This paper tells of just such a case.

Travelocity started 2004 as a little-known travel brand, overshadowed by its more established, higher-spending rivals and without any sense of differentiation.

However, after just 15 months, Travelocity had boosted brand awareness by 54%, brand consideration by 36%, visits by 123%, unique visitors by 86%, sales by 135% and market share by 44%. All achieved with the most efficient adspend in the category, and a return on investment of £5.60 for every £1 spent.

This paper demonstrates how famous advertising has been responsible for this overnight success story. And it gives hope to fellow upstarts, in fast-moving marketplaces, that you don't always need to wait to reap the rewards of your communications investment.

BACKGROUND

Travelocity.co.uk is an online travel agent, which launched in the UK in 1998, following the success of Travelocity.com in the USA. At that time, only 9% of UK households had internet access, let alone any interest in booking travel online. However, by 2003, 48% of households were online, and 59% of these had purchased travel, accommodation or holidays over the net.[2]

In fact, travel was one of the fastest-growing categories in the entire e-commerce arena, increasing its share of spend year on year (Figure 1).

Travelocity had benefited from this market boom, steadily building up a small band of users (Figure 2).

Sales showed a similar pattern, with a gradual uplift over 2002–03 (Figure 3).

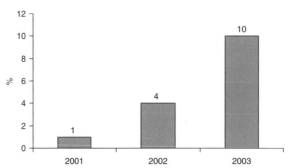

Figure 1: *The travel market's share of consumers' online spending*
Source: Interactive Advertising Bureau

---

1. For example, PG Tips (1990), BMW (1994), Stella Artois (2000).
2. *E-tourism trends*, Visit Britain, Autumn 2003.

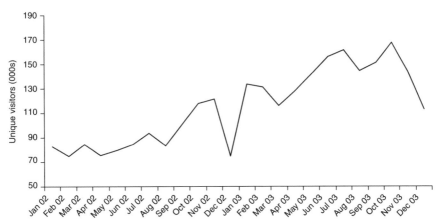

Figure 2: *Unique visitors*
Source: Travelocity

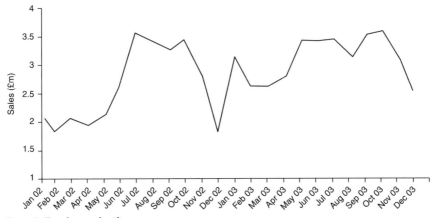

Figure 3: *Travelocity sales (£)*
Source: Travelocity

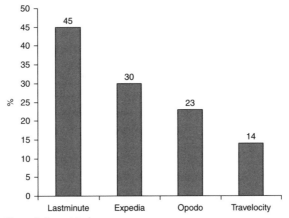

Figure 4: *Ever visited*
Source: Hall & Partners, Tracking, November 2003

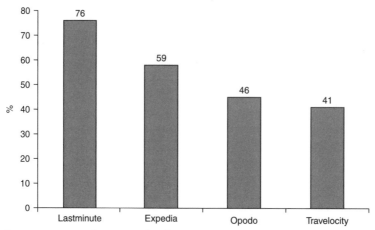

Figure 5: *Active consideration (top three boxes)*
Source: Hall & Partners, Tracking, November 2003

However, for all its success, Travelocity was still a relatively minor player in the grand scheme of things. Not only did it have far fewer visitors compared to its competitors (Figure 4), it was also less likely to be considered by most consumers (Figure 5).

In late 2003, Travelocity called an advertising review, with the brief to create a dramatic step-change in the brand's fortunes. MCBD won the pitch based on the following strategic thinking and creative idea.

DEFINING THE PROBLEM

We identified three interrelated problems that were holding Travelocity back – each was serious in its own right, but all three were potentially deadly in combination.

1. Low salience
2. Low share of voice
3. No differentiation.

Low salience

There is a strong correlation in this category, between salience and success (Figure 6).

On this note, Travelocity lagged far behind its competitors (Figure 7).

In a nutshell, Travelocity wasn't famous enough in a marketplace where fame counts for a lot.

Low share of voice

A key reason for Travelocity's lack of salience was its low share of voice. Other online travel brands had piled marketing money into the category, and were reaping the benefits (Figure 8), but Travelocity hadn't invested significantly or consistently

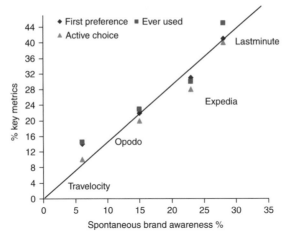

Figure 6: *Brand awareness vs key metrics*
Source: Hall & Partners, Tracking, November 2003

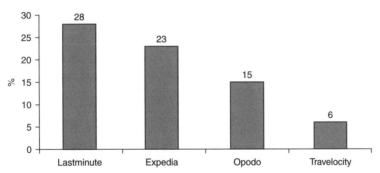

Figure 7: *Spontaneous brand awareness*
Source: Hall & Partners, November 2003

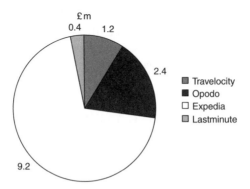

Figure 8: *Media spend, 2003*
Note: although Lastminute spent very little on advertising in 2003, it had spent heavily in previous years; indeed, in the heady days of the 2001 dotcom boom, it was one of the heaviest spenders of all
Source: MMS

behind communications. For example, in 2003 alone Expedia spent over seven times more than Travelocity.

Again, the implication was clear: this was becoming a bruising battle, and if we couldn't match our heavyweight rivals pound for pound, we would need to punch above our weight.

No differentiation

Finally, Travelocity lacked any sense of differentiation. To be fair, this was also true of its main competitors (consumers felt there was little to choose between any of the operators) but Travelocity fared worst of all (Figure 9).

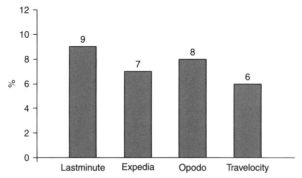

Figure 9: *People agreeing that site 'stands out as being different to the rest'*
Source: Hall & Partners, Tracking, November 2003

Now, the other players could arguably get away without any differentiation because they enjoyed greater salience and share of voice. But, as will be apparent from the previous two points outlined above, Travelocity did not have these factors in its favour.

The doomsday scenario

Taking these three challenges together, there was a danger that Travelocity's small size might become self-perpetuating. In the absence of a famous brand, a noisy presence or any sense of differentiation, consumers would never have a reason to consider Travelocity and would always defer to the bigger, more familiar, more established sites.

DEFINING THE TASK

Based on the three challenges above, we outlined the task for 2004 as follows:

- punch above our weight
- dramatically increase Travelocity's salience
- differentiate the brand
- thus force our way onto consumers' shortlists
- and create an immediate step-change in visits and sales.

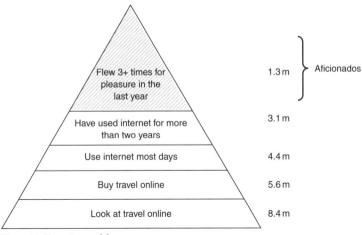

Figure 10: *Targeting model*
Source: TGI, 2003

DEFINING AN AUDIENCE

Using TGI, we created a rough targeting model for the marketplace (Figure 10).

Given our ultimate business objective (create a step-change in visits and sales), the obvious strategy would have been to focus on those 'novices' at the bottom of our pyramid. After all, there were lots of them (8.4m), they hadn't formed any strong brand preferences yet and they might therefore be easier to attract than hardened, regular travellers.

However, after further consideration, we decided to take exactly the opposite approach, and focus on 'aficionados' instead. These were typically 25–35-year-old urban types with money to spend and the confidence to spend it online. We decided to target them for two reasons.

1. First, we realised that a focus on 'aficionados' would make our money work harder: not only do they account for a disproportionate amount of sales, they also influence less knowledgeable consumers via word of mouth.
2. Second, we observed that most of our competitors were preoccupied with recruiting 'novices'.[3] In fact, the entire online marketplace seemed to be ignoring experienced users in their desperate quest to reassure beginners.[4] We realised that we could win over an important audience that everyone else was neglecting.

OUR STRATEGY

Having decided to target 'aficionados', we now needed to position the brand to appeal to this group's adventurous mindset, and to differentiate it from the gentle

---

3. For example, Expedia was using a cartoon man, climbing effortlessly through postcards, to spell out the site's ease of use. Meanwhile, Ebookers was appealing to beginners by imitating a high-street travel agent.
4. For example, AOL's Connie was busy teaching grandmothers to surf. Meanwhile, Self-trade was reassuring people that 'We make share trading a doddle.'

approach of our competitors. So, instead of using conventional focus groups, we commissioned a series of dinner parties in city-centre hotels, and encouraged our 'aficionados' to share their 'travelling' adventures with us. We noted their unbridled sense of confidence, their desire to discover new places and their taste for original marketing approaches. Excited by their attitude, we resolved to position Travelocity as nothing less than:

'The inspirational travel experts'

OUR CREATIVE IDEA

Our creative expression of this positioning was to feature Alan Whicker in unusual places around the world, commentating on Travelocity's expertise (Figure 11).

Figure 11: *Alan Whicker creative*

Although, on a superficial level, Whicker's age made him an unusual choice to talk to 25–35-year-old travellers, he was actually ideally suited to this role.

First, he was universally liked and regarded as the original expert in the field. Second, he was seen as a genuine travel 'aficionado' and not a marketing puppet. And third, precisely because he had been off the public radar for some time, he could acquire a cult cachet that our sophisticated audience would really appreciate.[5]

OUR MEDIA APPROACH

With less money than our competitors, it was vital to adopt seamless communications throughout, from the moment of inspiration to the point of booking.

Thus, we used TV (eight ads so far) to drive awareness and reach quickly (Figure 12).

---

5. As the *Independent* noted, in a three-page special devoted to Whicker and the campaign: 'He's an icon, the person we'd most like to sit next to on the plane. He changed the way we think about holidays. He has an extraordinary following among the travelling generation of twenty- and thirty-somethings, who see him as a pioneering adventurer, the man who got to their favourite destinations first.'

Figure 12: *TV ad*

Figure 13: *Outdoor creative*

We used radio (17 ads so far) to multiply the effect of the TV, with specific messages about the website's superiority.

We used outdoor (seven executions so far) to build awareness of the brand name and web address in travel-related locations (e.g. around tube/train stations and airports) (Figure 13).

We used press on a tactical basis, most notably with a one-off 'Whicker for Mayor' ad around London's elections (Figure 14).

Naturally, we used the idea online, in everything from customer emails to the website itself, to help clinch the sale (Figure 15).

Finally, we used guerrilla marketing to create a buzz around the campaign. From viral ads[6] to stunts at airports[7] to Whicker dolls,[8] we're always looking for new ways to engage 'aficionados' with the campaign.

---

6. We emailed our 'Ironing' commercial to travel 'aficionados' prior to its airdate.
7. We paid people to stand in airport arrivals lounges holding signs for 'Alan Whicker'.
8. We distributed thousands of dolls to 'aficionados' for them to photograph in unusual locations – for the chance to win Travelocity vouchers.

Figure 14: *Topical press ad*

Figure 15: *Online ad*

We launched the campaign on 4 January 2004, spending £3.7m in 2004 and £2.7m so far in 2005.

BUSINESS RESULTS

Within days of the campaign's launch, the business experienced a dramatic surge across all key measures.

A step-change in visiting

Almost immediately, visits to the website more than doubled. Although the new year is a key season for all travel brands, this was way out of proportion to any 'seasonal' blip: in January 2003, visiting was up 67% on the previous month, whereas in January 2004, we saw an uplift of 168% versus the previous month. By the end of 2004, visiting was up 123% versus 2003 (Figure 16).

The number of unique visitors shot up even more dramatically, virtually trebling in the first month. In fact, total unique visiting over 2004 was 86% higher than in 2003 (Figure 17).

The vast majority of these visitors have been new to Travelocity, although we have also held onto our existing customers (Figure 18).

And as more people have discovered Travelocity, and begun visiting more often, they have explored more of the site too: by our most recent burst (January 2005), page views were about eight times the levels of two years ago (Figure 19).

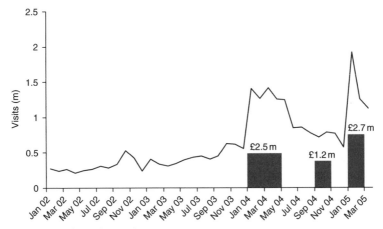

Figure 16: *Total visits by month*
Source: Travelocity

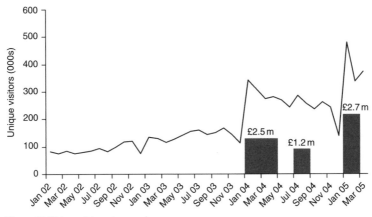

Figure 17: *Unique visitors by month*
Source: Travelocity

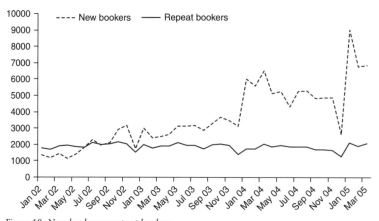

Figure 18: *New bookers vs repeat bookers*
Source: Travelocity

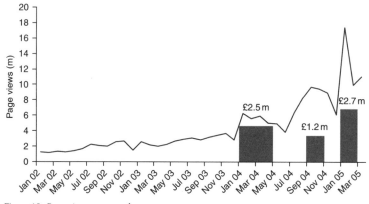

Figure 19: *Page views per month*
Source: Travelocity

A step-change in sales

As you'd expect from the preceding charts, there was also a huge and immediate surge in sales. In fact, 2004's sales ended up 135% up on 2003 and have continued to rise in 2005 (Figure 20).

A step-change in market share

Given the buoyancy of this market, it is important to emphasise that our massive uplift in visits and sales did not simply reflect category growth.

In fact, Travelocity also saw an immediate rise in market share[9] (from 10% to 18% in the first month). Although this extraordinary surge subsequently receded, our average share still held up at over 13% over 2004, versus 9% the previous year (Figure 21).

This was the biggest shift in market share in the category (Figure 22).

---

9. There is no readily available measure of value share in this market, hence these figures relate to volume share – i.e. of visitors.

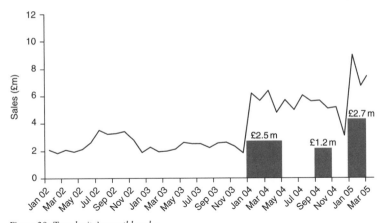

Figure 20: *Travelocity's monthly sales*
Source: Travelocity

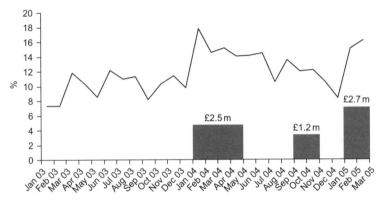

Figure 21: *Market share of online travel category*
Source: Nielsen

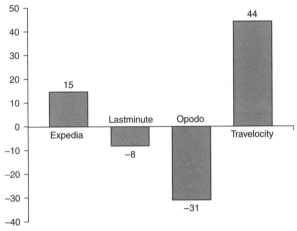

Figure 22: *Percentage shift in market share, 2003–04*
Source: Nielsen

WHAT ROLE DID ADVERTISING PLAY?

Having established that Travelocity experienced an immediate and dramatic step-change in its business, we will now demonstrate that advertising was responsible for this uplift. In particular, we will demonstrate that the campaign worked just as intended ...

We punched above our weight

After the first burst, Travelocity was catapulted from last place in the advertising awareness stakes, to first place. We have stayed in that position ever since (Figure 23).

With campaign recognition at 78%, we have by far the best-known campaign in the category.

By comparing advertising awareness against spend, we can prove that our campaign was over four times more efficient than Expedia's in generating cut-through (Figure 24).

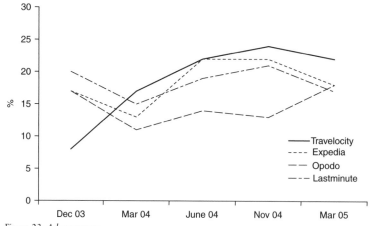

Figure 23: *Ad awareness*
Source: Hall & Partners, Tracking

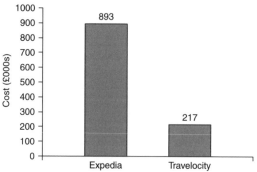

Figure 24: *Cost per ad awareness point gained November 2003–March 2005*
Note: this exercise cannot be conducted for Lastminute or Opodo as both saw a decline in ad awareness
Source: Hall & Partners, Tracking/MMS

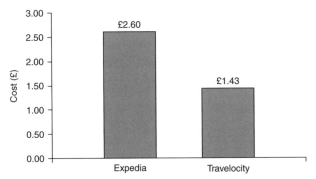

Figure 25: *Cost per additional visitor gained between 2003 and 2004*
Note: this exercise cannot be conducted for Lastminute or Opodo as both
saw a decline in visitors
Source: Nielsen

Similarly, we can prove that our campaign was almost twice as efficient in acquiring visitors (Figure 25).

We dramatically increased Travelocity's salience

The campaign also had an immediate effect on brand awareness (Figure 26).

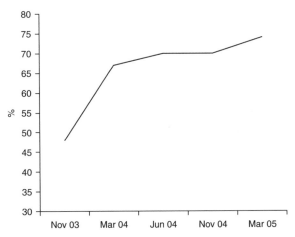

Figure 26: *Total brand awareness*
Source: Hall and Partners, Tracking

Again, this increase was far greater than those experienced by our rivals. Travelocity became more famous more quickly than anyone else (Figure 27).

Due to the advertising, Travelocity is now a brand all sorts of people are talking about.

Travel marketers have voted it the best campaign of the year, calling it:

'Brilliant ... memorable... engaging ... amazing for Travelocity's brand awareness'[10]

---

10. CIMTIG (Chartered Institute of Marketing Travel Industry Group) Travel Awards, 2004, Judges' Comments.

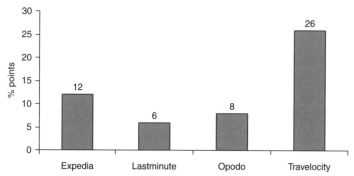

Figure 27: *Percentage points gained in brand awareness, March 2003 to March 2005*
Source: Hall & Partners, Tracking

Other online players have named it the most successful case of brand-building by an online brand.[11]

Business advertisers have shortlisted it, on two different occasions, as one of the top five most effective campaigns of the year.[12]

Media owners have fallen in love with the idea, and donated free space to the campaign.[13]

Creatives have hailed it as 'A work of genius',[14] 'A wonderful creation'[15] and 'Strategically smart and genuinely funny',[16] while festooning it with awards.[17]

The trade press has identified it as one of the top ten campaigns of the year, and the best use of a celebrity.[18]

Most importantly, the campaign has attracted huge amounts of coverage in the consumer world, in titles as diverse as *heat* and the *Daily Telegraph* (Figure 28).

Figure 28: *Consumer PR*

---

11. Revolution Awards, 2004.
12. National Business Awards 2004; Marketing Society Awards, 2005.
13. For example, the *Evening Standard* loved our 'Whicker for Mayor' ad so much that it donated a free DPS, worth £18,000.
14. Will Awdry, Creative Director, DDB London.
15. Paul Cardwell, Creative Director, Doner Cardwell Hawkins.
16. Nick Hastings, Executive Creative Director, Partners BDDH.
17. Awards include: Creative Circle – two Golds, two Silvers, two Bronzes, CIMTIG – four Golds, one Silver, Aerial – Grand Prix and Best Leisure Ad, Kinsale – one Silver, BTAA – one Bronze.
18. *Campaign*, Review of the Year, 2004.

Not bad for a brand that, a few months previously, had been worried that it wasn't famous enough.

We made Travelocity stand out as different

As we established earlier on, one of Travelocity's key challenges was that virtually nobody felt there was anything different about the brand or site. Again, this situation was changed overnight and we continue to perform strongly on this measure (Figure 29).

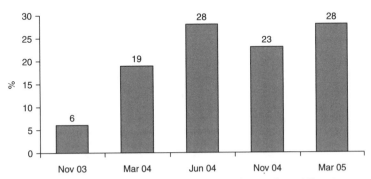

Figure 29: *Percentage of people claiming Travelocity 'stands out as being different'*
Source: Hall & Partners, Tracking

In particular, we have made huge progress in terms of positioning Travelocity as 'the inspirational travel experts' (Figure 30).

Once again, it's clear that advertising has contributed massively to this sense of differentiation (Table 1).

In particular, Whicker's own role in building our expert credentials is clear. And his contribution continues to grow each year (Figure 31).

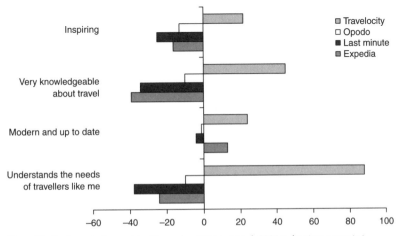

Figure 30: *% change in key metrics (December 2003 to March 2005 in key image metrics)*
Source: Hall & Partners, Tracking

TABLE 1: ADVERTISING STANDOUT

	% agreeing that the advertising
Stands out as different	60
Makes me pay close attention to it	61
Really sticks in my mind	46

Source: Hall & Partners, Tracking

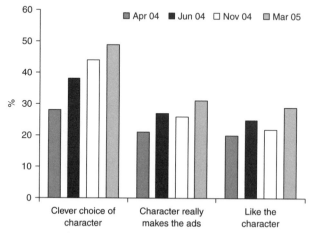

Figure 31: *% of respondents giving opinion on Alan Whicker as advertising spokesman*
Source: Hall & Partners, Tracking

The following quote nicely sums up Travelocity's newfound success at standing out in a crowded marketplace:

'They are the first people in history to make the words 'ATOL protected' sound interesting.'[19]

Advertising forced Travelocity on to consumers' shortlists

Finally, by punching above its weight, boosting Travelocity's salience and making the brand stand out as different, advertising has massively increased consumer involvement with Travelocity (Figure 32).

In fact, it is the only brand to increase involvement over 2004 (Figure 33).

Boosted by this new sense of involvement with the brand, Travelocity also increased active consideration consistently over the campaign period (Figure 34).

Yet again, Travelocity increased this measure more than any of its competitors (Figure 35).

---

19. Damon Collins, *Campaign*, 30 July 2004.

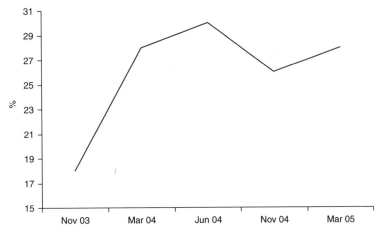

Figure 32: *'Involvement' top two boxes (Definition: 'how close do you feel to the brand')*
Source: Hall & Partners, Tracking

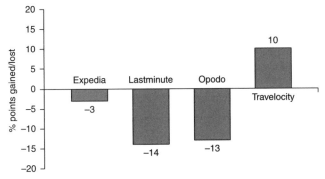

Figure 33: *Percentage points gained in 'involvement', from November 2003 to March 2005*
Source: Hall & Partners, Tracking

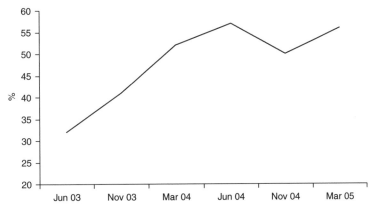

Figure 34: *Active consideration (top three boxes)*
Source: Hall & Partners, Tracking

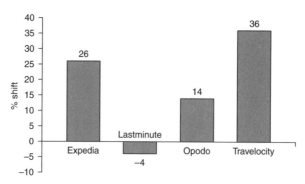

Figure 35: *Active consideration, percentage shift from November 2003 to March 2005*
Source: Hall & Partners, Tracking

ELIMINATING OTHER FACTORS

Improvement to the product

While the basic product has been regularly updated (as with any website), these changes have been incremental and certainly no more radical than those made by our competitors.

Pricing strategy

There have been no major changes to Travelocity's pricing policy over the period. Indeed, during 2004, Travelocity's competitors reduced their booking fees to £4 to undercut the £10 fee charged by Travelocity. Even though we have since reduced this to £6, clearly we operate at a price disadvantage on this measure.

Promotional strategy

Travelocity is not pursuing more, or deeper, promotions than in the past. And, if anything, as we have built a strong, differentiated brand, our association with constant deals has fallen (Figure 36).

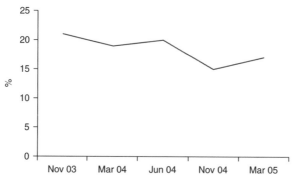

Figure 36: *% agree that 'Travelocity has great deals'*
Source: Hall & Partners, Tracking

Other communications

As with most websites, Travelocity has an ongoing CRM programme. However, this is relatively limited in scope and, in any case, we have established that growth has come almost entirely from attracting new visitors.

Market growth

We have already established that Travelocity has significantly increased its market share, thus eliminating growth as the key driver of success. Similarly, we have demonstrated that Travelocity has outperformed its key rivals on almost all measures.

However, it would be disingenuous to discount market growth entirely. As the market grew by 39% over 2004, and Travelocity grew by 135%, it is reasonable to acknowledge that 29% (39/135) of Travelocity's growth may be due to market growth. The remaining 71%, we would argue, is due to advertising.[20]

QUANTIFYING ADVERTISING'S RETURN ON INVESTMENT

Based on our calculation that advertising has been responsible for 71% of Travelocity's growth, in sterling terms this equates to £26.3m.[21]

On a total spend of £4.7m,[22] this equates to a return on investment of £5.60 for every £1 invested.

Now Travelocity has a strict policy of not disclosing its margins, but it is happy to confirm that, 'even in the short term, this has been a very valuable investment'.[23]

CONCLUSION

Travelocity has (appropriately enough) been on quite a journey in the last year. From a bit-player to the market's thought-leader; from a recessive advertiser in its category to one of the most famous in any sector; from an undifferentiated product to a brand with a distinct point of view; and finally, from a business that was just doing OK, to one that has grown very dramatically, very quickly. We agree with the wisdom of past IPA papers, which have argued that advertisers should think of themselves as being in it for the long haul. But we hope we've proved that, with the right vehicle, advertising can make brands travel at supersonic speed too.

---

20. Actually, even this calculation is probably conservative. After all, even in a growing market there is no guarantee of growing in line with the market, a truth Travelocity learned prior to the 'Hello World' campaign.
21. Year-on-year sales grew £37m in total – from £27m in 2003 to £64m in 2004. Advertising-generated growth was 71% of this (37/100 × 71), hence £26.3m, giving a ROI of £5.5957 for every £1 spent.
22. Including gross media cost, production, agency fees, VAT.
23. Ned Booth, MD.

3

Inland Revenue – Self Assessment

How a change in advertising direction proved that tax doesn't have to be taxing

Principal author: Andy Nairn, Miles Calcraft Briginshaw Duffy
Media agency: ZenithOptimedia

EDITOR'S SUMMARY

The Inland Revenue's Self Assessment campaign has long been labelled one of marketing's most difficult tasks. However, a dramatic change of advertising direction over the last three years has made this unenviable reputation a thing of the past.

This paper tells how the Inland Revenue borrowed from theories of behavioural psychology, to take a more positive approach in their communications. The results have been impressive. Record numbers of taxpayers are now filing their tax returns on time, and more and more of them are doing it online, thereby reducing processing costs. Perhaps most remarkably, there has been a dramatic uplift in the sense that the Inland Revenue is changing for the better, and that self assessment is getting easier.

Altogether, the campaign has helped to recover £185m of tax revenue – impressive given expenditure of £22.5m.

The judges felt that this paper showed sound thinking and good use of data. In particular, they felt that other public information campaigns could learn from the Inland Revenue's research into how to get people to tackle unpleasant tasks (like filling in a tax return).

INTRODUCTION

In 2002, *Marketing* magazine described the Inland Revenue's[1] self-assessment task as 'one of advertising's poisoned chalices'.[2] However, three years on:

- 'the most irritating ads in the country'[3] have been replaced by a highly engaging campaign
- record numbers of people are now filing their tax returns on time
- targets for internet filing have been shattered three years running
- taxpayers increasingly believe that the Inland Revenue is changing for the better
- and even *Marketing* now lauds the role of advertising as a success story, shortlisting the campaign for its 2005 Marketing Excellence Awards.[4]

This paper tells how a dramatic change in advertising direction brought this turnaround about, and demonstrates how it has more than paid for itself.

BACKGROUND TO SELF ASSESSMENT

Self assessment was introduced in 1997, as a way of getting taxpayers to complete their own tax forms, instead of the Inland Revenue. There are several reasons why it represents one of marketing's trickiest challenges:

- the size and diversity of the audience[5]
- the inherent complexity of the subject matter[6]
- the low interest shown to advertising in this sector[7]
- the inherently delicate relationship between taxpayers and the Inland Revenue
- the vast sums of money at stake.[8]

SELF ASSESSMENT'S LAUNCH: HELLO HECTOR

In order to meet these challenges, the Inland Revenue created a character who soon became dubbed 'Hector'[9] (Figure 1).

Hector did his best to communicate the intricacies of the new scheme, and the launch was generally considered to be a success.[10] However, after a couple of years, three key challenges emerged.

---

1. In April 2005, the Inland Revenue merged with HM Customs and Excise, to form HM Revenue & Customs. However, since this paper relates to the period prior to the merger, we will refer to the organisation by its previous name throughout.
2. *Marketing*, 2 May 2002.
3. *Marketing*'s annual consumer survey of 1000 adults, 4 January 2002.
4. For 'Best Customer Insight'.
5. Self assessment affects over 8 million people united only by their relatively complex tax affairs. These include the self employed, higher-rate taxpayers, partners, directors, certain pensioners, landlords and construction workers.
6. Even Gordon Brown freely admits he needs help with his tax form!
7. According to TGI, only 2% of consumers are 'very interested in financial services advertising'.
8. Self assessment garners over £16 billion for the nation's coffers every year. In addition to this, a further £40 billion is collected from self-assessment taxpayers through the PAYE system and other forms of deduction at source. Source: National Audit Office Report 5 July 2001 (latest data available).
9. It is a popular misconception that this name was given by the Inland Revenue: in fact, it was the *Sun* newspaper that came up with the moniker. However, since it has stuck, we will use it throughout.
10. See, for example, *Accountancy Age*, 'Many happy returns', 21 March 1998.

Figure 1: *Hector the inspector*

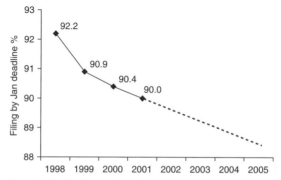

Figure 2: *Timely filing trend and projection (at 2000–01 decay rate of 0.44% p.a.)*
Source: Inland Revenue

The timely filing challenge

First, the percentage of taxpayers filing by the key deadline (31 January) began to decline. If this trend continued, the level of on-time filing might be as low as 88.4% by 2005 (Figure 2).

Now although this shift might appear small, one has to remember the vast sums of money at stake. In fact, the National Audit Office (NAO) estimated that even with on-time filing at 90%, up to £300m in tax was already at risk of being lost.[11] Clearly, this was a situation where every percentage point – indeed every fraction of a percentage – mattered: things could not be allowed to deteriorate any further.

The online challenge

The second challenge was that, since 2000, the Inland Revenue had been trying to persuade taxpayers to file their returns over the internet. It was estimated that £3 would be saved for every return received online.[12] However, despite Hector's efforts, the service was well behind target (Figure 3).

---

11. National Audit Office report, 5 July 2001.
12. *Accountancy Age*, 19 April 2002.

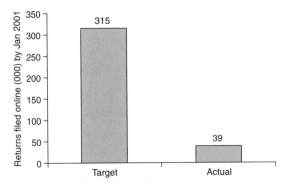

Figure 3: *Online filing vs target (2001)*
Source: National Audit Office Report, 14 February 2002

To be fair, a succession of much-publicised technical difficulties was partly to blame for this.[13] But Hector's old-fashioned image also did not feel right for the online era.

The brand challenge

The final challenge was that the Inland Revenue was itself changing, and Hector was hampering this transformation. As a service organisation, with 76,000 staff and ever increasing responsibilities, the Inland Revenue was understandably keen to position itself as a modern, customer-friendly brand. And yet the image of a bowler-hatted bureaucrat was quite at odds with this vision, let alone reflective of the Inland Revenue's diverse workforce.[14]

Taking these three challenges together, Hector was retired in 2001, without much complaint.[15] Then, while the Inland Revenue mulled over the long-term response to the three challenges outlined above, it commissioned an interim campaign, to run for one year only ...

THE INTERIM SOLUTION: MRS DOYLE

The Inland Revenue's interim campaign featured 'Mrs Doyle' from the Channel 4 sitcom *Father Ted* (Figure 4).

Mrs Doyle was even more persistent than Hector, urging taxpayers to 'Go on, go on, go on' and to 'Go on, go on, go online.'

However, this hardline approach had only mixed success against the challenges outlined above.

---

13. For instance, in 1999/2000, only c.20% of attempted online submissions succeeded first time (National Audit Office, 11 February 2002).
14. *Accountancy Age*, 7 February 2002, 'Hector, in pinstripes and bowler hat, was viewed as male, middle-class, white ... not the profile the Inland Revenue wanted to project.'
15. The following comment, by the independent taxation website Taxbuddies.com, was typical: 'A fresh campaign is clearly called for, Hector having lost his momentum some time ago.'

Figure 4: *Mrs Doyle*

Some progress on the timely filing challenge

Sure enough, the percentage of people filing on time rose again, to 90.6% (Figure 5).

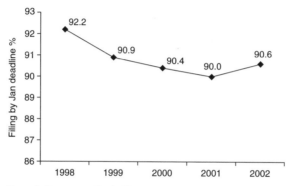

Figure 5: *Progress on timely filing*
Source: Inland Revenue

No progress on the online challenge

Unfortunately, online filing was still way below expectations, despite the target having been significantly lowered (Figure 6).

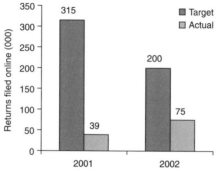

Figure 6: *Online filing vs target (2001–02)*
Source: National Audit Office Report 14/02/02

Now, by this stage, most of the major technical problems had actually been eradicated.[16] However, perception lagged behind reality, and security concerns in particular abounded. Unfortunately, Mrs Doyle, with her gung-ho approach had not addressed these concerns. Some began to question whether communications could ever salvage the situation.[17]

No progress on the brand challenge

Finally, Mrs Doyle did little to position the Inland Revenue as a modern, customer-friendly organisation. In fact, the ads were actually voted the most irritating in the country.[18] In addition, industry observers were scathing about the fit with the organisation's new customer service ethos.[19]

At this point, Mrs Doyle was retired to some rather unkind headlines,[20] and a pitch was called.

THE PITCH BRIEF

Faced with the three challenges outlined above, the Inland Revenue set some very demanding objectives for 2003 onwards.

- Continue to hold back the trend towards later filing, by ensuring that 90.5% of all returns issued were filed on time. This would be especially difficult going forward, as the absolute number of self assessment taxpayers was also set to rise significantly over the next three years.[21] Hence, by 2005, this would really mean generating an absolute increase of over 660,000 forms (+8%).
- Double the take-up of online filing (from 75,000 in 2002 to 150,000 in 2003); double it again in 2004 and once again in 2005.
- Achieve these hard-nosed business aims while reflecting the Inland Revenue's new customer service ethos.

A DRAMATIC CHANGE IN ADVERTISING DIRECTION

Conventional wisdom suggested that the only way to meet these demanding targets was to nag people – even more persistently than before. For instance, *Marketing* warned that:

---

16. For instance, by the end of 2001, at least 70% of submissions succeeded first time – up from 20% the previous year (National Audit Office, 11 February 2002).
17. For example, under the heading 'Revenue's net returns give no satisfaction, *Accountancy Age* (24 July 2002) complained that, 'The Revenue is wasting millions of pounds of taxpayers' money to persuade us to file our tax returns online.'
18. *Marketing*'s annual consumer survey of 1000 adults (4 January 2002).
19. For instance, John Whiting, President of the Chartered Institute of Taxation, commented in *Accountancy Age* (7 February 2002) that, 'If the ad is about raising the Revenue's profile and showing how consumer friendly it is, I'm not sure Mrs Doyle was the right character.'
20. 'Go home, go home, go home Mrs Doyle', *Accountancy Age*, 2 January 2002; 'Go on, go on, get out', *Accountancy Age*, 11 January 2002.
21. There has been a gradual increase in the number of people brought into self assessment because of changes to the taxation system (e.g. a widening of the definition of 'self-employment') and in the employment market (e.g. salary increases that have risen faster than income tax thresholds, thus pushing more people into the higher-rate tax band).

'Some brands are meant to be unpopular and are all the better for it ... MCBD should be aware that hectoring works ... as a nation we respond to nannyish, unambiguous tellings off.'[22]

However, we took completely the opposite approach.

We reached this radical decision via an unusual route: speaking to behavioural psychologists. They explained that hectoring people typically serves only to entrench negative behaviour. Many cited the example of smoking: shouting at someone to quit won't work, whereas supporting them and reassuring them about the difficulties might just do the trick.[23]

We applied this thinking to self assessment and won the pitch with a completely different advertising model, namely:

- grab attention (obviously, this was still crucial).

But, *just as importantly*:

- address taxpayers' concerns
- provide support
- hence prompt action.

THE 'TAX DOESN'T HAVE TO BE TAXING' CAMPAIGN

Our new campaign used the enthusiastic TV presenter Adam Hart-Davis – the perfect choice for a more supportive take on self assessment.

Using analogies with other apparently difficult tasks (e.g. learning to play the piano, abseiling down a building, asking someone out for a date), Adam grabs our attention, addresses our natural concerns and emphasises that plenty of help is available (Figure 7).

Figure 7: *Adam Hart-Davis shows how to tackle difficult tasks*

---

22. *Marketing*, 20 May 2002.
23. For example, Assoc. Prof. Joseph Ferrari, De Paul University, Chicago.

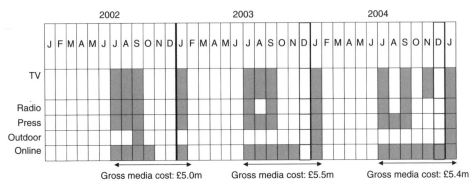

Figure 8: *Media plan*

As he points out in the ad, 'Tax doesn't have to be taxing', particularly if you file early and/or online.

Because self assessment taxpayers are relatively light consumers of media, we had to deploy a broad array of channels to reach them. These included TV, radio, press, posters and online, with the creative idea integrated seamlessly throughout.

The campaign broke in July 2002 and has run every autumn and January (the two main filing periods) for the last three years (Figure 8).

DID THE ADVERTISING WORK AS PLANNED?

Yes, our innovative approach worked just as we had intended.

The advertising grabbed taxpayers' attention

Awareness of this campaign has been consistently high since launch (Figure 9).

Although the Inland Revenue doesn't track ad awareness for other financial brands, data from past IPA papers show that this is well above the category norm, despite a relatively small spend (Figure 10).

Partly this has been aided by our multi-stranded media approach, which has helped to reach a difficult-to-reach audience (Figure 11).

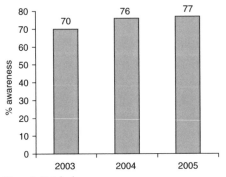

Figure 9: *Total ad awareness*
Base: SA taxpayers
Source: Synovate Tracking, January data

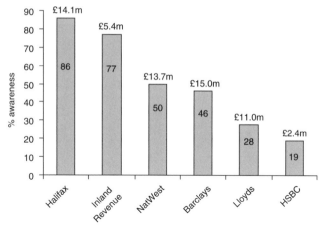

Figure 10: *Ad awareness vs other financial services brands*
Note: Figures shown for competitors are their highest scores
Source: *Advertising Works*, 2002, Halifax case-study

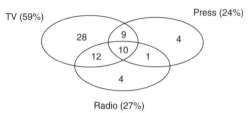

Figure 11: *Ad awareness by media*
Base: SA taxpayers
Source: Synovate Tracking, January 2005

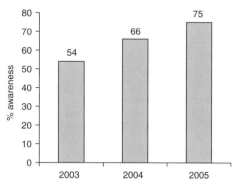

Figure 12: *Slogan recognition*
Base: SA taxpayers
Source: Synovate Tracking, January data

But it has also been helped by a powerful central thought – 'Tax doesn't have to be taxing' – which has increasingly embedded itself in taxpayers' minds (Figure 12).

And, of course, by a consistent campaign vehicle, which has become more and more memorable with every year (Figure 13).

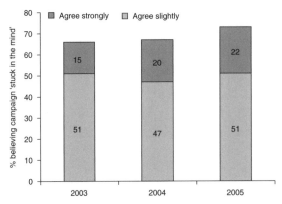

Figure 13: *Campaign memorability*
Base: all recognisers of ads
Source: Synovate Tracking, January data

The advertising addressed taxpayers' concerns

A total of 53% of respondents agreed that the main message of the advertising was that 'self assessment doesn't have to be hard work'.

Sure enough, people's concerns about the filing process have eroded over the campaign period (Table 1).

TABLE 1: CONCERNS ABOUT FILING

	% shift 2002–05
I dread compiling all the information	−12
Compiling the information is a chore	−18
Filling in the return is very/quite difficult	−21

Base: SA taxpayers
Source: Synovate Tracking

Overall, there has been a marked (19% point) increase in the belief that self assessment is becoming easier (Figure 14).

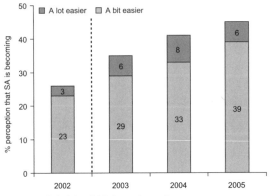

Figure 14: *Belief that SA is becoming easier*
Base: SA taxpayers
Source: Synovate Tracking, January data

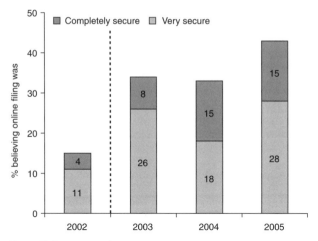

Figure 15: *Decreasing online concerns*
Base: SA taxpayers with online access
Source: Synovate Tracking, January data

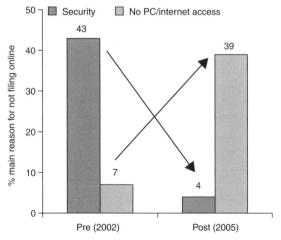

Figure 16: *Security no longer an issue*
Base: SA taxpayers who would not consider filing online
Source: Synovate Tracking

Similarly, the advertising helped allay long-standing (but groundless) worries about the online service's security (Figure 15).

Most rejecters of the online service now do so simply because they don't have a PC or internet access (Figure 16).

The advertising provided support

Taxpayers found this a very helpful, supportive campaign (Table 2).

TABLE 2: CAMPAIGN RESPONSE

Prompted statement	% agreeing
They told me something worth knowing	66
The ads are for people like me	61
They are supportive and encouraging	55
They are really good ads	49
They are patronising	19

Base: all recognisers of ads (January 2005)
Source: Synovate Tracking

What's more, they appreciated the broader implications of this new approach:

'The campaign's messages about help and support were very well received and created a sense that the Inland Revenue may be trying to lighten up.'

Researchworks, 2002

In fact, this unusually supportive approach was welcomed across the board. Whereas previous advertising had been pilloried, this campaign was named 'Pick of the week' in titles as diverse as *Campaign* and the *Telegraph*. Even independent taxation websites (never the Inland Revenue's greatest fans) were gushing in their praise.[24]

The advertising prompted activity

Finally, an unusually high number of people (47%) stated that the advertising had directly made them take action. Moreover, this effect was particularly pronounced among last-minute filers – the key people we needed to persuade (Figure 17).

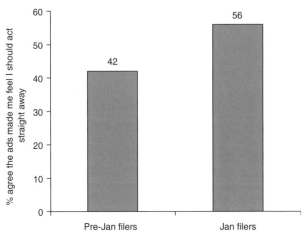

Figure 17: *Advertising's effect on action – late filers vs early filers*
Base: SA taxpayers
Source: Synovate Tracking, January 2005

---

24. For example, Tax Buddies: 'After trying the humorous approach with the little lamented Hector, and badgering us with the infinitely annoying Mrs Doyle, the Inland Revenue appear to have seen sense. At Tax Buddies, we support the aims of this campaign and wish it every success.'

So, according to the claimed data, the campaign did indeed work as planned.

But what actually happened? Did the advertising address the three challenges facing the Inland Revenue?

KEY 'BUSINESS' RESULTS

Significant progress on timely filing

As predicted, more returns were issued than ever before (Figure 18).

But, despite this influx, we managed to hold the percentage of on-time filers at over 90.5%, for three years running, thus avoiding the shortfall predicted in 2001 (Figure 19).

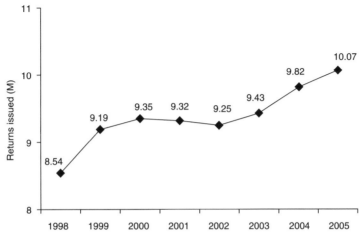

Figure 18: *More returns were issued*
Source: Inland Revenue

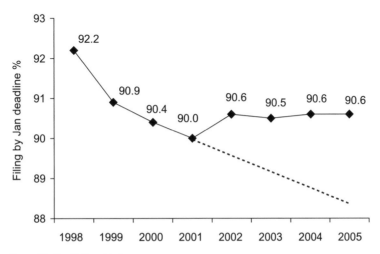

Figure 19: *Shortfall avoided*
Source: Inland Revenue

57

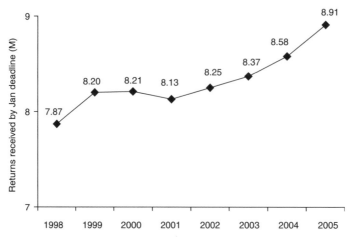

Figure 20: *Record-breaking response*
Source: Inland Revenue

This meant that the absolute volume of response has risen to an all-time high (Figure 20).

Based on the National Audit Office's estimate that up to £300m would be lost if 10% of self assessment taxpayers did not file on time, we can extrapolate that each 1% point represents at least[25] £30m. We can therefore estimate the incremental savings generated, by stemming the natural downward trend, as follows (Table 3).

TABLE 3: REVENUE SAVED BY AVOIDING TIMELY FILING SHORTFALL

Filing by 31 January	Projected %	Actual %	Revenue saved
2003	89.2	90.5	£39m
2004	88.8	90.6	£54m
2005	88.4	90.6	£66m
		Total	£159m

A massive improvement in online filing

After only three months of advertising, the annual target had already been achieved and *Accountancy Age* was grudgingly admitting, 'Revenue finally records a hit.'[26]

The numbers continued to rocket, so that by the end of the first year, we had actually quadrupled the previous year's result and doubled our target. Although this meant that subsequent years' targets were also pushed upwards, we met these easily too (Figure 21).

---

25. We believe that, if anything, this is a conservative estimate. The NAO estimate dates from 2001 and so does not take into account the combined effects of inflation, an increased tax burden and the significantly larger number of people now affected by self assessment.
26. *Accountancy Age*, 26 September 2002.

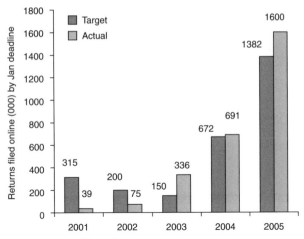

Figure 21: *Online filing uplift*
Source: Inland Revenue

By late January 2005, we were receiving over 30,000 online returns every day – almost as many as Hector had generated in a year. The only technical issue now was whether the website could cope with the demand.[27]

Based on the estimate that every online return saves the Inland Revenue £3, we can quantify the contribution made as shown in Table 4.

TABLE 4: ANNUAL SAVINGS FROM ONLINE FILING

Filing by 31 January	Number of online filers (000s)	Annual saving (£)
2003	336	£1.0m
2004	691	£2.1m
2005	1600	£4.8m
Total		£7.9m

However, this doesn't take into account the 'lifetime' value of these online filers.

If one makes the fairly conservative assumption[28] that each online filer will remain in self assessment and file online for five further years, the long-term savings of recruiting them become even more apparent (Table 5).

The Inland Revenue's brand has significantly improved

Finally, and perhaps most remarkably, there was a dramatic uplift in the sense that the Inland Revenue was changing for the better (Figures 22 and 23).

---

27. See, for example, *Accountancy Age*, 25 April 2005 where this point is discussed.
28. Since SA is still relatively young (eight years old) and online filing younger still (five years old) it's difficult to predict exactly how people will behave over the long term. However, research from TNS Interactive shows that 93% of online filers say that they will 'definitely' file online in future. And given that the typical SA taxpayer is a thirty-something high earner or self-employed, it is likely that many will stay in the self assessment system for at least a decade. Hence using a five-year time-frame is conservative.

TABLE 5: FIVE-YEAR SAVINGS FROM ONLINE FILING

Filing by 31 January	Number of online filers (000s)	Five-year savings (£)[29]
2003	336	£4.1m
2004	691	£6.3m
2005	1600	£15.7m
	Total	£26.1m

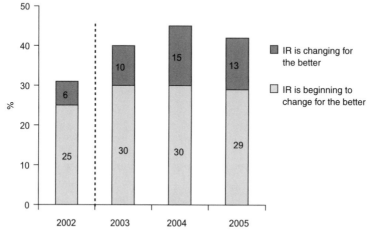

Figure 22: *Perception that the IR is changing*
Base: SA taxpayers
Source: Synovate Tracking

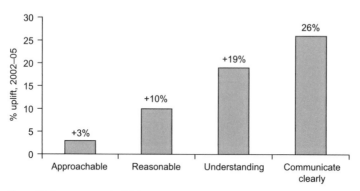

Figure 23: *Improvements in IR's image*
Base: SA taxpayers
Source: Synovate Tracking

29. We have taken care to avoid double-counting in our calculation. For any five-year period, the first four years will contain taxpayers who have already been counted in the previous year's five-year calculation and so need to be stripped out. To achieve this, we have used the formula of: (4 years × incremental online filers × £3 saving) + (1 year × total online filers × £3 saving) = 5 year total. For example, in 2005 the incremental total of online filers is 909K (2005's total of 1600K – 2004's total of 691K). So the five-year saving is: (4 years × 909K × £3) + (1 year × 1600K × £3) = £15.7 million.

ELIMINATING OTHER FACTORS

Other communications

The only other communications taxpayers receive from the Inland Revenue are the fairly functional forms and guidance they get with their tax returns. These mailings are sent from spring onwards, far in advance of the critical January filing period. Hence, their direct influence is much less pronounced than that of the advertising (Figure 24).

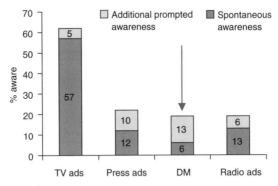

Figure 24: *Awareness*
Base: SA taxpayers
Source: Synovate Tracking

Improvements to the basic product

A four-page tax form (as opposed to the normal 16 pages) was trialled during the campaign period. This will be a significant improvement going forward. However, so far it has been sent to only a relatively small number of people (300,000 by January 2005). Moreover, it has been sent only to taxpayers with relatively simple affairs who already file on time. Crucially, it appears to have had little effect on making these 'good' filers even better (Table 6).

TABLE 6: SHORT TAX FORM PILOT RESULTS

	Filed by 31 January
Short form pilot	95.49%
Control sample	95.24%

Source: Inland Revenue

Improvements to the online filing service

The most obvious change to the online service has actually made advertising's job harder: the removal (one year before our campaign broke) of a £10 incentive to file online.[30]

---

30. It is often asserted that re-introducing a financial incentive would be the single greatest boost to online filing (e.g. *Accountancy Age*, 2 October 2002).

Less obviously, it is true that the online service's functionality has been upgraded. However, taxpayers still need to visit the site, register and wait one week for password details before they can discover these improvements. If advertising had not doubled demand every year, and addressed taxpayers' concerns, these enhanced features would have remained unknown.

Changes to the self assessment customer profile

There were three significant shifts in the self assessment profile over the campaign period, but they all made the task harder rather than easier. First, there was an influx of construction workers (who are typically 9% less likely to file on time). Second, there was an influx of new taxpayers (who are also 9% less likely to file on time). And, third, there was a 'weeding out' of people with simpler tax affairs (who collectively were 7% more likely to file on time).[31]

CONCLUSION

Self assessment is one of the most difficult tasks in marketing. However, this paper has demonstrated how a new advertising approach has helped:

- save at least £159m in tax revenues, which would otherwise be lost
- save at least £26m through massively increasing the take-up of online filing
- significantly improve the Inland Revenue's reputation at the same time.

All at a total cost of £22.5m over three years.[32] In other words, a return of £8.22 for every £1 of investment.

The critics said this couldn't be done, but we hope we've shown that, with a powerful new insight, even the most difficult marketing task doesn't have to be taxing.

---

31. Inland Revenue.
32. Including all media, production, research, agency fees, COI fees, VAT and ASBOF.

4

Roundup Weedkiller

Making a killing

How advertising delivers profits for Roundup Weedkiller

Principal authors: Guy Abrahams and Kate Williams, BLM Media
Creative agency: Flint

EDITOR'S SUMMARY

In 2002, Monsanto launched a new campaign for their weed-killer, Roundup. While other brands pussyfooted around the subject, BLM's ads, from its creative division Flint, were straight talking. Roundup was a killer, and BLM weren't afraid to say so.

This no-nonsense approach paid off. Spontaneous brand awareness tripled, taking the brand from relative obscurity to the forefront of gardeners' minds. Roundup quickly established its killing credentials, making its competitors look weak by comparison. As a result, sales rose by 86% in a single year, and Roundup became the undisputed market leader.

All of this was achieved without distribution gains, price changes, promotions or NPD. There was no complex multi-media strategy – just some great TV ads.

The judges enjoyed this paper's tough, gutsy approach and its firm focus on profit, and so awarded it the prize for Best Read. If you want to find out how to harness the power of TV to kill your competitors, give it a read.

INTRODUCTION

From 2002, Roundup began promoting the benefits of weedkiller with straight-talking advertising, taking it from a failing third-ranked outsider to undisputed market leader in volume and value (Figure 1).

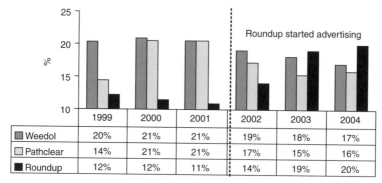

	1999	2000	2001	2002	2003	2004
■ Weedol	20%	21%	21%	19%	18%	17%
□ Pathclear	14%	21%	21%	17%	15%	16%
■ Roundup	12%	12%	11%	14%	19%	20%

Figure 1: *Volume share by year of the total weedkiller market*
Source: GfK top three brands in the weedkiller market

This new Roundup advertising:

- helped grow the market by nearly 50% and drove an 86% rise in volume sales (Figure 2)

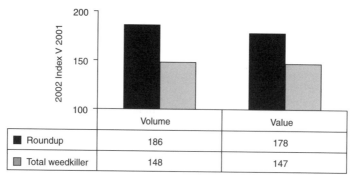

	Volume	Value
■ Roundup	186	178
▦ Total weedkiller	148	147

Figure 2: *How Roundup grew the market*
Source: GfK, 2002 (as the advertising featured the smallest pack size, hence value sales rose by less)

- delivered Roundup's five-year plan by 2003 and nearly doubled targeted sales by 2004 (Table 1 and Figure 3)

TABLE 1: CHANGES IN PROFIT, 2001–04

Versus 2001	2002	2003	2004
Change in gross profit (excluding the cost of advertising)	+$2.2m	+$3.9m	+$4.4m
Change in net profit (including the cost of advertising)	−$0.36m	+$1.1m	+$1.4m

Source: Monsanto

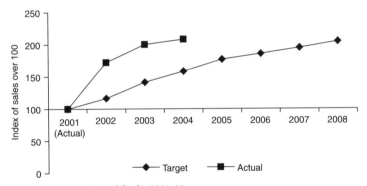

Figure 3: *Target and actual £ sales 2001–08*
Source: Monsanto (actual numbers confidential)

- delivered payback on advertising investment by 2003 with over $1m of additional net profit in that year and further profit growth in 2004.

This was achieved despite the odds being stacked against the brand, as Roundup had:

- a premium price and, as a young brand, very low awareness compared with two household names (Figure 4)

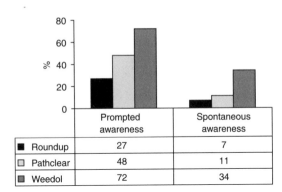

	Prompted awareness	Spontaneous awareness
■ Roundup	27	7
□ Pathclear	48	11
■ Weedol	72	34

Figure 4: *Roundup awareness levels compared with household names*
Source: NEMS pre wave 2002

- only marginally more total media budget than the competition – yet still took share from advertised and unadvertised brands (Table 2)

TABLE 2: WEEDKILLER ADVERTISING EXPENDITURE

	2000	2001	2002	2003	2004
Roundup	£0	£0	£2.09m	£1.66m	£2.01m
Weedol	£0.1m	£0	£1.42m	£1.83m	£1.59m
Pathclear	£1.2m	£0	£0	£0	£0

Source: Nielsen Media Research

TABLE 3: WEIGHT OF ADVERTISING

Actual TVRs	2002		2003		2004	
	Adults	ABC1Adult	Adults	ABC1Adult	Adults	ABC1Adult
Roundup	614	502	647	508	647	508
Weedol	573	436	840	694	840	694

Source: BARB; Weedol used shorter time lengths, hence higher ratings on lower spend

TABLE 4: DIRECT MARKETING SPEND

Direct marketing spend	2001	2002	2003	2004
Index on 2001	100	54	72	44
% of annual marketing budget	51%	12%	16%	11%

Source: Monsanto

- a similar weight of advertising (Table 3)
- no sales promotion, no price reduction, no significant PR and no change in formulation packaging or NPD
- a reduction in direct marketing (Table 4), which funded more TV advertising
- no major change in distribution and the same distributor as the competition. In 1999, Scotts became the agent for Roundup. Scotts managed a portfolio of competitive products including its own brands, Weedol and Pathclear
- no category product superiority.

HOW ROUNDUP GOT TO NUMBER ONE

The test: where it all began

Roundup's assault on the market had been long in coming. Its five-year plan to dominate the consumer weedkiller market was based on a regional test of the effectiveness of advertising in Granada in 1998 (Table 5).

TABLE 5: THE 1998 PLAN

Region	TVRs	Spot length	May 1998 w/c (Fri)			
			1	8	15	22
Granada	712	30"	150	150	150	150
Coverage 1+ 86% of target audience						
Coverage 4+ 53% of target audience						

Source: BARB, 1998

This confirmed advertising's ability to generate significant uplifts in awareness (Table 6) and massive uplift in sales (Table 7).

TABLE 6: UPLIFTS IN AWARENESS

	Pre	Post
Prompted brand awareness	16%	56%
Total advertising awareness	4%	41%
Consideration 1st choice	3%	19%

Source: Laser 1998

TABLE 7: IMPACT ON SALES 1998 VS 1997

Volume sales	Granada	National ex Granada
Roundup 1-litre pack	+109%	+12%
Roundup 3-litre pack	+69%	+11%

Source: Leading national retailer, 1998; a leading retailer was used as GfK does not split regional data by brand

Figure 5: *Similarity to other leading UK brands. Middle: Weedol gun II (launched March 1999). Right: Pathclear gun I (launched March 2000)*

For the next three years, Roundup focused its efforts entirely on the US market. In that time, the UK market changed with the two leading brands marketing similar-looking and similarly performing ready-to-use products (Figure 5).

Roundup sales were decimated as a consequence (Figure 6).

For this reason, Roundup had to refocus on the UK and try to replicate the success of the Granada test in 2002.

The difference this time was that Roundup had fierce competition.

Target audience: Garden sloths and psychopaths

In 1998, BLM had used a segmentation of the gardening market to identify 'Proud Warriors' as the core audience. Typically older, upmarket and male, the Proud Warrior was not differentiated demographically from your average garden owner.

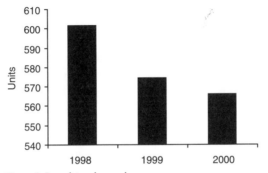

Figure 6: *Roundup volume sales*
Source: GfK (2001 not representative due to change in methodology)

Under his unassuming exterior, however, lay a different kind of beast. This garden 'perfectionist' had cleansed his garden of weeds. He had regimentally neat beds, a perfect striped lawn and spirit-level hedges. This character enjoyed the power of life or death he held over living organisms in his domain. While everything in the garden looked natural and rosy, the shed hid his secret arsenal. Weeds, slugs and moss were removed by any means necessary. Chemical and biological options were key to his mission of having the best garden in the neighbourhood.

By 2002, following the growth of the ready-to-use gun, BLM recommended stretching the targeting to another, altogether different, type of gardener. Demographically similar, this lazy gardener was after maximum effect for minimum effort. A horticultural cheat, he tended to be pushed into 'cleaning up' the garden by a persuasive spouse.

Despite being psychologically on different sides of the fence, we found four clear insights that related to both audiences.

1. They will spend money on the right solution.
2. A lot of garden products fail because people cannot exactly follow the instructions: bulbs fail to flower, moss, weeds, slugs and bare patches on the lawn always seem to return. Both groups were therefore cynical and needed convincing.
3. In shopping terms, weedkiller is an also-ran. They wouldn't go to B&Q especially to get it. It's something they would get next time they went or something they would add to the trolley when in the store.
4. They did not want to hug the weedkiller. They wanted it to do the job and go back to the shed where it belonged.

Our integrated approach

It wasn't until March 2002 that Monsanto, on its return to the UK, briefed BLM. With the gardening season fast approaching, lead times eliminated trade marketing and with television's previous stellar performance, it was quickly identified as the medium of choice.

While Monsanto initially thought that this was simply about repeating the 1998 test nationally, BLM realised that time had moved on. To take on this new competition, we knew that we had to get the most out of both media and message, to build the proposition that Roundup was the deadliest weedkiller in the market – even if, technically, it wasn't. We quickly recognised an obstacle on the path to glory. For us, delivery of media superiority was not an issue. The message, however, was a different story. The TV commercial may have worked in 1998 but in 2002 it looked dated and lacked the killer edge.

To take the message to the new level required new advertising. With a relatively low weight and awareness, we needed a direct, unequivocal, benefit-driven message to appeal to our gardening audience's psyche, by using a single minded proposition of:

'WEED KILLER!'

Monsanto needed a creative agency with this intimate knowledge, capable of going from brief to finished creative in less than six weeks, without demonstrably affecting the media budget. BLM had recognised this client need and had developed a creative capability, Flint, accordingly. By using Flint's unique offering, Monsanto no longer required a separate creative agency. The insight had already been done for the communication strategy, so BLM's Flint could deliver the creative quicker and more cost effectively.

We kill weeds, we don't persuade them to die

By 2002, the two leading brands had been advertising similar-looking and similarly positioned products to Roundup. The market leader, Weedol, chose to underplay the destructive side of the product by initially using animation and the strapline 'You'll be amazed, in just two days weeds will fade away', then subsequently quirky humour and the line 'Weedol. No mercy.'

In contrast, Pathclear maximised the claim to say, 'Clears weeds for up to six months.' To convince these gardeners, we needed to prove that Roundup didn't just temporarily clear weeds, bully them or make them fade, but prove it killed weeds dead. They had to believe failure was not in Roundup's vocabulary.

We didn't design the campaign to build dialogue or entertain our audience. Nobody wants to be friends with a weedkiller. It was designed to work in conjunction with media to be a clear visual reminder so that it was Roundup rather than the competition that fell into the trolley in B&Q.

As weeds are a serious problem for our audience, and to make the communication as credible as possible, BLM avoided using humour or metaphors, emphasising instead how Roundup annihilates weeds at the root, so they never return.

While other brands feared using the word 'kill', Roundup had been happy to use it before. We persuaded Monsanto to go further and grasp it with both hands. Hence, in 2002, we retained the hard-hitting sinister sentiment of the successful 1998 commercial, but modernised the advertising, making it darker – almost chilling – and added the new double-death end-line:

'KILLS THE ROOT, KILLS THE WEED' (Figure 7).

In 2004, this was adapted to feature the larger pack variant, 'Pull & Spray'.

Getting more out of media

In 2002, BLM had to find a way to recreate the overwhelming force of the 1998 test activity but without the privilege of an overwhelming budget. Key to the success in 1998 had been the density of activity and direct creative, which helped to convince customers of the veracity of the Roundup claim.

For BLM to recreate the 1998 effect the founding principle of 2002's and future campaigns was as follows.

- To maintain the 1998 weekly burst weight of the activity to those exposed to the campaign. This would not be continuous. We needed to take into account the vagaries of the weather and also had to allow time for restocking if the 1998 level of uplift was repeated.
- To make these on/off bursts more effective by timing the Roundup advertising to:

If you're not using Roundup

That perennial weed you thought was dead

Could still be alive

And it's going to come back

Again and again

Most weedkillers only kill the leaves

Roundup kills the root

Roundup: kills the root, kills the weed

Figure 7: *Roundup TV execution*

– pre-empt the competition's advertising
– coincide with key garden shopping days – weekends and bank holidays.

- To achieve overwhelming force over the competition's 'drip' strategy and to ensure dominance in the majority of the country in the short and long term. As London represented only 19% of weedkiller sales (Table 8), but over 30% of the cost of a terrestrial campaign (Table 9), we chose to sacrifice advertising on London terrestrial TV to deliver 25% more exposure elsewhere (Table 10).

TABLE 8: WEEDKILLER SALES BY REGION

Region	% purchasers	% value share
Scot	9	7
SWest	3	3
Yorks/NE	16	14
Lancs	12	11
Anglia	7	8
Midlands	18	18
South	10	11
London	**16**	**19**
Wales & W	7	8

Source: TGI 200102; GfK does not measure brand by region

TABLE 9: COST OF REGIONAL CAMPAIGNS

Region	% cost
Scot	5
SWest	2
Yorks/NE	10
Lancs	8
Anglia	8
Midlands	15
South	12
London	**33**
Wales & W	7

Source: ITVA 2002 BARB ABC1ADS

TABLE 10: WEIGHT IN ACTIVE REGIONS VS NATIONAL

	2002 regions ex London terrestrial	2002 national including London
ABC1 Adult TVRs	634	503

Source: BARB/BLM

- To reach more target gardeners: unbeknown to most media practitioners, BARB undertook a survey into the purchasing behaviour of panel members. From this, BLM identified a sample of 919 who spend over £100 per year on their gardens. Via this virtually secret minute-by-minute viewing data, we studied programme performance against gardeners, outwitting the competition, who looked only at demographics (Table 11). This improved the targeting of the campaign by up to 25%.

TABLE 11: KEY PROGRAMMES FOR THOSE SPENDING OVER £100 PER
YEAR ON THEIR GARDENS

ABC1 Ads vs £100+ on gardening products per annum	
Coronation Street	125
The Bill	124
UEFA Champs	115
Inspector Morse	111
Where The Heart Is	123

Source: BARB April–June 2001 (programme over five TVRs)

The resultant campaign pre-empted and overwhelmed the competition outside London at key times (Figure 9).

We ran the same strategy in 2003, overwhelming Weedol with significantly longer time lengths (Figure 10) and in 2004 (Figure 11).

But what difference did all these efforts make?

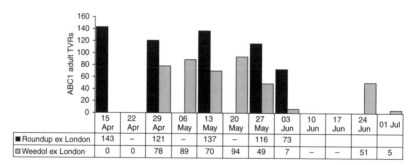

	15 Apr	22 Apr	29 Apr	06 May	13 May	20 May	27 May	03 Jun	10 Jun	17 Jun	24 Jun	01 Jul
■ Roundup ex London	143	–	121	–	137	–	116	73				
▢ Weedol ex London	0	0	78	89	70	94	49	7	–	–	51	5

Figure 9: *2002 weekly strike rates*
Source: BARB April–July 2002

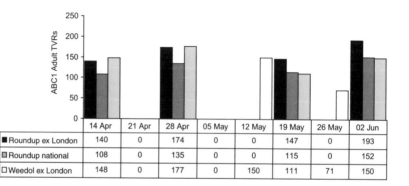

NB
18 Apr – Good Friday
21 Apr – Easter Monday
5 May – BH
26 May – BH

	14 Apr	21 Apr	28 Apr	05 May	12 May	19 May	26 May	02 Jun
■ Roundup ex London	140	0	174	0	0	147	0	193
▢ Roundup national	108	0	135	0	0	115	0	152
▢ Weedol ex London	148	0	177	0	150	111	71	150

Figure 10: *2003 weekly strike rates*
Source: BARB April–July 2003

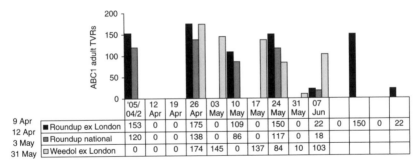

9 Apr
12 Apr
3 May
31 May

	'05/04/2	12 Apr	19 Apr	26 Apr	03 May	10 May	17 May	24 May	31 May	07 Jun				
■ Roundup ex London	153	0	0	175	0	109	0	150	0	22	0	150	0	22
■ Roundup national	120	0	0	138	0	86	0	117	0	18				
□ Weedol ex London	0	0	0	174	145	0	137	84	10	103				

Figure 11: *2004 weekly strike rates*
Source: BARB April–July 2004

THE RESULT – KILLER PROFIT

Despite spending only 19% more than our nearest competitor, in three years £5.76m[1] of advertising was responsible for an increase in sales of £19m (Table 12).

TABLE 12: INCREASE ON 2001 SALES, 2002–04

	2002	2003	2004	Total
Value £000s	£4.7m	£6.6m	£7.7m	£19.0m

Source: GfK

By 2004, total unit sales had more than doubled (Figure 12) and net profits, including the cost of advertising, were rising (Table 13).

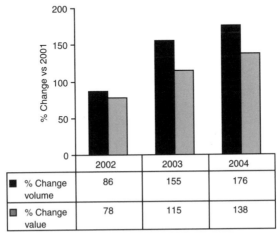

	2002	2003	2004
■ % Change volume	86	155	176
■ % Change value	78	115	138

Figure 12: *Roundup sales more than doubled*
Source: GfK
NB Difference in volume share is a function of greater increase in sales of smaller pack sizes. There was no discounting.

---

1. Reported Nielsen Expenditure – actual figure is less and confidential.

TABLE 13: NET PROFIT INDEX

	2001	2002	2003	2004
Net profit (index)	100	88	134	138

Source: Monsanto

That, however, was only the beginning of the story. The sales effect of advertising extended beyond a single year.

- 2002 unit volume sales were up 86% year on year, 2003 up a further 37% and in 2004 still managed another 5%.
- In 2004, the advertising focused on the Pull & Spray larger pack format, leading to a value sales increase of 9% year on year.
- This either means that some 2002 customers were buying again in 2003 and 2004, or that the advertising effectiveness was improving year on year.

It doesn't take a statistician or econometrician to see the potential increase in profitability that advertising could bring to the business in the future.

- For the period 2002–04 every £10 spent on advertising delivered £13 more profit than 2001.[2]
- In 2003 every £10 spent delivered £15 more profit than 2001.[3]
- In 2004 every £10 spent delivered £16 more profit than 2001.[4]

While some success had been predicted, its scale was unprecedented. All targets were continuously broken:

- vs target – £ sales +48% in 2002, +42% in 2003, +31% in 2004
- vs target – net profit +113% in 2002 and +38% in 2003.

Competition killing awareness

The advertising has not only driven sales and profits today, it has increased the knowledge of Roundup amongst future customers.

Roundup's spontaneous awareness tripled, making it the second best-known brand in the market (Table 14) and second in prompted awareness (Table 15), which more than doubled to 66%.

TABLE 14: SPONTANEOUS AWARENESS OF BRAND

Spontaneous	2002 pre	2002 post	2003 pre	2003 post	2004 pre	2004 post
Roundup	**7%**	**17%**	**15%**	**24%**	**14%**	**21%**
Weedol	34%	47%	46%	58%	45%	54%
Pathclear	11%	15%	17%	17%	15%	15%

Source: NEMS Market Research

---

2. Actual spend vs actual additional profits.
3. Actual spend vs actual additional profits.
4. Actual spend vs actual additional profits.

TABLE 15: PROMPTED AWARENESS OF BRAND

Prompted	2002 pre	2002 post	2003 pre	2003 post	2004 pre	2004 post
Roundup	**27%**	**53%**	**41%**	**60%**	**47%**	**66%**
Weedol	72%	82%	81%	88%	81%	89%
Pathclear	48%	55%	50%	55%	52%	59%

Source: NEMS Market Research

Weedol's advertising also increased brand awareness: prompted to 89% by 2004 and unprompted up to 58% in 2003. The competition's problem, however, was that people's perception of its permanent effectiveness fell when Roundup advertised, thereby putting it in the shade (Table 16).

TABLE 16: 'IT'S THE MOST EFFECTIVE'

Pre/post change	2003	2004
Roundup	+71%	+9%
Weedol	−12%	−23%
Pathclear	−48%	−44%

Source: 2003/2004 NEMS Market Research

This is why Roundup, by the end of 2003, was first choice for one in four gardeners versus one in ten prior to the campaign. In that same time, Weedol as first choice had fallen from 39% to 33%. This is also why, by the end of 2004, Roundup was beating all the competition on key root-killing scores for the first time (Table 17).

TABLE 17: KEY ROOT-KILLING SCORES

	2004 pre	2004 post
'Kills the roots to the weeds'		
Roundup	**22%**	**28%**
Weedol	42%	25%
Pathclear	17%	10%
'Kills weeds so they never come back'		
Roundup	**20%**	**23%**
Weedol	38%	22%
Pathclear	20%	12%

Source: 2003/2004 NEMS Market Research

Roundup might be number two in brand awareness but it was number one in consumer perception of its ability to kill weeds.

Imitation is the sincerest form of flattery

The effect of our media and message has not been lost on the competition. In 2003 the historical market leader changed its media strategy, started earlier and went from drip to burst (Figure 13), and changed its creative so that it used the word 'kill' (Figure 14).

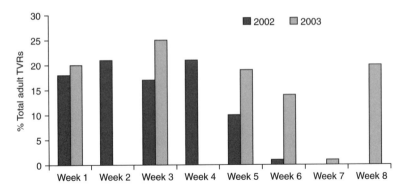

Figure 13: *2003/2003 competitor schedule*
Source: BARB

Figure 14: *Changed competitor creative, using the word 'kill'*

The proof

Most campaigns use a regional strategy as a way of proving the effectiveness of advertising. In this market, however, regional data is not available at a brand level. In its absence, the evidence is still overwhelming, making this an open-and-shut case of a television campaign that simply worked. Not just because of money spent, although if all money spent on advertising worked this well there would be a lot more advertising. No, the competition had spent similar levels of money without our success. It was down to BLM's demonstrably deeper understanding of the consumer, brand, market and media, and our joined-up approach to communication strategy.

Weakness in the competition wasn't to blame either. The two leading brands in the market were better known before we started (Figure 15), with a better reputation (Figure 16).

Roundup had no advantage in terms of formulation. Pathclear gun, for example, has more weedkilling ingredients than just root-killing glyphosate. In terms of price, Roundup per litre was, and still is, significantly more expensive than its core competitors (Table 18).

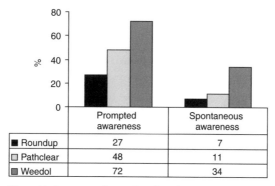

	Prompted awareness	Spontaneous awareness
■ Roundup	27	7
□ Pathclear	48	11
▣ Weedol	72	34

Figure 15: *Awareness of major brands in the market*
Source: NEMS pre wave, 2002

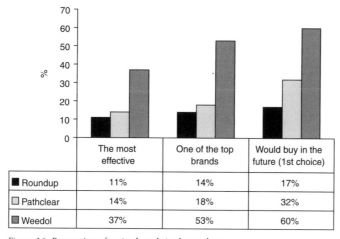

	The most effective	One of the top brands	Would buy in the future (1st choice)
■ Roundup	11%	14%	17%
□ Pathclear	14%	18%	32%
▣ Weedol	37%	53%	60%

Figure 16: *Reputation of major brands in the market*
Source: NEMS pre wave, 2002

TABLE 18: RETAIL PRICE – ROUNDUP
43% HIGHER THAN THE
ADVERTISED COMPETITOR

Roundup	£4.99
Pathclear	£3.99
Weedol	£3.49
Tumbleweed	£2.99

Source: Leading national retailer
(2002–04), 1-litre ready to use

In terms of marketing, the competition had successfully launched numerous garden products. They hadn't skimped on spend or creative talent – the advertising for both Weedol and Pathclear was well produced and properly funded. Until Roundup came along, sales were rising – albeit slowly (Table 19).

TABLE 19: RISING COMPETITOR SALES – VOLUME (000s) AND
VALUE (£000s)

	1999	2000	2001
Weedol volume	993	1051	1063
Weedol value	5163	5405	5971
Pathclear volume	705	1030	1062
Pathclear value	4918	6182	6754

Source: GfK

It's just when it came to a fight, Roundup beat them dead.

Between 2001 and 2004, the marketing mix remained the same, except for a decline in direct marketing. Packaging, pricing and formulation were constant. No PR was paid for and nothing came for free.

As for any other elements of the marketing mix, like distribution, it was a level playing field as Roundup had the same agent as both key competitors. There was no change in the 2002 distribution, and the small changes (less than 3% in total) in 2003 and 2004 were a direct result of the success of the 2002 activity. The sales figures speak for themselves (Figures 17 and 18).

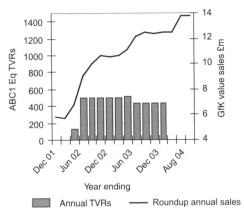

Figure 17: *Value sales vs advertising weight*

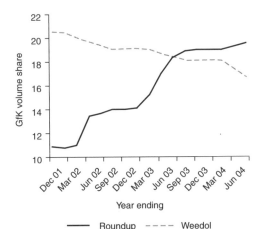

Figure 18: *Changing share in weedkiller market*

With over £3m of new advertising in the category, it's no surprise sales grew. The difference is that Roundup grew far ahead of the market, taking share from the advertised competition, because gardeners believed it was more effective.

Finally, neither the weather nor growth in gardening can be credited for Roundup's success. Market share as well as sales climbed significantly. At the end of the day, Roundup only had advertising to get it to number one in volume and value.

Final thought: it's not the size that matters but how you use it

In 2002, you couldn't have asked for a worse scenario – nothing was working in Roundup's favour: falling sales, falling profits, low awareness, little product advantage, declining DM expenditure, with the same distribution channel as the competition and a price point at 25% above the most expensive competitor.

Briefing in March meant a normal agency would have been able to start in May at the earliest with an existing commercial.

Instead, BLM's unique set-up delivered new advertising in six weeks, which used the word 'kill' to speak the unspeakable, demonstrating product efficacy. Despite having passed AB deadlines, we pre-empted the competition by launching at Easter, while still buying at an audited market discount. By speaking to the right gardeners, loudly enough at the right moment, we redefined the market, forcing the competition to play catch-up.

By leaving no stone unturned, BLM's advertising has not only delivered increased profits every year but leadership in the weedkiller market.

Section 2

Silver Winners

5

Broadband for Scotland

Turning Braveheart into Blade Runner

How the Broadband for Scotland campaign took Scotland into the 21st century

Principal author: Giles Moffatt, The Union
Contributing authors: Wayne Oxley, Scottish Enterprise,
and Stewart Laing, Parallel 56
Media agencies: Feather Brooksbank/MediaCom

EDITOR'S SUMMARY

This case is unusual, in that it shows how, by using advertising and other marketing communications as lobbying tools, they can increase supply, as well as demand.

Prior to the campaign, Scotland lagged behind the rest of the UK in the adoption of broadband, with serious implications for the competitiveness of the Scottish economy. The Union's task was to encourage BT to make broadband more widely available in Scotland by stimulating demand.

They achieved this using a cleverly integrated campaign that clearly explained the benefits of broadband to consumers and then, crucially, got them to actively demand that BT wire up their local exchanges.

The judges felt that the insight into 'internet rage' that emerged from research led to an advertising campaign that resonated with consumers. An innovative 'product sampling' approach drove the message home even harder, and direct response channels then turned interest in broadband into active calls for BT to act. This is not only a good example of an integrated campaign, but also a great example of how communications can help boost a whole economy.

PROLOGUE: BEWARE OF THE LUDDITE ...

'Luddism began on the night of 4 November 1811, in the little village of Bulwell, some four miles north of Nottingham, when a small band of men gathered in the darkness, counted off in military style, hoisted their hammers and axes and pistols, and marched to the home of a "master weaver" named Hollingsworth. They posted a guard, suddenly forced their way inside through shutters and doors, and proceeded to destroy a half-dozen weaving machines of a kind they found threatening to their trade. They scattered into the night, later reassembled at a designated spot, and at the sound of a pistol disbanded into the night, heading for home.

'That, at any rate, was the first attack on textile machines by men who called themselves followers of General Ludd, who would convulse the countryside of the English Midlands for the next 14 months – and would go down in history, and into the English language, as the first opponents of the Industrial Revolution and the quintessential naysayers to odious and intrusive technology.'

Kirkpatrick Sale (1999) A brief history of the Luddites, The Ecologist 29(5), August/September

INTRODUCTION

There has always been a certain amount of resistance to new technology. Ned Ludd remains the most notorious exponent. We are now in an age where innovation and new technology dominate our lives more than ever before. The irony is that despite a rich tradition of invention and innovation, Scotland's future was recently threatened by its national reluctance to embrace a new technology.

Broadband is recognised by all advanced and developing economies as being a key technology for economic growth and future prosperity. Governments around the world are investing billions in developing bandwidth and availability.

Before this campaign was devised, Scotland lagged well behind.

You may ask why a government body like Scottish Enterprise should spend taxpayers' money on promoting a product that is already widely advertised by the likes of British Telecom, AOL, Freeserve and Wanadoo. What is the motivation? What is the gain?

The purpose of this paper is to demonstrate how an integrated and impartial campaign was the differentiating factor in stimulating availability and take-up of broadband in Scotland. We will also demonstrate why this was of major economic importance in the first place. Lastly, we want to show why a successful outcome hinged on getting the communications message right, and using a multichannel approach in a strongly integrated way.

BACKGROUND

The internet took off properly in the mid-1990s. By 2000, as broadband began to flourish, governments around the world recognised the importance of this new technology. In the UK, the Broadband Steering Group (BSG) was set up to promote availability and take-up, and to give advice on the Government strategy to meet its target for the UK to have the most extensive and competitive broadband market in the G7 by 2005.

Similarly, the Scottish Executive and Scottish Enterprise took on the task of developing and promoting broadband in Scotland, where coverage and usage were both well below the UK average. This was done under the banner of Broadband for Scotland (BFS).

Many of us think of broadband as a means of entertainment, or simply 'posh internet access'. It is worth pointing out the serious economic benefits at this stage, to put the whole initiative in context.

TABLE 1: WHY IS BROADBAND IMPORTANT FOR THE ECONOMY?

Macro-economic

Increased GDP: the BSG reports that, by 2015, successful adoption of broadband in the UK will boost productivity by 0.5–2.5% and increase GDP by £22 billion. Accenture has calculated that, from 2003–10, broadband adoption has the potential to contribute $300–400 billion to European GDP.

Employment benefits: in the USA it is estimated that broadband technologies will directly create an additional 2.7 million jobs by 2012 (Criterion Economics, 2003).

Regeneration of rural areas: especially important for Scotland where the population is less than 14 per square kilometre.

TABLE 2: BENEFITS TO BUSINESS

- Time and cost savings
- Enabling teleworking
- Improved productivity
- Facilitate collaborative projects regardless of geography
- Reduction in overhead costs through increased teleworking
- Opportunity to hire people who are well qualified but do not want to relocate
- Reduction in absenteeism (up to 63%)
- E-learning: increased training opportunities
- Procurement: efficiency gains through streamlining supply chains
- Improved inventory control
- More effective communication
- E-CRM: lower cost of ongoing marketing
- Increased workforce collaboration
- Access to intelligence: news, research, competitive data

TABLE 3: BENEFITS TO CONSUMERS

- Communication: lower bills, simultaneous services
- Entertainment: increased download speeds and access to music, video, gaming
- Free software updates to optimise your PC/defend against viruses
- Educational aspects – the world's largest information database
- Shopping: fast, easy, safe transactions for cheaper products and services
- E-tourism: 'visit' places before you go there
- Managing utility bills – facilitating domestic administration

---

Tables 1–3 list the hard economic benefits of broadband adoption, which should explain the need for the public sector's intervention.

Scotland needed intervention more than other nations and more than any other region in the UK. Before the campaign, in 2003, coverage (availability) stood at only 57%. The take-up figures were even worse: 96% of homes were without broadband and, even more significantly, 87% of Scottish businesses *did not have broadband in the workplace.*

We outlined the *benefits* of broadband earlier. It's also worth considering the consequences of *failure* to achieve sufficient adoption (see Table 4).

TABLE 4: NEGATIVE OUTCOMES:
NATIONS WITH LOW BROADBAND ADOPTION

Business
- Productivity will trail that of other broadband-enabled economies
- Lack of bandwidth will discourage inward investment and relocation
- Workforce will leave – 'brain drain' to more competitive nations

Consumer
- Individuals' quality of life will be worse than elsewhere
- Social fragmentation: greater divide between urban and rural economies

Source: KPMG 2005

In short, big problem ... and big challenge.

THE BUSINESS STRATEGY

There are three distinct stages to the Broadband for Scotland initiative.

1. Achieve a marked increase in coverage – the target was availability to 90% of Scotland by 2005.
2. Increase take-up among business (target 30%) and domestic users (target 18%) by 2005.
3. Address the availability issue in rural/remote areas (the remaining 10%).

Stages one and two are the subject of this paper. Stage three is being dealt with in the next 12 months.

A total marketing budget of £5 million was made available. As the initial priority was to boost coverage, the first task was to persuade the telecoms network (BT wholesale) to enable telephone exchanges across the country.

Other regions of the UK (particularly the north-east of England) opted to use their budget to incentivise the telecoms company to do this (i.e. pay a set fee per exchange enabled). Scottish Enterprise chose to take a demand-led route: in other words, convince enough consumers and businesses to register their interest in broadband, and thus meet targets set by BT.

This approach was deemed to be more cost-effective in creating the coverage, but also had the added benefit of stimulating take-up. This was subsequently validated by a KPMG report in 2005.

To generate all this demand, a group of agencies was briefed to develop a comprehensive through-the-line campaign.

THE MARKETING CONTEXT

Broadband is to the 'noughties' what the mobile phone market was to the 'nineties'. The technology is still in the adoption phase, there are a myriad of suppliers offering different packages, performance, pricing and products. Many of them advertise heavily, and there is no shortage of direct marketing from ISPs (internet service providers) promoting their own broadband products. In short, the market is emergent, but already highly cluttered.

And like the mobile phone market in the mid-1990s, this clutter has led to a huge degree of confusion. The result of this confusion: paralysis and inertia. Consumers are faced with too much choice; too many packages; too many tariffs; too many suppliers – and all for a product they barely understand in the first place. The ISPs in the UK spend over £70 million a year promoting their products.

Our job was to stimulate demand for broadband, and the task was literally to cut through the clutter and noise. Perversely, the more active the suppliers were in their efforts to seduce consumers with deals, features, tariffs, packages, the harder our job would be. Our activity would have to complement their efforts by making the whole decision-making process clearer. An impartial website would form an important part of this.

THE STRATEGIC SOLUTION

We knew we had to stimulate demand. We knew we had to eradicate a lot of the confusion to achieve this. What we didn't know was how the public would react to a government body 'advertising' what was effectively a commercial product. As a result, there were several stages of research.

The first step involved two key pieces of insight work: a quantitative opinion poll and some qualitative groups across Scotland.

The findings confirmed our hypotheses on the market. Although heavy users of the internet had frustrations with slow speeds and blocked phone lines, the majority of people claimed they 'felt they could live with it' (Scott Porter, October 2003). The quantitative opinion polls corroborated the levels of inertia in Scotland. When asked, 'What's stopping you getting broadband?' over 14% of people without broadband claimed the main reason was that they had 'never got round to it'. A significant proportion of Scots (35%) legitimately claimed 'lack of availability'.[1]

The agency's brief was becoming clearer. If advertising was going to succeed in enabling exchanges, it was going to have to *provoke* the public enough to shake off their apathy. It would also have to be populist and accessible, given the breadth of the audience and the levels of confusion out there.

A number of initial routes were tested in December 2003. The first played on the Scots' reputation for inventiveness and intelligence, and questioned why, despite this, they weren't smart enough to get broadband. Although humorously treated, the idea alienated many (with hindsight, not surprisingly!).

The second route focused on speed, and lampooned 'slow' characters. People warmed to it, but felt it didn't tell them anything new about broadband. Everybody knew it was faster.

A third idea was entitled 'Why are you waiting?' It was designed to highlight the absurdity of using the internet in sub-optimal form. This came out as the strongest

---

1. Source: MRUK.

of the three routes. It touched a raw nerve, without making people feel foolish or backward.

However, we got more from the groups than we expected. At one point, one of the respondents launched into a major rant about how useless his computer was when going online. Others joined in, and there followed a freeform discussion on 'bad experiences' on the internet. We were amazed at the levels of 'internet rage' we could see, even in groups of seemingly reasonable people. ('Internet rage' subsequently became the theme for a major PR initiative, and received substantial press coverage.)

We realised that if you pushed the right buttons, people would confess to having 'lost it' with their computer at some point in their recent lives. Despite claiming earlier in the groups that dial-up was 'good enough', when the confession finally came it unleashed a tirade of abuse at inferior technology and an inferior experience.

As none of the routes we had researched fully tapped in to this, we amended our creative proposition to:

'Don't get mad, get broadband.'

Three more creative routes were developed along the lines of this proposition, including the Ford Kiernan 'Angry Man' idea (see Figure 1), which used the 'Ballistic Bob' character from the BBC's hugely popular sketch show, *Chewin' the Fat*. Populist and accessible, we thought he would be a great vehicle for building awareness rapidly.

The 'Angry Man' route dominated in the next round of research. Many people identified with the scenarios: one where Kiernan is trying to get through to someone whose dial-up connection is blocking the line; another where he waits patiently for a file download only for it to crash. In both instances, he loses the plot completely and trashes everything around him in a frenzy of rage.

People said things like:

'Been there, done that. Had to get a new laptop.' (Male, Glasgow)

'It's so true – there are times when you just want to punch the screen.' (Female, Edinburgh)

(*MRUK qualitative research*, December 2003)

We were pleased that we had found a very strong solution. It clearly tapped into something that would help break up the inertia. It also bore no resemblance to anything the suppliers were doing. While they were battling it out with claims on pricing, megabytes, ADSL, we took the high ground and concentrated on a fundamental consumer insight.

THE COMMUNICATION ACTIVITY

The whole Broadband for Scotland programme was quite an elaborate one, involving many media and many channels. Each channel had a slightly different role.

The first phase was designed to boost availability of broadband in Scotland. The chosen strategy was to build enough interest and physical registrations (businesses or consumers in all areas registering their details) (see Table 5).

Figures 2–5 show examples of the creative used in different media.

TABLE 5: PHASE 1 – TARGET: BOOST COVERAGE IN SCOTLAND FROM 57% TO 70% (NOVEMBER 2003–JULY 2004)

Media	Role
TV	Consumer awareness (and visibility to suppliers)
Press	Consumer and business education
Posters	Consumer awareness
Radio	Consumer awareness
Online	Traffic to website
Website	Impartial advice, postcode checker and registrations
Other channels	
Field marketing	Capture business and consumer registrations
Door-drops	Lobbying consumers to register for broadband locally
Business incentives	Encouraging take-up of broadband in SMEs

Figure 1: *'Angry Man'*

Figure 2: *'Billy' press ad*   Figure 3: *'Thinking Cap'*

Figure 4: *Mailing*

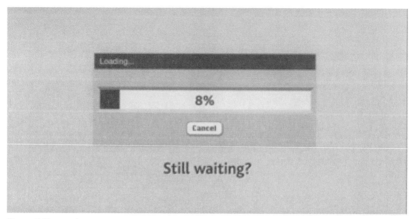

Figure 5: *Postcard*

THE RESULTS

The first objective (phase 1) was to increase coverage to 70% of Scotland (Table 5). The combined impact of 38,000 registrations and the scale of the activity convinced BT to enable far more exchanges than expected.

By the end of 2004, 92% of the country had the potential to access broadband through land-based services. This exceeded the 2005 target of 90% a year early.

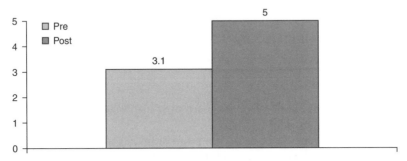

Figure 6: *Pre-/post-campaign population with access to broadband (millions)*

Figure 6 shows how many million Scots had potential access to broadband as a result of the campaign – about 95% of the population.

The efficiency of the demand-led strategy can be quantified. If you divide up the total marketing budget, the cost of enabling the exchanges works out at approximately £7000 per exchange. At the same time, that investment created widespread consumer and business awareness (as detailed below).

Other regions paid BT *significantly* higher sums to enable exchanges. This with absolutely no impact on consumer awareness or behaviour.

With the coverage job achieved so comprehensively in phase 1, the ongoing challenge was now to convince Scots businesses and home users to trade up to broadband. The take-up figures speak for themselves. Across the period measured, Scottish Enterprise data showed the increases illustrated in Figure 7. These figures show that business usage more than doubled.

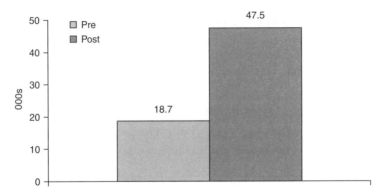

Figure 7: *Business users pre-/post-campaign (pre = December 2003, post = January 2005)*

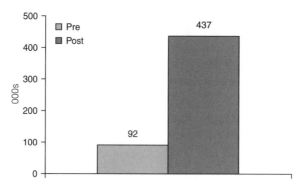

Figure 8: *Domestic users pre-/post-campaign*

A total of 33% of Scotland's businesses now use broadband daily. This is now higher than the UK figure of 25%.[2]

The increase in domestic users is even more dramatic, as is illustrated in Figure 8. The number of home users in Scotland increased almost fivefold across the period.

To put this particular growth figure in context, the figure for the UK as a whole for the period is only 191%.[3] The growth rate in Scotland was therefore *2.8 times that of the rest of the UK.*

HOW DO WE KNOW THE CAMPAIGN ACTIVITY WAS RESPONSIBLE FOR ALL THIS?

To demonstrate that the Broadband for Scotland campaign was the primary force behind these results, we will look at two other factors.

1. Supplier 'competitive' activity: we want to be sure that supplier advertising in Scotland had no greater effect than activity in the rest of the UK.
2. Proof that the individual parts of the campaign were effective in their own right, increasing the likelihood of a cumulative effect.

Pricing of broadband packages must also be taken into account. The cost has decreased slightly throughout the UK since the campaign started. Ofcom states that prices in July 2004 were between £20 and £40 per month, depending on the supplier and the package. By February 2005, prices were £15–£40, making entry-level packages marginally more accessible. Most importantly, broadband pricing is decided nationally. There is no evidence that pricing in Scotland was unduly lower than in any other area of the UK. Price variation can therefore be excluded from the results.

Supplier 'competitive' activity

Total UK spends are obviously considerably higher than Scotland-only activity. NMS figures for Scotland show a gradual increase in overall spending from 2001

---

2. Source: Ofcom.
3. Source: Ofcom, January 2005 Quarterly Update, pp. 5, 38.

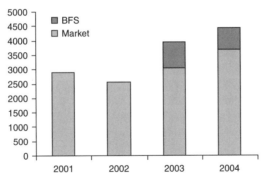

Figure 9: *Media expenditure Scotland (£000s) NMS*

through to 2004. However, the major significant increase in media expenditure in 2003 and 2004 came directly from the Broadband for Scotland campaign. Figure 9 demonstrates that the lion's share of incremental activity was actually ours. There was no sudden or massive increase in spending by suppliers that can be deemed to have influenced the marketplace any differently from previous years. Tiscali and Wanadoo did increase their spending by £500,000 (total for both brands) in response to the increased coverage that resulted directly from our activities.

Adoption of broadband in the UK

It is a key fact that the rate of broadband adoption in Scotland was 2.8 times greater than the rate for the UK as a whole (Figure 10).

This demonstrates that the stimulus provided by the campaign created a significant difference versus other 'control' regions. It's also worth noting that other regions of the UK *did* have supply-side programmes in place to stimulate broadband growth – none of them were *doing nothing*.

Campaign results

Advertising

The advertising clearly cut through and captured people's imaginations. Indeed, towards the end of the campaign, we got an unexpected indication of just how

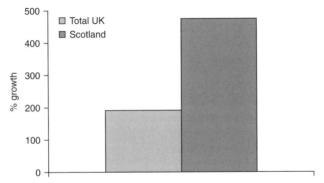

Figure 10: *Growth of broadband adoption, UK vs Scotland during campaign period*

Figure 11: *Media coverage of the Ford Kiernan road rage incident*

popular the campaign had become. The media had a field day when Ford Kiernan (who played all the characters, including the Angry Man) was involved in a road rage incident in January 2005 (see Figure 11).

In December 2004, tracking from TL Dempster puts overall awareness of the campaign in excess of 70%. A recent quantitative survey conducted by BD Network's field marketing team showed an even higher result of 87%. Although the main media clearly served to drive awareness, other channels were critical in fulfilling key objectives. Each of them performed phenomenally well individually.

Field marketing
The field marketing conducted on a local basis in phase 1 allowed us to target specific areas where broadband was not available. Promotional teams visited the areas and captured registrations in a way that no conventional direct-response activity could have; 176 new areas were triggered as a result.

The second phase of field marketing was designed to create a broadband 'experience' – we knew from focus groups that 'until you've tried broadband, you probably won't buy'. The field marketing offered interactive demonstrations to 310,176 people, including 10,000 businesses. Data show that interactions lasted an average of six to seven minutes on bespoke broadband terminals. This kind of quality experience is usually unheard of in sales promotion. When surveyed on exit, 74% said they were 'more likely to get broadband' and 97% said they 'would get broadband within the next three months'.

PR
PR also contributed to the overall success. Early in the campaign it was used to support the 'anger' message. The PR agency seeded the media with stories of internet rage along with statistics. The resulting press coverage achieved just under 13 million opportunities to see.

Website

From the outset the website (www.broadbandforscotland.co.uk) was an essential tool. It was created to be an impartial resource providing comparisons of the different options, as well as a postcode checker and a facility for registering your interest in broadband if it happened not to be available in your area.

Since the campaign started, 170,000 people have visited the site meaningfully, with about 65% of them going on to use the postcode checker. On average they viewed six pages, and the 54% of them who weren't already set on broadband said they were 'more likely to get broadband' as a result of viewing the site.

Direct marketing

Direct marketing to industry sectors with low broadband penetration (retail, tourism and leisure) adapted the above-the-line ideas to reinforce the hard business benefits of broadband.

PAYBACK/RETURN ON INVESTMENT

The total spend on marketing was in the region of £2.5 million per annum over two years. The price of increasing coverage through a demand-led strategy was a fraction of that spent by other regions. So the strategy was cost-effective, but what about the return on investment?

We cannot measure ROI the traditional way – we were selling a category and not a product. The real measure of the campaign's value is its contribution to 'Scotland plc'.

By 2015, the value of broadband adoption will be 1.5–2.5% annual growth in GDP.[4]

Scotland's current GDP is £64 billion. Effectively the contribution of broadband and broadband-related businesses will be upwards of £960 million to £1.6 billion growth *per year*. These figures absolutely dwarf the initial investment. They also show how essential the programme was in the first place. We are talking about future payback in hundreds of millions, if not billions.

Using an integrated and holistic approach to communications, the Broadband for Scotland campaign made this technology available to the majority of Scotland's population and businesses. It also made them realise the value of trading up from dial-up, and shook them out of their apathy and inertia. Domestic use quadrupled during that time period, at over twice the rate of the rest of the UK. Business use doubled. Overall adoption of broadband outpaced the rest of the UK by almost three times the rate.

Could we have done it without this campaign? We could have 'bought' coverage, but this wouldn't have stimulated take-up or achieved any kind of shift in cultural attitudes towards technology. We could have focused on businesses alone, but that's what other regions did, with less success. We might even have chosen a different advertising idea, but then again, would it have resonated so strongly with the Scottish public? As one respondent said in the recent field marketing survey, 'the ads are so close to reality it's scary'.

Not as scary as a future without broadband.

---

4. Source: KPMG.

6

Fire Authority for Northern Ireland

Writing on the wall

Principal authors: Orla Ross, John Keane and Stephen Roycroft,
Ardmore Advertising

EDITOR'S SUMMARY

Trying to reduce the deaths, injuries and damage caused by fire is an ambitious job for advertising, but Ardmore's campaign for the Fire Authority for Northern Ireland succeeded, thanks to a number of key ingredients.

Firstly, the campaign set very precise behavioural goals, such as getting people to not only fit smoke alarms, but also to test them regularly.

Secondly, a powerful creative idea was used to confront people with the reality of fire in a way that couldn't be dismissed with 'It'll never happen to me'.

Thirdly, analysis of the common causes of fires was used to guide choice of advertising messages and use of media.

As a result of the campaign, public awareness of the five key causes of fire and how to deal with them improved. The number of household fires in Northern Ireland fell by 14%, and injuries fell by 12%.

Proving hard results in a case like this is always difficult, but the evidence impressed the judges. The data showing how the situation improved in Northern Ireland compared to the rest of the UK is particularly compelling.

INTRODUCTION

This case study sets out to demonstrate how advertising can effect significant change in habitual behaviour. It will show how advertising succeeded in educating the public to think about fire safety behaviour and how it moved people to make positive changes in the home to prevent fire. It will also isolate the advertising effectiveness against the campaign period.

BACKGROUND

Our ultimate objective in our Fire Authority work is to save lives and property, and to prevent injury. Clearly this is a vital task. Northern Ireland as a region, after years of successful campaigning, has one of the highest levels of smoke alarm ownership per household in Europe[1] and yet most fires and fatalities point to the fact that smoke alarms have failed to act as the life-saving devices they have the potential to be. Why?

Post-fire examinations of various scenes indicate that, while people have smoke alarms, the batteries are not always tested and changed as required. We quickly identified this as a central element to address in the campaign creative. Previous advertising campaigns had established Mondays as the day on which all households should check their smoke alarms. We decided to build on this established habit through our campaign planning. Together with the Fire Brigade we analysed the other main hazards causing fires, injury and death, and we identified that our audience needed to be educated across five key areas.

1. *Candle safety*: extinguishing candles properly, not placing them near soft furnishings. In 2003/04, candles were the fastest rising cause of fire in the UK.[2]
2. *Escape plan*: having a viable and rehearsed escape route from the home in case of fire. Most people cannot navigate through their own home as smoke is so dense and disorienting.
3. *Chip pan safety*: not leaving them unattended nor filling more than one-third full with oil.
4. *Doors safety*: many people fail to close potentially life-saving doors at night as part of their bedtime routine; an ordinary household door can contain a fire for up to 15 minutes.[3]
5. *Battery maintenance in smoke alarms*: although fire incidents throughout the year can be subject to slight variation, historically the highest risk period is October–February. This is due to a combination of factors: the winter months result in more people staying in their homes for more sustained periods of time; there are more electrical appliances on, such as heaters, fires etc., and decorations at Christmas time account for a significant amount of incidents resulting from overloaded plugs. As outlined already, failure to maintain batteries in smoke alarms can lead to tragic consequences if any other precautions have been overlooked.

---

1. Fire Authority for Northern Ireland internal data.
2. Fire Authority for Northern Ireland internal data.
3. *Ibid.*

CAMPAIGN OBJECTIVES

- Raise public awareness of the causes of fire.
- Raise awareness of safety practices and routines.
- Reduce fatalities/injuries.
- Effect behavioural change.
- Reduce fire and injury in line with national reductions.
- Overturn the view 'It could never happen to me.'

THE TASK

We felt that our biggest challenge was to penetrate the life-threatening apathy born of 'it could never happen to me/my family/in my house' among our audience. We wanted to avoid sensationalising the experience of a fire and being in a fire, but rather focus on how to avoid this happening. The ability to simultaneously deliver precise audience targeting and value for money was another vital element of the task in hand. All of our work came under the highest levels of scrutiny from external committees and auditors.

Communicating the battery message and prompting weekly checks was critical to the campaign. Having a working smoke alarm in a fire situation is the biggest contributing differentiator to the outcome of that fire.

THE STRATEGIC SOLUTION

We agreed that, by creating the widest sphere of creative relevance to as many demographics as possible, the campaign would work most efficiently. We also decided to create a dedicated treatment to deal with each of the five key hazards. We made this decision based on Fire Brigade data, which showed a propensity for certain hazards to occur in specific geographical regions/demographic groups. This would ultimately allow us to target selected audiences with the most relevant messaging. We also made a strategic decision not to feature characters as appearing protagonists in the TV advertisements. Our research (internal focus groups) suggested that such personification can alienate sections of an audience through a failure to identify with the character. It is critical that any public conscience messaging captures as much of the population as possible without alienating them from the message.

THE IDEA

As part of our familiarisation process, we felt that it was important to understand the human experience of being in a fire. We arranged for our brand team to undergo fire behaviour training in real fire situations at the local recruit training facility. We also viewed forensic footage that revealed horrific post-fire scenarios. We were all struck by a prevalent tragic feature: human handprints desperately strewn across the walls of the home by those desperately seeking a way out as a means to escape the smoke and flame. This formed the creative basis of our campaign. We developed a series of messages left by the dying, with finger-written messages scratched desperately into charred walls. This device was deliberately designed to play upon the potential for guilt in our audience, reinforcing that they should take responsibility for fire prevention *before* they personally become responsible for the death of someone who had perhaps placed their trust in them. The tone of voice was personal and yet relevant to a broad audience in their various roles in life – parent, son, daughter, neighbour, friend – allowing us to directly challenge the apathy of 'It could never happen to me.'

The creative allowed us to achieve this by never showing any of the fire victims or target individuals, therefore removing the possibility of the viewer disengaging with the creative merely because the person in the advertisement is not like them.

THE COMMUNICATION ACTIVITY

The strategy we devised to reach the identified target audiences included strategic and integrated media planning to ensure optimum coverage of, and connection with, the mass Northern Ireland target audience.

We recognised that it would be necessary to deploy an extensive, but also complementary, mix of media initiatives, to ensure complete coverage of our target: the entire population of Northern Ireland.

In addition to mass-targeting media initiatives, it was also necessary to pinpoint and specifically target clearly identifiable at-risk demographics with fire safety messages particularly relevant to them.

Television

This was effective in facilitating the targeting of each individual fire safety message to a specific audience through extensive programme research and daypart analysis. For example, the chip pan safety message was upweighted at dinner time and late at night to target those returning hungry from pubs and clubs. The television activity was planned to provide a constant presence throughout the high-risk period.

Recognising the power of local news programming and our need to communicate on television for 12 months of the year we created and deployed a news initiative with Ulster Television. This consisted of a 30-second commercial running in each of the three local news breaks every Monday for 52 weeks, allowing us to achieve much needed repetition of the 'check your battery' message. This activity facilitated the placement of a fire safety message in breaks adjacent to local news bulletins that would inevitably cover any fire-related tragedies, but also highlight Fire Brigade successes over the key weekend period.

Key efficiency
- TV deal negotiated at significant discount achieving repetition of battery message three times on Mondays.
- This commercial also secured a private-sector sponsor contributing 50% of the production fees.
- Benign tone encouraging the weekly checking of smoke alarms.

Radio

Radio was also selected to cost-effectively deliver repetition of the campaign messages to the target audience while in the home; where fire prevention is essential. The radio activity was planned to run during the winter, in the midst of the extremely upbeat Christmas and January sales retail activity. This was to demonstrate a creative contrast between the stark reality of the Fire Brigade creative and the retail buzz, maximising recall and catching the audience off-guard with an unexpected sombre creative style.

Key efficiency
- 64% of radio listening in Ireland takes place at home with an average listening time of 3.5 hours each day.[4]
- The creative treatment for each spot was precisely planned to ensure that the five creative treatments were placed in the day-parts most relevant to the message and target audience. For example, the bedtime routine message was aired only after 8pm on all stations.

Press

The *Belfast Telegraph* is Northern Ireland's only indigenous evening title with a daily audited circulation of 94,540. This title provides an efficient advertising platform. This enabled the Fire Authority to work in partnership with the *Belfast Telegraph* and to effectively target all of its readers by placing a rotation of advertisements (Figure 1) in various sites in the newspaper including the front page, the television page, Christmas TV guides and also free-of-charge advertisements when possible.

Figure 1: *Press ads*

4. Source: Independent Radio Sales, 2002.

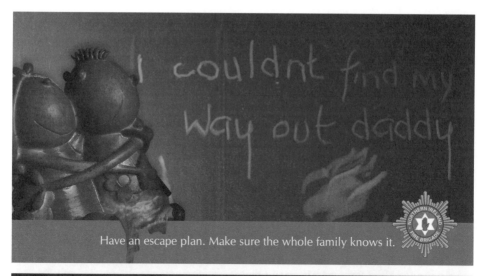

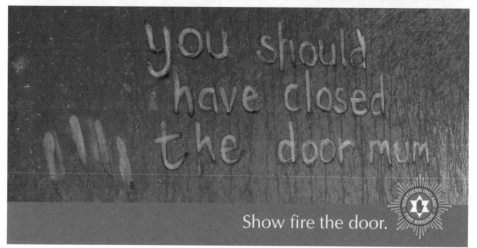

Figure 2: *Outdoor ads*

Key efficiency

- An extremely cost-effective initiative was devised to provide a 52-week press campaign on ad sites created specifically for the campaign.[5]
- Press was the ideal vehicle to allow us to convey a greater amount of detail on best fire safety practices.
- Monday title corners were secured in support of the Monday TV messaging.

Outdoor

Due to their sheer scale the 48-sheet panels delivered the emotive fire safety images and, with precise geographical targeting, provided coverage of the main population conurbations throughout Northern Ireland (Figure 2). This activity was deployed in January 2005, at a traditional heightened time of fire incidents.

Key efficiency

- 48-sheet posters were used for the campaign as 72% of people questioned recall outdoor advertising campaigns one week later.[6]
- Through internal Fire Brigade data we strategically bought sites where each creative would appear in the most relevant risk-group catchment areas by postcode.

THE RESULTS

How the advertising worked

Unquestionably, the advertising worked. The campaign consistently delivered advertising awareness when independently researched and, more importantly, it prompted action.

The campaign showed extraordinary results:

- 14% decrease in the total number of household fires year on year[7]
- 12% decrease in overall fire injuries year on year[8]
- 60% of respondents were influenced to take action and do something practical to prevent fire in the home as a direct result of the advertising.[9]

The research clearly showed an awareness based on the five fire hazards advertised and a change in behaviour as a result of each.

1. *Candle safety*: 39% decrease in fires caused by candles.[10]
2. *Escape plan*: 18% of respondents had prepared a fire safety plan.[11]
3. *Chip pan safety*: 18% decrease in chip pan-related fires.[12]
4. *Door safety*: 38% of respondents said that they now closed their doors before going to bed at night, an 11% increase on 2003.[13]
5. *Battery maintenance*: as a result of seeing the campaign, 17% said they fitted a smoke alarm and 42% said they tested their smoke alarm.[14]

---

5. This deal was struck following a fire at the Belfast Telegraph, during which the Fire Authority was instrumental in saving the press hall. An excellent rate was negotiated at this time.
6. Outdoor Media Association.
7. Fire Authority for Northern Ireland internal data/Northern Ireland Social Omnibus Survey
8–14. *Ibid.*

As such, there is no 'competitor' factor in this instance – all fire safety messaging is centralised through the Fire Authority for Northern Ireland. Historically, fires conform to a particular seasonality: incidents are higher October–February. The campaign was live across this period; it has therefore been measured against the highest-risk period and still shows a decrease in incidents across all hazards (Figures 3–16).

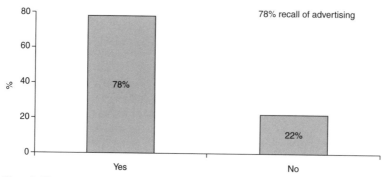

Figure 3: *Have you seen any advertising relating to fire safety in the last six months?*
Source: Northern Ireland Social Omnibus Survey

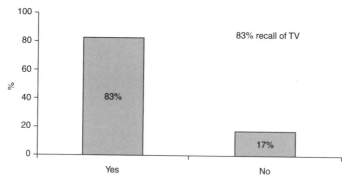

Figure 4: *Have you seen any TV advertising relating to fire risks within the last six months?*
Source: Northern Ireland Social Omnibus Survey

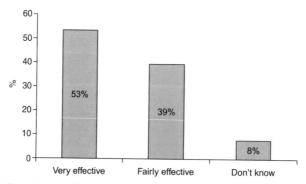

Figure 5: *How effective was the advertising?*
Source: Northern Ireland Social Omnibus Survey

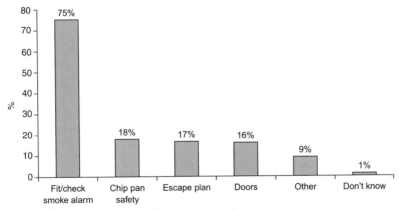

Figure 6: *What was the key message being communicated?*
Source: Northern Ireland Social Omnibus Survey

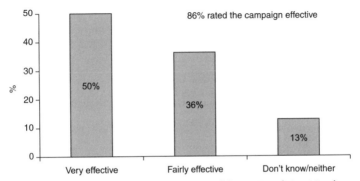

Figure 7: *How do you rate the overall effectiveness of the Fire Brigade in raising the public's awareness of fire safety/fire risks?*
Source: Northern Ireland Social Omnibus Survey

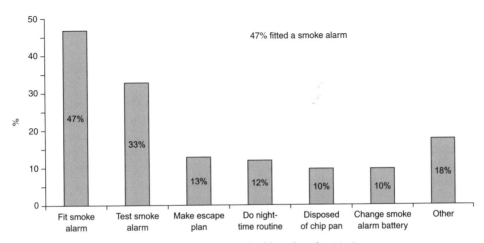

Figure 8: *What household changes have you made as a result of fire safety advertising?*
Source: Northern Ireland Social Omnibus Survey

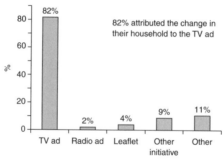

Figure 9: *What triggered the change in your household?*
Source: Northern Ireland Social Omnibus Survey

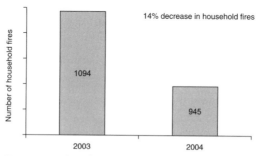

Figure 10: *Total number of household fires*
Source: Fire Authority Statistics

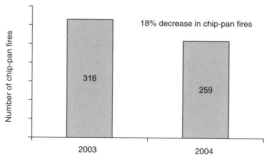

Figure 11: *Total chip pan-related fires*
Source: Fire Statistics Monitor

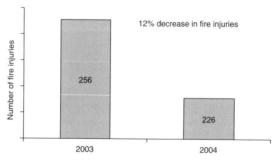

Figure 12: *Overall fire injuries*
Source: Fire Statistics Monitor

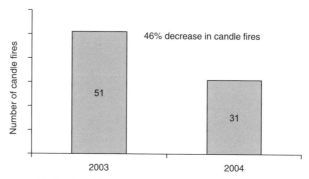

Figure 13: *Number of fires caused by candles*
Source: Fire Statistics Monitor

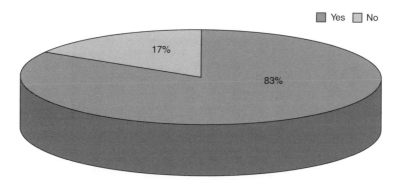

Figure 14: *Percentage of respondents who agreed the advertising had improved their awareness of fire safety issues, including the causes of fires*
Source: Northern Ireland Social Omnibus Survey

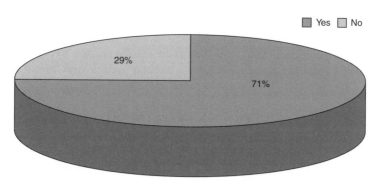

Figure 15: *Percentage of respondents who agreed the advertising changed how they think about fire safety*
Source: Northern Ireland Social Omnibus Survey

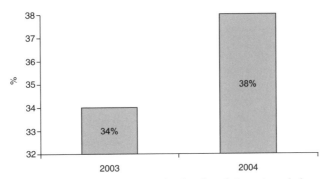

Figure 16: *Percentage of respondents who close doors before going to bed*
Source: Northern Ireland Social Omnibus Survey

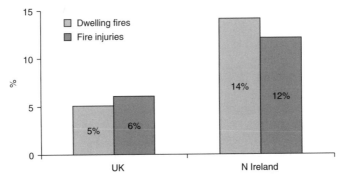

Figure 17: *Northern Ireland shows double the decrease in fires and injuries against the rest of the UK*
Source: Fire Statistics Monitor

It is worth noting that 2004 did show a general decrease in both dwelling fires and fire injuries nationally, a generic fire safety advertising campaign ran nationally at this time also. However, the targeted approach we took in Northern Ireland focusing on five fire hazards was clearly more effective in generating results; both measurements show that the decrease in Northern Ireland was more than double the national level of decrease (Figure 17).

More results
- 15% recalled seeing chip pan advertising, an increase of 6% from 2003.[15]
- A third of respondents (32%) checked their smoke alarms 'every week' with a further 20% checking alarms 'every two to three weeks' and 'monthly'.[16]

RETURN ON INVESTMENT

Clearly, the true value of this campaign's success is beyond financial measurement. The 12% reduction in injury year on year is the most significant return on -

15. Awareness of Fire Safety (Northern Ireland Social Omnibus Survey). Conducted by Research and Evaluation Services.
16. *Ibid.*

investment desired and would, reasonably considered, equate to many hundreds of thousands of pounds saved in medical cover and rehabilitation, as well as impact upon the labour market. An overall decrease in fires results in fewer appliances being called out and ultimately a reduction in operational costs. Other cost savings included:

- Private-sector sponsorship money secured to the value of £45,000.
- Sponsorships in kind delivered in excess of £280,000.
- Average media discount negotiated across campaign was 40%, a life-saving £110,000 off campaign costs.

The campaign was so successful that the agency was asked to produce Cantonese versions of the TV and outdoor to address Northern Ireland's largest ethnic community, the Chinese. We worked with the Chinese Welfare Association for Northern Ireland to achieve this. The National Safety Council has also expressed an interest in adopting the campaign for national rollout throughout Ireland as have a number of GB brigades.

CONCLUSION

In short, the results of this campaign were exceptional – there is clearly a definitive link between the advertising, the behavioural response and the decrease in fires and injury.

Each and every client objective was met and delivered.

Client Objective 1: To raise public awareness of the causes of fire.

Result
57% of respondents said that they remembered fire safety advertising campaigns in the last year.

Client Objective 2: To raise awareness of safety practices and routine.

Result
83% said the campaign resulted in improved awareness of fire safety issues including the causes of fires.

Client Objective 3: To reduce fatalities/injuries.

Result
Year-on-year reduction in injuries of 12%.

Client Objective 4: To effect behavioural change.

Result
71% said the advertising resulted in a change in how they thought about fire safety and 60% were influenced to do something practical about fire in the home.

Client Objective 5: To reduce fire and injury in line with national reductions.

Result
Northern Ireland decrease was 26%, 15% higher than the national figure of 11%.

7

Hidden Treasures of Cumbria

How to make £13.9m by marketing an overlooked destination

Principal authors: Annett Pecher and Lesley Deer, Alcazar
Media agency: MediaVest Manchester (Newcastle office)

EDITOR'S SUMMARY

Cumbria includes one of Britain's most popular tourism destinations – the Lake District. The areas outside the central Lake District area are much less visited by tourists due to existing negative perceptions. The Hidden Treasures of Cumbria campaign utilised a ground-breaking approach to destination marketing to overcome those negative opinions and attract new visitors to forgotten areas of Cumbria.

Through clever targeting, a single-minded strategy, and a distinctive creative execution, the Hidden Treasures campaign generated substantial results.

Unusually, the campaign used inserts to stimulate requests for a luxuriously printed 'coffee table' style brochure. This efficiently achieved generated responses, thereby stimulating interest in the region and ultimately increasing visitor numbers.

The result was that tourism grew significantly faster in the 'Hidden' regions of Cumbria than it did in the more famous Lake District. It is estimated that this added £13.9m to the local economy, for a marketing budget of only £315,000. Proof indeed that small budgets don't necessarily mean small effects.

INTRODUCTION

This paper will demonstrate how a groundbreaking approach to destination marketing overcame negative perceptions and attracted new visitors to forgotten areas of Cumbria. On a total campaign spend of £315,000 over two years this campaign generated £13.9m economic benefit for the regional economy.

BACKGROUND

In 2002 Cumbria Tourist Board (CTB) received funding to promote the lesser-known areas of Cumbria, and sought an agency to develop and implement a strategy that would have a profound economic impact. The campaign has been running successfully since spring 2003.

THE CHALLENGE

Cumbria includes one of Britain's most popular tourism destinations – the Lake District. The Central Lake District area is very successful in attracting large numbers of visitors every year. This is not surprising as Cumbria was, prior to this campaign, marketed with a positioning that the Lake District *is* Cumbria.

Before this campaign commenced, the impact of tourism in areas outside the central Lakes was significantly less.

In-depth research by Cumbria Tourist Board showed that some people had negative perceptions of the outer areas of Cumbria and did not perceive it as a destination to visit.[1]

The campaign was about getting more consumers to visit the 'overlooked bits'. It was categorically not allowed to feature any of the popular Lake District attractions (such as Windermere Lake Cruises) as support.

The UK holiday and short break market is a very competitive marketplace. One of the most successful players is VisitScotland, dominating the marketplace with clear branding and (for the tourism industry) a big budget. To put it into perspective, the annual CTB budget for this project was less than 2% of the VisitScotland annual advertising spend.

This was clearly a difficult task, which required creative strategic thinking and a client who was open to new ideas within an industry that is not renowned for innovation.

THE GROUNDBREAKING APPROACH

A new audience

Like many tourist boards, Cumbria's was using socio-demographic profiling to identify and target consumers for marketing communications at the time. However, for this project, profiling the existing visitor postcodes and then targeting them was

---

1. CTB Branding and Perception Research, 2002.

not an efficient route. After all, the current visitors did not have a tendency to visit the outer areas.

The client agreed to depart from the 'tried and tested' industry-standard tool and apply lifestyle profiling using TGI[2] instead. At the time no other tourist board was using lifestyle segmentation and even Visit Britain, the industry body, was still recommending socio-demographic profiling as the standard segmentation tool.

The strategy considered three main factors in relation to the audience.

1. Target consumers who already have a tendency to take holidays/breaks in the UK. With the current budget, trying to change behaviour and convince people who traditionally don't go on UK breaks to do so would have been highly wasteful and ineffective.
2. Select consumers who prefer holidays 'off the beaten track'. This type of person shows an interest in discovering new areas, areas that are not commonly known as tourism hotspots, which fitted the area this campaign was promoting.
3. A holiday in Cumbria is an active holiday – ideally suited for people who like walking and sight-seeing. We therefore selected consumers who disagreed with the statement 'On holiday I just want to eat, drink and lie in the sun.'

Based on the TGI survey it was estimated that the audience that fitted all three criteria was made up of 13.8 million consumers. This was the target audience for this campaign.

A tantalising creative idea

The creative idea was founded upon understanding the motivations of the target audience (i.e. people with a preference for 'holidays off the beaten track'). It was recognised that this was a set of people who would enjoy discovering a new destination. This is why the campaign idea of 'Hidden Treasures of Cumbria' was so successful in appealing to this audience.

A fresh media strategy

The main marketing activity was a postcard insert in selected quality press, offering a free 'Hidden Treasures of Cumbria' guide and entry into a prize draw for a break in Cumbria. This was also an innovation; traditionally Cumbria Tourist Board had been using classified and display advertising in the press rather than inserts.

Consumers who responded to the postcard insert were then sent the guide.

A distinctive creative execution

Our profiling showed that the target audience was very upmarket, well educated and made discerning purchase choices. This was a group of people who were sophisticated. This is why the creative strategy departed from the design style of a holiday guide and changed to the format of a coffee-table book (Figure 1). By using a size smaller than standard A4, luxurious paper stock and a different design style, the

---

2. TGI is a continuous survey of 25,000 UK consumers carried out quarterly by research company BMRB. It includes information on consumer lifestyle, motivations and attitudes, as well as purchasing behaviour and media habits.

Figure 1: *The 'Hidden Treasures of Cumbria' guide*

guide appealed to this sophisticated, new audience. The copy in the guide was written in a conversational style, taking the reader on a poetic journey, which is unusual within a UK holiday guide. The postcard insert also reflected the design ethos.

RESULTS

Attitudinal shift

In order to get people to visit the area the perceptions of the target audience had to be shifted to Cumbria being a desirable destination. There are several research studies that prove that the campaign was successful in achieving this shift.

During the initial testing of the creative work it became clear that the campaign counteracted respondents' preconceptions of the area:

'Wow there's so much to do in Cumbria.'

'Cumbria, I just thought of factories and working things, it's really opened my eyes.'

Brochure testing, focus group comments, January 2003

The 'Hidden Treasures of Cumbria' guide contained a feedback card for respondents to complete and send in. Those cards that were sent in (293) were collected and analysed, and the results showed that the guide not only extended people's knowledge of the area but also radically improved perception of the area.

'I thought I knew the area until I read the guide. Well done – we have a treasure trove only two hours' drive away.'

Feedback card respondent, 2003

The feedback card also showed that the creative execution (glossy, coffee-table book) perfectly matched the taste and preferences of this new, sophisticated audience.

'A beautiful publication'

'... a pleasure to read'

'Of a high, attractive standard'

'... I will keep [it] on bookshelf'

Feedback card respondents, 2003

All of this qualitative feedback is nice – but did the activity actually generate responses, visits and an economic return?

Responses

This was not a promotional insert from a well-known, loved brand. This postcard insert was promoting breaks in an area of which people had strong negative perceptions, and to an audience also exposed to a vast array of advertising from well-known destinations.

Despite this setting the insert achieved a response rate in national press of 2.8% in the first year and 2.4% in the second campaign year (see Table 1). This was achieved by using a message in line with the attitudes of the target audience and selecting media targeted at the correct lifestyle segment.

TABLE 1: RESPONSES TO INSERT IN NATIONAL PRESS

	2003	2004
No. of inserts	1,770,224	1,401,000
No. of responses	50,000	33,000
Response rate	2.8%	2.4%

Source: Alcazar, Carrier Direct

Visitors

People who responded to the inserts in the national press then received the 'Hidden Treasures' guide. Conversion research[3] shows that this guide was very successful in converting readers into visitors.

The conversion research used a telephone survey with a statistically significant sample of respondents (1382 in 2003, 1472 in 2004) to identify how many respondents had in fact visited the area for a day visit or overnight stay after receiving the guide. This included number of trips, average length of stay, group size, money spent and various other statistics.

We all know that it is easier to generate a repeat purchase than to win a new customer; that's why, in 2004, a proportion of the guides was also mailed to the respondents from the 2003 campaign. This was in addition to the responses from the postcard insert.

---

3. Conversion research was completed by Carrier Direct Marketing, which is a specialist within this area of tourism research.

In year one, when the campaign was targeting the north-west region,[3] the guide converted 38% of its readers into actual visitors to Cumbria (see Table 2). Of those visitors, 58% came for overnight stays and 42% on day trips. The majority of people came for more than one day trip and 35% of the overnight visitors came on more than one break.

In year two, when the campaign was targeting the Tyne Tees and Yorkshire region, the guide converted 26% of the readers to actual visitors to Cumbria (see Table 2). Of those, 77% came on overnight stays and 23% on day visits. The majority of people came for more than one day trip and 33% of the overnight visitors came on more than one break.

TABLE 2: VISITS GENERATED BY 'HIDDEN TREASURES' CAMPAIGN

	2003	2004
Target area	North-West	Tyne Tees & Yorkshire
Number of responses to postcard insert	50,000	33,000
Number mailed to previous respondents	–	17,000
Total number of guides distributed	50,000	50,000
Conversion rate	38%	26%
Day visits		
Proportion of day visits	42%	23%
Average number of day visits	7.3	3.4
Average group size on day visit (no. of people)	2.7	2.7
Number of day visit days	159,535	27,909
Overnight stays		
Proportion of overnight stays	58%	77%
Average number of overnight stays	1.9	1.8
Average group size on overnight stay (no. of people)	3	3
Average length of stay (no. nights)	3.5	4.3
Number of overnight stays	225,068	237,366
Total number of core visits	**384,603**	**265,275**

Source: CTB

The differences in conversion rate between 2003 and 2004 are due to the fact that different areas were targeted. The travel distance for people from the Tyne Tees and Yorkshire area (targeted in 2004) explains why there was a lower conversion rate but a higher proportion of overnight stays.

Economic return

Cumbria Tourist Board carries out economic impact calculations for all its campaigns. Applying statistics for average spend per trip, it can be calculated that the 'Hidden Treasures' campaign generated an economic impact of £6.6m in 2003 plus £7.3m in 2004.

This means that a campaign investment of £315,000 over two years has generated £13.9m economic return for the region of Cumbria. This equates to a return on investment of £44.13 per pound invested in the campaign.

---

4. As the budget was limited it was decided to concentrate on one region at the time, starting with the near markets. This is why, in year one, the North-West region was targeted and, in year two, Yorkshire and Tyne Tees.

Visitor figures

The economic impact calculation is based on existing statistics and a statistically sound telephone conversion research project. However, it is still a calculation. What do the actual visitor statistics for the region tell us about the success of the campaign?

The number of tourists who visited Cumbria increased in 2003, the first year of the 'Hidden Treasures' campaign, compared to 2002. Visitor figures for 2004 are not available at the time of going to press.

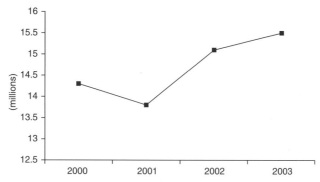

Figure 2: *Tourist numbers Cumbria overall, 2000–2003*
Source: CTB

However, this increase could be just a continuation of the increase in 2002, a positive continuation of a trend started much earlier than the 'Hidden Treasures' campaign.

When we compare the growth rates in visitor figures between the Lake District National Park area (Central Lakes) and the 'Hidden Treasures' area in Table 3, we can see that 2002 on 2001 the Lake District National Park area shows stronger growth than the 'Hidden Treasures' area. However, in 2003 compared to 2002, the 'Hidden Treasures' area shows stronger growth than the National Park. This proves that there is growth in visitor figures in the 'Hidden Treasures' area over and above any 'spillover' from growing visitor figures for the Central Lake District area.

TABLE 3: GROWTH IN NUMBER OF TOURISTS IN LAKE DISTRICT
NATIONAL PARK AREA AND 'HIDDEN TREASURES' AREA

No. of tourists Growth rates	Lake District NPA	'Hidden Treasures' area
2002 on 2001	11.0%	7.7%
2003 on 2002	1.2%	4.3%

Source: CTB

OTHER FACTORS

Tourism in general

There is a possibility that the response and conversion rate for the campaign has been influenced by a positive trend for UK holidays in general.

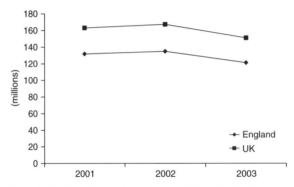

Figure 3: *Number of domestic tourism trips UK and England*
Source: UKTS

The contrary is the case: in both England and the UK, domestic tourism trips decreased in 2003 (Figure 3). So the 'Hidden Treasures' campaign achieved its success in the context of a difficult climate for domestic tourism. This makes the results even more impressive.

Weather

UK holidays and the weather – the two are intrinsically linked. A warm, dry summer can persuade more people to stay at home and explore their own backyard rather than go abroad. So was the weather particularly favourable for UK breaks in 2003 and 2004?

2003 proved to be a relatively dry and sunny year compared to the UK long-term average. Rainfall was below average for all months apart from May, June, July and December (see Figure 4). Sunshine for the North of England was average or above average for all months, but particularly for February and March (see Figure 5).

Looking at the weather charts one would expect more visits to take place in February, March, April or August, September, October. These were the periods that were sunnier and dryer than expected at that time of year.

However, when we look at the information from the CTB conversion research (see Figures 6 and 7) we can see that most people who received the 'Hidden

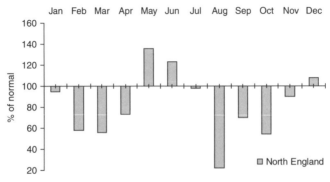

Figure 4: *Rainfall anomaly, 2003*
Source: Met Office

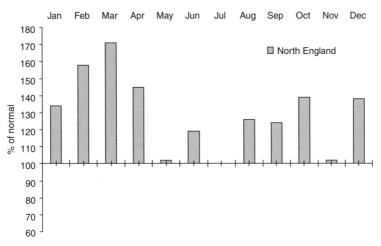

Figure 5: *Sunshine anomaly, 2003*
Source: Met Office

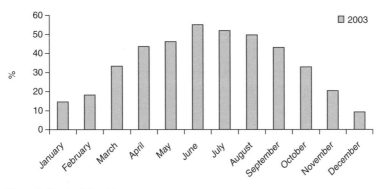

Figure 6: *Month of day visit*
Source: Carrier Direct conversion research, 2003

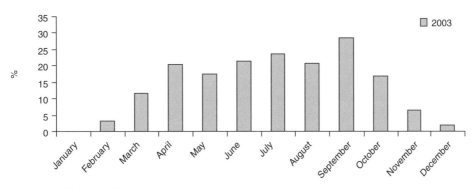

Figure 7: *Month of overnight visit*
Source: Carrier Direct conversion research, 2003

Treasures' guide actually went on day visits in June, July and August. This period does not match the strong 'fine weather' periods as it includes June and July, which were 'average' and wet. Most overnight visits took place in September, July and June – of which only September is one of the particularly good weather months. There is no visible link between periods of above average weather and the months when 'Hidden Treasures' guide readers visited Cumbria in 2003.

2004 was not favourable with regards to the weather in the North of England. The months with above average sunshine were February and December, neither of which are key periods for UK breaks. When we compare when 'Hidden Treasures' guide readers actually visited with the periods of above average weather there is no visible link.

CONCLUSION

This case study has proven that the 'Hidden Treasures' campaign broke the mould of UK destination marketing by applying industry-leading audience targeting, a single-minded strategy, distinctive creative execution and a commitment to research to generate substantial results. It demonstrates that tourism campaigns, when strategically planned and executed, are a very worthwhile investment and do generate economic benefits for a region. Most of all it illustrates that a small-budget campaign can be highly effective.

8

Northern Ireland Office – Community Safety Unit

Changing behaviour to help reduce theft from vehicles

Principal authors: Mike Fleming and Damian Donnelly,
AV Browne Advertising

EDITOR'S SUMMARY

One of the reasons why theft from vehicles is such a problem is that the public at large are so complacent about it. Too many people leave their valuables on display, providing temptation for opportunistic thieves.

In Northern Ireland, A V Browne tried to change that by highlighting the absurd way drivers practically ask for their valuables to be stolen. Great creative work was complemented with clever media thinking. The result was an integrated campaign that reduced reported thefts in the test region by 33%.

Proving effectiveness in cases like this is never easy, but the judges felt that a strong case was made. In particular, the use of outdoor to target high-crime areas allowed a 'test and control' approach that revealed the campaign's effects particularly clearly.

This is good, clear, simple exposition of how to use communications to help solve a pressing social problem.

INTRODUCTION

Where is your car right now? In the car park at your office? Parked in the street outside your house? In a multi-storey? Take a moment to think about it and then try to remember what you've left sitting on the passenger seat, on the rear seats or even in the footwells. A CD. A jacket. Even some small change. You're worried now, aren't you? Best go and check (reading this IPA paper can wait for a few minutes), because even the smallest item is enough to tempt an opportunist thief.

In a nutshell, that is the threat we had to combat in our ad campaign: the opportunist. And because thieves are not prone to be swayed by advertising messages, what we had to do was to change the behaviour of potential victims: the motoring public. Taking away temptation removes the problem.

BACKGROUND

The stealing of valuable items from parked vehicles doesn't just have an impact on the victims of the crime. Dealing with it takes up a considerable amount of police resource; paying for it hits insurance premiums for everyone; and fear of it affects retail trade in the worst affected areas. The effects are wide reaching and often traumatic. In its 2002 Community Safety Strategy report, 'Creating a Safer Northern Ireland through Partnership', the Northern Ireland Office (NIO) outlined its commitment to 'lessening the impact of crime by working with other criminal justice agencies to maintain and develop policies aimed at preventing or reducing the threat of crime'. To support this objective, HM Treasury set the NIO a series of crime reduction targets to be met by April 2007, one of which was to reduce theft from vehicles by 10%. Tasked with this target, the NIO approached AV Browne to roll out a pre-Christmas test campaign (15 November–31 December 2004) in the Greater Belfast, Lisburn City, Newtownabbey and Castlereagh areas, across seven Police District Command Units (total population: 1.2 million). These areas were the seven worst affected by this sort of crime according to the Police Service of Northern Ireland (PSNI) statistics for the previous 12 months, accounting for over 55% of *all* thefts from vehicles across Northern Ireland's 26 District Command Units. If this proved a success, the strategy would be adopted on a province-wide basis.

MARKETING OBJECTIVES

To achieve the stated 10% reduction in theft from vehicles the NIO set out a very clear marketing objective: 'To raise awareness of this type of crime and influence motorists to be less *laissez-faire* in their attitude towards it.' If successful, this behavioural shift would bring down instances of the crime by removing the temptation to commit it in the first place. At its core, it is a simple, logical crime prevention brief. To prove the success or otherwise of the campaign, independent post-activity awareness and attitudinal research was commissioned and would be augmented by the hard evidence contained in crime statistics for the period of the campaign – and hopefully beyond. It was also our intention to contribute positively to a downturn in the public's fear of crime, a hugely stressful and debilitating affliction in Northern Ireland.

'Crime and the fear of crime can destroy the lives of innocent victims.'

Paul Murphy, Secretary of State for Northern Ireland, 2004

If we could point out a way to beat the thugs we would give, for once, the upper hand to the general public. This empowerment was core to our thinking and drove the agency team.

THE TASK

People are, by nature, lazy. This is a huge generalisation and we mean no offence by it. But they are.

As part of our strategic formulation process we walked the streets, looking through the windows of parked cars, marvelling at the treasure trove of valuables left idly scattered on seats, parcel shelves and poorly hidden in footwells. We even got stopped by the police – our activity had aroused suspicion. We obviously wouldn't make great thieves, but our street research did confirm the unbelievable bounty sitting on the street just waiting to be nicked. Briefcases and handbags; mobile phones and Bluetooth headsets; CDs and iPods. We even saw wallets, laptops and golf clubs. Quite how people believed this stuff would still be there on their return defied logic. It takes less than a minute to put things in the boot; to remove the face of your stereo; to think. But do we do it? No, because it takes time. We didn't either until this campaign came along. However, we are now all ardent stashers, hiders and concealers. The challenge was to make the general public just as fastidious.

We also spoke to the police and, crucially, to local insurance companies to discover what items were generally targeted. The results were amazing. Items as small as a single pound coin, a packet of cigarettes and an old jacket were cited. Crazy to think that by leaving small change on view in your car you could end up having to pay hundreds of pounds to replace a side window. To prick the public's conscience and make them aware of their invitational attitude was our biggest challenge. And we overcame it with humour, pointing out how ridiculous their current actions were. And we also did it with a very modest budget. Just £87,000 had been allocated to this test campaign. It's not much to cover such a large geographical area and target such a large proportion of the adult population.

THE STRATEGIC SOLUTION

We discovered on our walks around the streets that people were turning their modes of transport into display cabinets for all sorts of goodies. They were basically signposting their vehicles as potential targets.

What we needed to do was dramatise their behaviour. Exaggerate and bring to life in a big way that they were putting their valuable property at risk. If we could over-emphasise the ridiculousness of the situation it would bring home the reality.

They might laugh. They might think, 'that's ridiculous', but they would also hopefully relate it to their own behaviour and quickly change it. The simple insight we discovered in all our research with the NIO, the police and with insurance companies, was that thieves will pinch anything. This discovery shaped our campaign theme.

Our media strategy reflected the most appropriate opportunities to reach our target audience. As they were driving cars and vans around our geo-specific test area we could accurately target them in their vehicles with a combination of radio and Adshel executions. Rarely do we get the chance with both these mediums to elicit direct action, but in this instance we did. We also tailored the weighting of the outdoor campaign to be biased towards areas (even the specific roads and streets) that were particularly blighted by this type of crime. This information was drawn from 2003 NIO Crime Statistics.

Self-help also played a part. As mentioned above, we wanted to put the power back into the hands of the public and take it away from the thieves. We did this by creating a leaflet that drivers could put on their dashboards to tell potential thieves that there was nothing of value in their vehicle.

THE IDEA

Our creative strategy and subsequent iterations were drawn from the simple fact that thieves will steal anything and, by leaving valuables on view, you are giving them an open invitation. Quite simply, *if they see it, they'll steal it*. This unequivocal statement of fact became our campaign theme.

Adshels

Two simple, powerful visuals demonstrated the vehicle owners 'signposting' of their property (Figure 1). Graffiti and van graphics were used to point out how obvious valuables are to thieves. This was further reinforced with the bold statement 'Valuables on view are this obvious to thieves'.

Tactical press

In press we used a series of small classified ads in appropriate sections to highlight where the public's property could end up if they weren't vigilant (Figure 2).

Radio

On radio we translated our ridiculous signposting device into an aural comedy. Car drivers announced to the entire street through a megaphone exactly what they were leaving on view.

Leaflet

We developed an interactive leaflet (Figure 3), which detailed the most frequently stolen items, gave some simple practical crime prevention advice and also

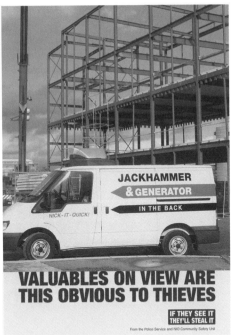

Figure 1: *Adshel executions*

Figure 2: *Press ads*

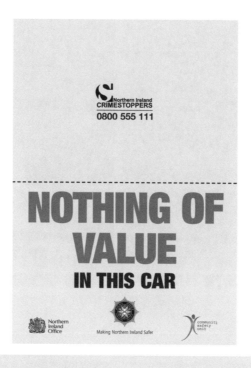

PROTECT YOUR VALUABLES.

EITHER LOCK THEM AWAY OR TAKE THEM WITH YOU.

Nothing attracts a thief more quickly than the prospect of easy pickings. And valuables left on view in parked vehicles are one of the easiest. A quick smash, a fast grab and before you know it your mobile phone, handbag or stereo is gone.

However, there are easy ways you can help to reduce the risk of becoming a victim of this kind of opportunistic crime.

Nothing attracts a thief more quickly than the prospect of easy pickings.

On the opposite page is a handy, detachable checklist of crime prevention measures. Keep it in your car to remind you of the easy ways to protect your property.

On the reverse side is a message that you can leave on display on the dashboard of your car. It will tell potential thieves that there is nothing of value in your car.

WHAT THIEVES ARE ON THE LOOK OUT FOR.

The 10 most stolen items from vehicles in Northern Ireland.

1. **Audio Equipment**
2. **Tools**
3. **Mobile Phones**
4. **Handbags/Purses/Briefcases**
5. **Cash (including small change)**
6. **Driving licences and other documents**
7. **Cheque Books and Cards**
8. **Clothing**
9. **Computer Equipment**
10. **Luggage**

Thieves will steal anything. So the simple rule is, don't leave anything on view.

TAKE 60 SECONDS TO PROTECT YOUR VALUABLES

- Park in a secure or well lit location
- If you can, remove the stereo or at least the face plate of it
- Remove valuables and personal possessions
- Lock bulky items in the boot
- If you can, leave the glove box open to show that there is nothing of value in it
- Lock all windows and doors

From the Police Service and NIO Community Safety Unit

Figure 3: *Interactive leaflet*

incorporated a tear-off section with the message 'Nothing of value in this car' – a card that could be left on the car dashboard, diverting unwanted attention away from the vehicle. This leaflet was distributed as an insert in local press and also through local policing initiatives.

Budget

As stated previously, the total creative, production and media budget for this campaign was just £87,000.

RESULTS

There is a simple logic to the way we measured the results for this campaign, based both on qualitative research and actual crime statistics. The qualitative research model (carried out independently by Millward Brown) took representative samples of Northern Irish households across 50 sampling points in Greater Belfast, which were selected with a probability proportional to the adult population for each point.

The results can be broken down into the following four sections.

1. *Did the target audience see the communication as planned?* Of the 700 people interviewed, 14% mentioned the Adshels unprompted (Figure 4) and 35% the radio campaign (Figure 5). To put these figures into context, the average and acceptable levels of awareness are benchmarked by Millward Brown as Normative Data Comparison (NDC) figures based on years of experience in the

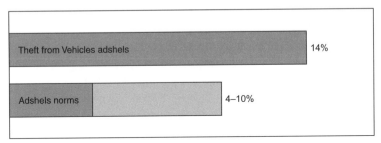

Figure 4: *Unprompted awareness, Adshels – 'Theft from Vehicles' campaign vs norms*
Source: Millward Brown, March 2005

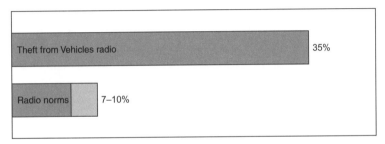

Figure 5: *Unprompted awareness, radio – 'Theft from Vehicles' campaign vs norms*
Source: Millward Brown, March 2005

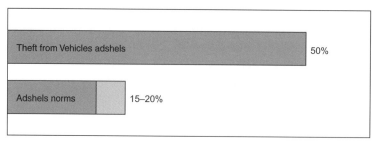

Figure 6: *Prompted awareness, Adshels – 'Theft from Vehicles' campaign vs norms*
Source: Millward Brown, March 2005

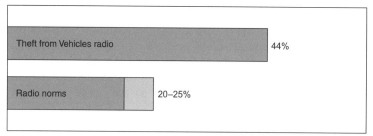

Figure 7: *Prompted awareness, radio – 'Theft from Vehicles' campaign vs norms*
Source: Millward Brown, March 2005

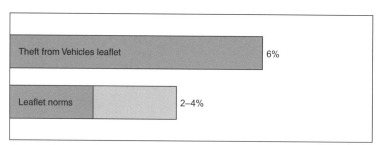

Figure 8: *Unprompted awareness, leaflet – 'Theft from Vehicles' campaign vs norms*
Source: Millward Brown, March 2005

market research industry. The unprompted NDC for Adshels is 4–10% (Figure 4) and, for radio, 7–10% (Figure 5). Our campaign outperformed these established benchmarks. Indeed, the margin grew even greater when the respondents were prompted with visuals and radio commercials. Against an NDC of 15–20% for Adshels, our campaign performed strongly at 50% (Figure 6), while our radio awareness rose to 44% when prompted, against an NDC of 20–25% (Figure 7). Unprompted awareness of our leaflet was just as credible resulting in a score of 6% against an NDC of 2–4% (Figure 8). Tactical press was not researched due to budgetary constraints. So it's a resounding 'yes' to our first measurement.

2. *Was the intended message conveyed?* A total of 89% of respondents, when shown the Adshels and on hearing the radio, said they 'got' the message with

67% actually stating that their understanding was that 'thieves will steal anything, so don't leave anything on view'.[1]

3. *Did this, in turn, cause a change in behaviour?* Of the respondents who were aware of the campaign before being interviewed, 68% said that it had made them change their behaviour; 33% said that they now made a conscious effort to remove valuables from their vehicles; 17% said they now locked valuables in the boot; the remainder stated that they either parked in well-lit areas or ensured that they locked all doors and made sure windows and sunroofs were closed tight.[2]

4. *Did this shift in behaviour fulfil the original marketing objectives?* Of course, the real test of this campaign was whether these attitudinal and behavioural changes actually translated into a downturn in thefts from vehicles. Comparing the same 46-day period from 2003, there were, on average, 33% fewer reported thefts across the seven District Command Unit (DCU) areas during our campaign. This translates into 70 fewer crimes.[3]

ISOLATING THE ADVERTISING EFFECT

Although all DCUs in Northern Ireland showed an average crime decrease of 20% during this period, our geo-targeted areas improved upon this figure by 13%. This is already 3% ahead of HM Treasury's target for 2007.

And bearing in mind that, while these seven DCUs represented 27% of the entire DCU complement in Northern Ireland, they accounted for over 55% of all thefts from vehicles in 2003, our campaign can be judged a success.

LONG-TERM EFFECTS

Although much too early to judge accurately, it is perhaps (and hopefully!) indicative of the memorability of our message that thefts from vehicle crime rose only 2% in the 46 days after our campaign, compared with a rise of 24% in the previous year. Only time will tell.[4]

CONCLUSION

The figure of 70 fewer crimes in a 46-day period is not quite two per day, but it is close. It is 70 fewer windows to replace; 70 fewer insurance claims; 70 fewer ruined Christmases; 70 fewer cases for police to spend time on; and 70 fewer people who fall under the title 'a victim of crime'. Our campaign will roll out again across Northern Ireland in the next few months. Testament indeed to our client's confidence in its success. Perhaps the last word should go to them:

---

1. Source: Millward Brown, March 2005.
2. Source: Millward Brown, March 2005.
3. Source: NIO crime statistics, May 2005.
4. Source: NIO crime statistics, May 2005.

'The aim of the project was to raise awareness of the problem of thefts from vehicles and to reduce incidents in the target areas. In comparison to the previous year, and taking into account the expected reduction due to overall decreasing crime levels, there has been a notable fall in theft from vehicle crime.'

PSNI Analysis Centre Report, May 2005

9

Oral Cancer Awareness

How Henry helped save lives (and save the NHS £695k)

Principal author: Margaret Byrnes, The Bridge
Media agency: The Media Shop

EDITOR'S SUMMARY

Oral cancer, though just as deadly as other kinds of cancer, is much less well known and understood by the general public. This campaign aimed to raise awareness of the disease, and persuade people with possible symptoms of oral cancer to get them checked out early on.

However, a campaign like this is a delicate balancing act. Scare people too much, and you risk swamping the NHS with 'the worried well'. Careful development research led to a campaign that hit exactly the right note.

The results were just what the doctor ordered. Awareness of the disease and understanding of its symptoms increased, leading more sufferers to present their symptoms at an early stage.

Comparison of advertised versus non-advertised regions makes it clear that this shift was definitely due to the campaign. The payback is clear too. Simply getting patients to present earlier on saved the NHS around £695,000 in medical costs – nearly three times the cost of the campaign. And the true long-term payback, in terms of lives saved, will be priceless.

Figure 1: *Henry*

WHY ORAL CANCER?

The man pictured in Figure 1 is Henry – a typical west of Scotland middle-aged man – drinks a bit too much, smokes, avoids going to the dentist or doctor, and had never heard of oral cancer, much less the signs or symptoms. Henry had a sore spot in his mouth that wouldn't go away, he ignored it for a while and eventually went to the doctor. He was diagnosed with oral cancer. Because Henry presented late, the cancer was large and deep, his treatment lifesaving but invasive. Nowadays, Henry has difficulty speaking and swallowing, but he owes his life to the doctors. Left untreated any longer Henry would have died.

Each year over 530 people in Scotland are told that they have mouth cancer – only half of them survive for more than five years, often because the cancer has been detected too late. Although it is a debilitating disease, it can be treated successfully if it is detected early and survival rates could improve by up to 30%.

The West of Scotland Cancer Awareness Project (WoSCAP) hypothesised that a successful oral cancer campaign could save the lives of people like Henry.

WoSCAP is a partnership between five west of Scotland NHS Boards and is funded by lottery money. In July 2003, WoSCAP commissioned the Centre for Social Marketing (CSM) at Strathclyde University to conduct research to inform the strategic development of a mouth cancer campaign. The key learnings from this stage of research were as follows.

- Spontaneous awareness of types of cancer focuses most commonly on breast, lung, prostate and skin cancers, with bowel, cervix, throat, pancreas and testicular cancer mentioned less frequently.
- Among the target audience low awareness is equated with low prevalence – so mouth cancer was not on the radar.
- The concept of early detection of cancer, and hence early treatment leading to improved outcomes, is relatively familiar. While the benefits were accepted at a

logical and objective level, at an emotional and personal level cancer-related fears meant there was considerable reluctance to confront the issue.

- While keen to advise 'others' to go forward with symptoms, many would be much more hesitant to do so themselves.

An additional study of 1000 people by MRUK found the following.

- Awareness of mouth cancer was negligible, with only 6% spontaneous awareness and only 45% prompted.
- A high proportion of individuals could not name any symptoms of oral cancer at all (54%).

RISK OF RUNNING AN ADVERTISING CAMPAIGN

At face value, the evidence collected provided a strong case for running an advertising campaign. However, a mass-media communication strategy was not without risk. There was widespread concern among all stakeholders that a poorly devised campaign could cost lives, not save them.

The big worry with this campaign was that we might swamp the health service. The everyday nature of the signs and symptoms risked that large numbers of the 'worried well' would descend upon their GP or dentist, meaning everyone would have to wait that much longer for an initial appointment, then that more cases would be referred to the hospital services where, again, waiting time would be affected. The knock-on effects to diagnosis and treatment times would be terrible.

The creative development and media-planning processes had to address this concern.

DEVELOPING THE ADVERTISING

The advertising objectives were:

- to raise awareness of mouth cancer and the importance of early detection
- to arm people with what signs to look out for and what action to take should they find something.

Five creative routes were developed to explore the appropriate approach, appropriate tone of voice and appropriate language.

1. 'Survival' sought to challenge the fatalism around cancer and help give hope to the people with symptoms. The importance of getting help early was established through testimonials from people who have gone through it.
2. 'Niggling worries' are part of the mindscape when it comes to cancer. We explored a route that examined this and how we play games with ourselves and bury our heads in the sand.
3. 'Humour' explored the language, the excuses we use and how to talk about symptoms. It was explored for its ability to break through the barriers.

4. 'Here comes the science bit'. We tried to use science in a detached and rational way to explore whether detachment could lead to the required change in behaviour.

5. 'Habits' explored the quirks of human nature and the ceremony that some people have when looking at themselves in the mirror. The idea was to show them how easy it can be to self-check as part of what is already a routine.

The research found that survivor testimonies had most impact because they provided a compelling way of linking the symptoms with the health consequences. Cancer is a frightening disease and this campaign was seen as presenting 'new' information about a disease that the target audience had little or no knowledge about. There had been an underlying disbelief that the symptoms, which often appeared trivial, could be cancer. The use of real people added a credibility that helped overcome this underlying disbelief. A 40-second TV commercial and radio ad formed the core of the campaign, with noticeboard posters, leaflets and PR supporting the broadcast work.

The implications of ignoring your symptoms were dramatised by the endline 'If in doubt, get it checked out' (see Figure 2) and in the contrast between the first two survivors, Robert and Harvey, who went to the doctor early and who have had successful treatment, and Henry who left it very late and had most of his jaw and tongue removed, resulting in speech difficulty.

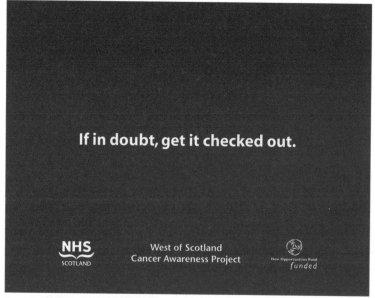

Figure 2: *Endframe of the television ad*

THE RESULTS

The campaign was evaluated using two studies. First, CSM at the University of Strathclyde conducted pre- and post-campaign research. The research took place in the campaign and control areas, and took the form of semi-structured in-home interviews. The sample reflected the age and social class of the key targets for the campaign. A baseline was taken in July–August 2003 before the campaign, with the follow-up in March–April 2004.

To claim success we would need to demonstrate not only that people had seen the advertising, but that they had understood it, that it had made them more aware of the symptoms of oral cancer, and that they had taken some action as a result of that knowledge. This increase in knowledge and understanding would be among those with symptoms but also among the wider at-risk population.

Awareness of the campaign

Were people aware of the advertising? Prompted awareness of the TV commercial in the intervention area reached 83%. Given that those in the research sample were all over 40 years old this is a particularly high awareness figure as advertising awareness notoriously tails off among the 45+ age group as they tend to be less engaged with advertising in general. This compared to 23% prompted awareness in the control area (see Figure 3).

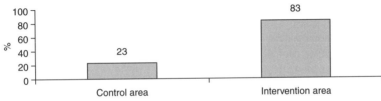

Figure 3: *Prompted advertising awareness*

Understanding of the advertising message

The spontaneous responses in Table 1 suggest that people understand the subject matter: They:

- understand the need to raise awareness of mouth cancer
- feel an emotional involvement with the testimonials
- can relate this back to themselves and their family.

TABLE 1: SPONTANEOUS RESPONSES TO TV AD

Base: (483) all respondents in the campaign area who have seen the TV ad	%
Raises awareness of mouth cancer	50
'Makes you think about mouth cancer'	19
'Get it checked out'	35
'Watch out for changes'	5
Emotional response	35
Sympathy for the people in the ad	18
Relief	2
Shock that the symptoms are so everyday	4
Worried for [Henry]	5
Frightened how serious mouth cancer is	5
Personalisation of the message	32

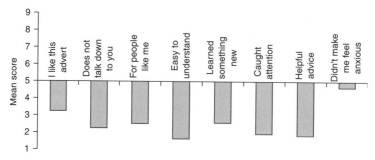

Figure 4: *Prompted responses to TV commercial*

At a prompted level we can also see that respondents understood the content of the advertising. A nine-point semantic differential scale was used to ask respondents to rate the advert, with 1 being 'totally agree' and 9 being 'totally disagree' with a range of statements. Figure 4 shows very positive ratings for all criteria. The bottom half of the chart is positive and, the nearer to 1, the more positive.

We can see that respondents found it likeable, easy to understand, for people like them, and not patronising. They also felt that it caught their attention and that they learned something new.

The anxiety rating of 4.65 is where we would want it to be: well short of panic but enough for people to feel some concern about the message and the need to act.

Knowledge and awareness of mouth cancer

So they had seen the commercial and they thought that it was impactful and easy to understand. But what had happened to their knowledge about oral cancer?

Table 2 shows awareness of cancers. Baseline awareness of mouth cancer was very low. Both spontaneous and prompted levels have increased in the intervention area.

TABLE 2: AWARENESS OF VARIOUS CANCERS

Base: all respondents	Unprompted awareness				Prompted and unprompted awareness			
	Campaign area		Control area		Campaign area		Control area	
	Baseline (571) %	Follow-up (583) %	Baseline (351) %	Follow-up (351) %	Baseline (571) %	Follow-up (583) %	Baseline (351) %	Follow-up (351) %
Lung cancer	68	66	65	62	99	98	100	98
Breast cancer	66	60	61	64	99	99	98	99
Bowel/colorectal cancer	45	36	51	47	96	97	97	98
Skin cancer	27	18	27	21	97	97	97	97
Prostate cancer	25	22	23	32	92	94	93	96
Stomach cancer	20	16	20	23	90	90	87	91
Cervical cancer	20	17	17	18	91	91	89	89
Testicular cancer	17	8	12	12	87	88	88	86
Mouth/oral cancer	**12**	**16**	**11**	**12**	**82**	**92**	**80**	**85**
Ovarian cancer	11	9	10	15	84	85	84	83
Bladder cancer	3	3	5	5	61	65	58	65

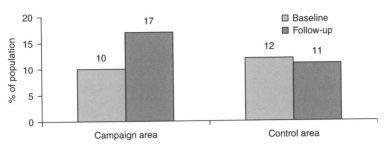

Figure 5: *Saliency of mouth cancer (conversations)*

And, though too complex to show in Table 2, prompted awareness of mouth cancer among those who have seen the TV advert reached an almost universal level of 94%.

Not only were people more aware of mouth cancer, they were more willing to talk about it. After the campaign, almost twice as many people in the intervention area held a conversation about mouth cancer as had done so before the campaign (see Figure 5). In the control area the figure reduced marginally.

What about detailed knowledge of the symptoms? Figure 6 shows that we not only improved awareness of the signs but that the persistence message also penetrated. This was not seen in the control area, where ulcers remained at 34%, sores 11%, any patch 7% and persistence 11%.

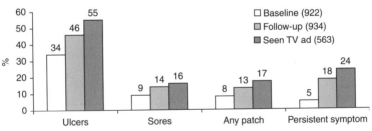

Figure 6: *Awareness of symptoms in campaign area*

Campaign impact on primary and secondary care

A second study of the effects of the campaign was conducted post-campaign among patients attending the 11 secondary care rapid referral clinics across the campaign area. This would be the acid test. The advertising objectives were to raise awareness of mouth cancer and the importance of early detection, and to tell them what action to take should they find something. Quantitative independent research measured the impact of the campaign on primary and secondary care.

The research took the form of a self-completion questionnaire. The results of this study were very encouraging.

- A total of 64% of the sample (583) had heard or seen a campaign about mouth cancer.
- Of the 343 patients who said they had seen a campaign about mouth cancer, 92% reported having seen a TV advert and 7% having heard a radio advert.

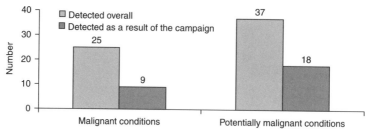

Figure 7: *Analysis of cancers and pre-malignant conditions detected*

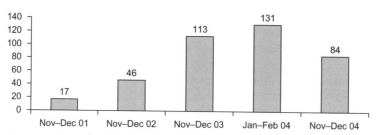

Figure 8: *Referrals to Oral Medicine (Dental School) for suspicious lesions*

• Of those who had seen the campaign, 68% responded that it had encouraged them to seek advice more quickly. Given people's usual tendency to discount the effect of advertising on their behaviour, this figure is very high.
• Critically the campaign had not generated the numbers of 'worried well' that had been feared at the planning stage.

Figure 7 shows the analysis of the cancers and pre-malignant conditions that were presented. Pre-malignant conditions are conditions that can be treated successfully and monitored to prevent cancer developing in the future.

Research suggests that 68% of people presented earlier than they would have done – that's 42 people (68% of 25 plus 37) who are likely to require less expensive, less invasive treatment. It also suggested that 27 (9 plus 18) malignant or potentially malignant conditions would have presented later or not at all had it not been for the campaign.

When compared to previous years we can see the very real impact the campaign has had and continues to make. Figure 8 compares the number of referrals to Oral Medicine (Dental School) for suspicious lesions. The campaign resulted in a 185% increase in numbers and, long after the campaign had ended, numbers remain at almost double.

We would argue that we demonstrated clear success: in awareness, in understanding, in knowledge and in action.

DISCOUNTING OTHER FACTORS

The WoSCAP campaign is the first of its kind in Scotland, and has been carefully examined and analysed with the use of data collected pre- and post-campaign in both the campaign area and the control area.

These data allow us to conclude that the only difference between the two areas was the campaign.

Additionally, we can confirm that no other factors were at play (e.g. storyline about mouth cancer in a TV soap or a famous person being reported as diagnosed with mouth cancer).

RETURN ON INVESTMENT

The real return on investment is to be measured in lives – the lives of people like Henry. However, it is still important to look at this project from a financial perspective.

The total advertising campaign budget was £250,000, which divided by 27 people equals £9259. Treatment costs to the NHS are complex and vary by individual, but the average cost of hospital care and operation alone for a single patient with advanced oral cancer is £25,000 with oncology costing a further £10,000. This does not include costs for diagnosis, radiology, intensive care, ongoing outpatient care, speech therapy, restorative dentistry and the cost of recurring disease. On this basic cost analysis we may have saved 27 (the cases that would not have presented early had it not been for the campaign) multiplied by £25,741 (the average cost of treatment minus the average cost of advertising), which equals a saving of £695,000 – an ROI of 278% in six months. In addition, there are the savings generated by the 41 cases that presented earlier than they would otherwise have done.

We are confident that, given the ongoing reported positive impact of the campaign by service providers, the NHS will see a continued return.

CONCLUSION

Has the campaign been a success? A patient from the Southern General Hospital who presented early and is now doing well, says, 'I saw that man on the telly and I thought I'd better go and see about this sharpish.' True story.

10
Tizer

Tizer turns teenage but won't change its colour!

Principal author: Lorna Hawtin, BDH\TBWA
Contributing authors: Chris McDonald and Peter Harris, BDH\TBWA

EDITOR'S SUMMARY

Tizer used to be a minor player in the carbonated drinks market, mainly bought by mums for their children. Kids themselves were much less likely to buy it – it wasn't cool enough for them. To them, Tizer was the odd kid hanging out at the edge of the gang, rather than one of the in-crowd.

BDH\TBWA decided to make a virtue of Tizer's 'oddness'. In particular, they decided to exploit the brand's unusual colour. Several new flavours were launched, but, against convention, each new flavour was red. The relaunch was supported with an integrated campaign that proudly proclaimed Tizer's redness.

As planned, kids started to re-appraise the brand, and began to try the new flavours. Sales increased in the impulse sector, proof that they were buying it for themselves.

The paper proves that the campaign drove those impulse sales. But more importantly, there is evidence that it helped to increase distribution in supermarkets as well. The judges felt that this provided a good basis for long-term growth, and a brighter future for the brand.

INTRODUCTION

This paper describes how Tizer, a tertiary brand in the competitive carbonated soft drinks market, became re-energised in the eyes of a difficult teenage audience, using the power of integrated communications and disruptive thinking.

BACKGROUND

When this story begins, there was only one flavour of Tizer: Original. It was a long-established carbonated soft drink with a 'blended' fruit flavour. Its vibrant red colour was its only differentiator and many consumers still saw the brand in the context of its 'jelly and ice cream' heritage.

It had always been consistently overshadowed by the influence and investment levels of key competitors. Brands such as Coca-Cola, Fanta, Dr Pepper and Tango had used heavy investments to launch new variants, run promotions and ensure their brand imagery kept up to date:

'They've seen adverts on the TV or their friends are talking about it, and you go into a shop and they say "Can I try this?"'

Mum of a teenage boy, Clarity Research, 2004

And when a brand isn't at the forefront of consumers' minds, it's rarely a priority for the trade. Tizer suffered from distribution pressures across both the grocery multiples and impulse channels, increasingly struggling to maintain facings and promotional resilience in the face of heavy competition and a noisy marketplace.

Tizer's traditional strategy had been to maintain its 1.3% share of the flavoured carbonates market, by focusing on the major-multiples channel. Heavy promotional tactics were used to court the big-volume soft drinks buyers: mums of teenagers. Mums were familiar with the brand and could be targeted at point of purchase, leaving the limited marketing budget free to keep the brand 'ticking along' at a low level.

Meanwhile, the core consumers of soft drinks, young teenage boys, increasingly saw Tizer as a brand that mum bought rather than one they'd choose themselves. As a result, they only tended to drink it in the home. It wasn't viewed as a 'cool' brand you'd drink in front of your mates. In functional terms, they often described it as 'non-descript' or 'a little too sweet' and, if at all present in a repertoire, it would be selected only infrequently (Figure 1).

During 2003 things began to change. Negative PR surrounding the 'health' issues of carbonated soft drinks began to prompt mums to choose alternatives[1] (Figure 2).

Perceived as one of the sweetest fizzy drinks, with a bright red colour, Tizer was at a disadvantage relying on mums for its volume. So the team set out to find an alternative strategy.

---

1. This was reflected in the strong growth of waters, dairy-based drinks and fruit juice-based drinks at the expense of carbonated soft drinks like Tizer.

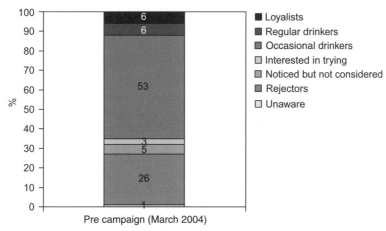

Figure 1: *Attitudes towards Tizer, 13–15-year-old boys*
Source: LaybourneValentine Tracking Research

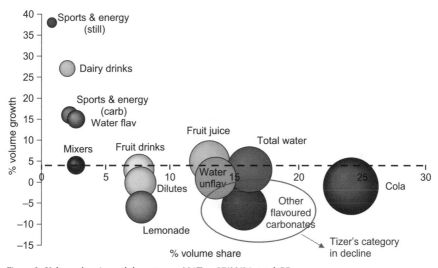

Figure 2: *Volume share/growth by category, MAT to 07/08/04, total GB*
Source: ACNielsen Scantrack

THE STRATEGIC OBJECTIVE

Analysis showed a market in overall decline, with the only category growth confined to the corner shops, forecourts and newsagents, where the teenagers themselves would purchase.

AG Barr set out to devise a strategy that would revitalise the impulse business and energise Tizer in teenagers' eyes.

THE STRATEGIC SOLUTION

Category marketing and communications assumed that 13–15-year-old boys associated themselves with 'big' brands, in order to bolster their position within the peer group. However, research showed that young teenage boys viewed Tizer as a category 'follower', with a slightly weird personality:

> 'The person on the edge of the group that hangs around with you … but he isn't really cool.'
>
> *Clarity Research, 2003*

This placed Tizer at a major disadvantage, given the importance within the psyche of teenagers of peer group belonging.

Competitor brands reinforced this concept of 'teenage belonging' by making themselves into 'big brands', thus associating themselves with peer group acceptance and 'success'. This message was invariably driven home by heavyweight TV campaigns, where 'bigger' spends were believed to result in 'better' campaigns (Figure 3).

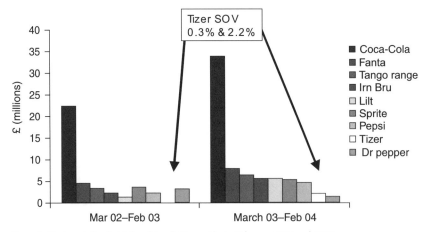

Figure 3: *Carbonated soft drinks adspend, 12 months to February 2003 and 2004*
Source: Nielsen Media Research

It was revealing to see that Tizer's lack of ATL visibility had been translated to mean 'outsider' in the culture of the media-savvy target audience of 13–15-year-old boys. And, with this tough teenage audience, 'outsiders' were most definitely 'losers'.

Insight

Our research validated that there was indeed a strong drive to be part of the crowd, but there was also a rejection of a 'sheep', or 'follower', mentality. Teenagers at this age were taking their first steps towards adult independence.

Tizer could capitalise on teenagers' underlying desire to be independent by making a virtue out of its 'outsider' position, while harnessing it to the product's only functional difference, its vivid red colour.

Tizer's new vision

We identified an opportunity to become the red, spirited challenger of the category
– celebrating our independent, irreverent stance, rather than apologising for it.
Several key goals were therefore agreed for 2004:

- deliver 50% growth in the impulse sector
- generate trial among non-drinkers and occasional purchasers (positioning Tizer
  as a complement to consumers' existing repertoires
- increase awareness and drive a reappraisal of the Tizer brand among teenage
  boys (13–15 years).

IMPLEMENTATION OF THE STRATEGY

The 500ml bottle would now become the strategic driver of the range, being the
format favoured by the teenage audience and the impulse sector. Its identity was
refreshed and refocused squarely around the 'red' equity that set Tizer's product
apart (Figure 4).

Figure 4: *Old 'blue' and new 'red' identities*[2]

We knew that to turn uninterested teenage consumers into Tizer advocates, we
would need to extend the flavour choices offered in a way that would be ownable
by the brand.

This led us to disrupt two of the key market conventions: product convention
and communications convention.

---

2. Developed in conjunction with 'the spirit of ...' design agency.

THE PRODUCT STRATEGY

Three new flavours would be launched, but rather than following category conventions by using the colour of the product to denote flavour, Tizer's new challenger position enabled us to think about the task from a different perspective.

Because Tizer was red and proud, all three variant products would remain red in colour, regardless of flavour. To further highlight this, the products were named as shown in Figure 5.

Itzred but tastes ORANGE
Itzred but tastes PURPLE
Itzred but tastes GREEN

Figure 5: *A broader range of tastes, but still anchored in our redness*

COMMUNICATIONS STRATEGY

With the launch of products in spring 2004, we planned our communications support to focus on the key summer months of June and July.

We needed to announce the arrival of the new variants, but do it in a way that only Tizer could.

The communications objectives were clear:

- to raise the salience of the brand and help put it on teenagers' maps
- to raise awareness of the new products and communicate their proposition
- to reinforce the brand's intrinsic link to its red identity and underpin the brand's new spirited challenger attitude – make Tizer cool.

CREATIVE STRATEGY

The creative strategy and execution needed to sum up our intention to be the category's red, spirited challenger, while effectively launching the new products.

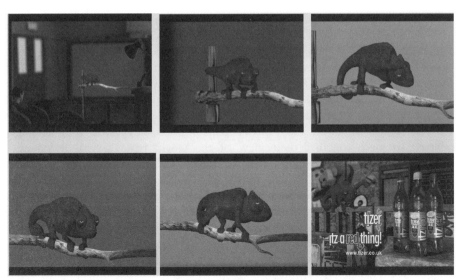

Figure 6: *The Tizer chameleon – screen grabs from the 30-second TV commercial*

We needed a vehicle that could embody the brand's new 'spirited challenger' attitude and reinforce our redness, while at the same time announcing that there were new flavours to try. Our solution was to harness a simple chameleon: the animal known for changing its colour at will.

But Tizer's irreverent chameleon won't change from his chosen red colour. He remains red, despite the manipulations of a very uncool lecturer, who is using him for a demonstration. The chameleon is clearly unimpressed, reflecting teenagers' attitudes towards figures of authority (Figure 6).

The execution concluded with the message:

'Yes, we have three great new flavours … No, we're not changing colour!'

The brand's core sentiment was encapsulated with the end-line:

A simple statement that captured our intent to be outwardly confident about who and what we were.

The strategy is summarised in Figure 7.

Single-minded proposition
Three great new flavours, one brilliant colour

tizer

Core creative idea | Creative execution
Tizer: itz a red thing! | *Red chameleon doesn't change his*
…we're red and we're staying red | *colour for anyone*

Figure 7: *Summary of Tizer's communication strategy*

CONNECTIONS STRATEGY[3]

To us, the 'bigger is better' approach was not appropriate behaviour for a category's spirited challenger, so we searched for a more suitable strategy.

The worst thing we could have done would have been to preach to our audience, so our campaign was designed to work from the bottom up, infiltrating Tizer into the grass-roots culture of the teenage audience.

Psychological research into media consumption suggested that teenagers preferred to piece together their view of the world from several independent sources. So rather than relying solely on heavy TV investment, we decided to supplement a relatively small-scale four-week TV campaign of 550 TVRs with a range of opportunities to raise awareness, develop the profile of the brand and offer opportunities to try the new products. The result was an integrated campaign that would hit them from several independent sources at once (Figures 8 and 9).

Sampling activity included under-18 club nights, sponsorship of the Urban Music Festival and, importantly, recruitment of 100 cool but independently minded teenage boys. They acted as brand ambassadors within their peer groups, spreading the word, distributing products and merchandise, and giving us a direct feed on what their friends were saying about the brand.

Other connection points in the campaign included:

- rebranded online presence at www.tizer.co.uk, to give the target audience a full brand experience
- in-store promotions to generate trial interest at the point of greatest competitive pressure
- branded merchandise, to help raise the profile and infiltrate the brand into the lives of the target audience

Figure 8: *Connections summary*[4]

---

3. By 'connections', we are referring to every point of contact a brand has with its consumers.
4. The agency partners involved in executing the overall plan included 23red, Cooke & Brand, the spirit of ..., PHD, Dubit & Henderson and Grime.

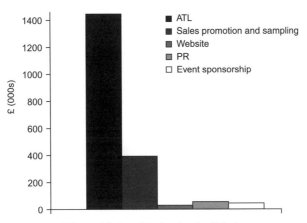

Figure 9: *Breakdown of the launch budget (total = £1.9m)*
Source: AG Barr

- a national six-sheet poster campaign, to create pack recognition and awareness; this time when teenagers were out in town centres and on public transport
- trade marketing to help build expectation of the launch, and thus distribution, in advance of the consumer campaign
- extensive consumer PR and sampling programmes
- plus a concentrated staff PR programme, which included competitions, posters and a Tizer 'Itzred' day.

THE RESULTS

We will set out to show that the campaign was successful against all its objectives. It:

- increased brand salience
- improved perceptions
- encouraged trial
- attracted new and lapsed users
- lowered brand rejection
- drove sales through the key impulse sector direct into the hands of the core audience of teenagers.

Salience

As a result of the campaign, advertising awareness among the target audience was significant, especially given the historical lack of investment (Figure 10).

Without prompting, teenagers were significantly more likely to recall having seen Tizer's campaign than that of any of its long-spending competitors (Figure 11).

Spontaneous brand awareness among the target audience increased to 27% (Figure 12), spontaneous awareness being the acid test of a brand's cut-through in this noisy category.

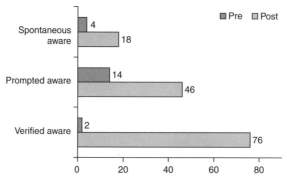

Figure 10: *Advertising awareness (post- vs pre-campaign)*
Source: Laybourne Valentine Tracking Study

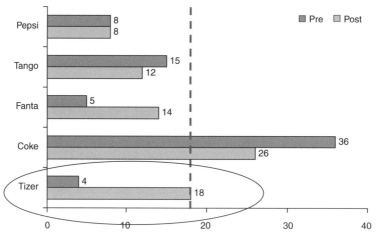

Figure 11: *Spontaneous advertising awareness (Tizer vs key competitors)*
Source: Laybourne Valentine Tracking Study

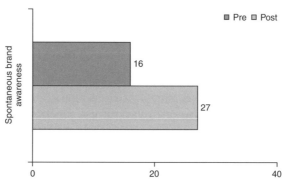

Figure 12: *Brand awareness (post- vs pre-campaign)*
Source: Laybourne Valentine Tracking Study

Perceptions

Significant favourable shifts were recorded on all positive brand imagery statements, most notably:

- Comes up with exciting new ideas
- Has cool advertising
- Has a good sense of humour
- Is a clever brand.

These shifts were attributable directly to the campaign. Teenagers recognised it in qualitative research:

'Tizer advertise on the TV now, whereas before, you never saw anything from them. That shows they are getting more popular.'

Boy, 12–13, south

'I've tried these after seeing this [Chameleon ad]. I wanted to taste them because they are new.'

Boy, 13–14, north

'I like the Tizer ad. It's strange because it's red but green flavour.'

Boy, 12–13, south

Clarity Research, post-campaign qualitative research

We've isolated it further by comparing the views of campaign-aware teenagers with those unaware of the campaign (Figure 13).

The most rewarding evidence of this shift came from the grass roots. Prior to the campaign, the team had been struggling to recruit the quota of brand ambassadors set. However, once we had the campaign materials as recruitment tools, we ended up having to turn people away. It appeared that we had started to present the brand in a way that teenagers could really identify with.

We also had feedback from the grass roots, via the Dubit website and the ambassadors themselves. In research terms this online feedback provided a direct

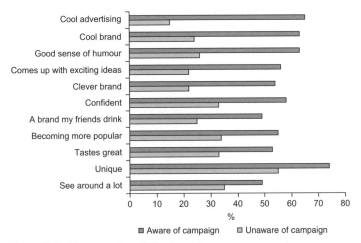

Figure 13: *Positive perceptions of Tizer (campaign aware vs unaware)*
Source: Laybourne Valentine Tracking (post-campaign data)

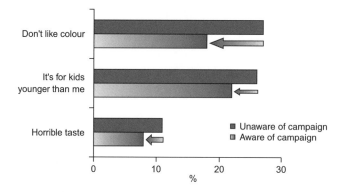

Figure 14: *Negative perceptions of Tizer (campaign aware vs unaware)*
Source: Laybourne Valentine Tracking (post-campaign data)

two-way dialogue with teenagers, in real time and on their own terms. We knew exactly what the audience was thinking of our work at every stage and the following quotes represent a sample of the feedback:

'Today our year went on a [school] trip to the beach. I had a new green-flavoured Tizer and about six or seven people came up to me and asked if I had seen the advert and telling me how good they think it is.'

'I've tried the purple one and the green one. When I saw the ad I just wanted to try the new flavours to see what they were like.'

Teenage boys, Clarity Research, post-campaign qualitative research

Positive online dialogue was also reflected in the tracking. We saw substantial reductions in negative perceptions associated with the brand, illustrated again by comparing those campaign aware to campaign unaware (Figure 14).

Although we were shifting the brand towards teenagers, we successfully did so without alienating mums. They understood and appreciated what we were trying to achieve:

'They are doing new flavours. They are keeping up with everyone else.'

'They are changing flavour but it stays the same colour. Red. It's their trademark. They are keeping up with everyone else.'

Mums, Clarity Research, post-campaign qualitative research

Rejection levels

A key benchmark for the success of the campaign was the proportion of the target audience who would reject the brand outright. Rejection dropped by 47% as a result of the campaign activity (Figure 15) and brand adoption increased by 33%.

Importantly, however, these perceptual shifts in attitudes towards the brand have proved lasting. A recent research study conducted in March 2005 showed that people still felt the brand was cool, despite no supporting activity since the previous summer (Figure 16).

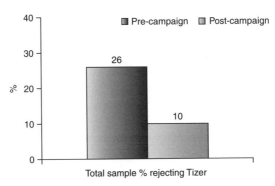

Figure 15: *Rejection of the brand among teenage audience*
Base: 13–15-year-old boys
Source: Laybourne Valentine Tracking Study

Figure 16: *Research results, March 2005*
Sample: 665
Source: Dubit

Trial and penetration

Ultimately this needed to translate into renewed trial among non-drinkers for the campaign to be successful on all measures.

Tracking measured a 52% increase in claimed purchasing levels, often a precursor of actual trial and an indicator of a brand's improving currency in the marketplace. A total of 27% of those claiming to have trialled were new or lapsed users and out of those who had trialled, 85% said they would buy the product again (Figure 17).

TNS panel data showed that in a depressed market, only Tizer and Dr Pepper saw penetration increases in the impulse sector in the 12 months to January 2005 (Figure 18).

Distribution

As a smaller player in the market, influence with the trade was critical. Following the trade launch, we tracked a sustained increase in distribution of the new products on a national basis that provided the necessary platform for a successful launch (Figure 19).

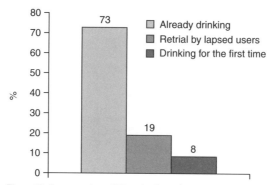

Figure 17: *Segmentation of Tizer drinkers, three months ending August 2004*
Source: Laybourne Valentine Tracking Research

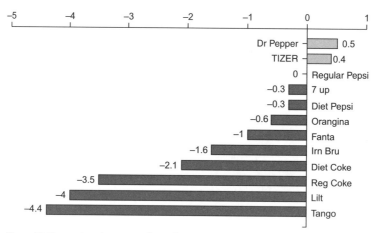

Figure 18: *Penetration changes, total impulse (MAT Jan 05 vs Jan 04)*
Source: TNS

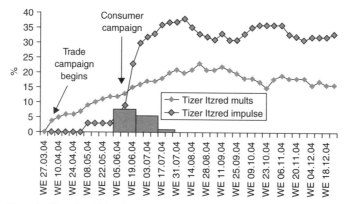

Figure 19: *Tizer 'Itzred' distribution build*
Source: ACNielsen Account weighted selling distribution

154

Sales

Analysis highlighted a radical improvement in impulse channel performance, with sales through the channel doubling in the period of the campaign and the core 500 ml product exceeding its turnover targets by an amazing 230%.

Figure 20 compares Tizer's performance with that of the category, and you can see a clear turnaround in performance year on year not reflected in the market as a whole.

In fact, despite lower distribution levels, Tizer's impulse volumes overtook its multiples volumes in 2004, turning Tizer into a truly 'impulse brand' (Figure 21).

This share growth came in the context of a significantly depressed market year on year, where even the key players were struggling to maintain sales (Figure 22).

Overall the brand achieved a share growth of 2%, owing singularly to the performance of the profitable 500 ml products and despite struggling sales in the

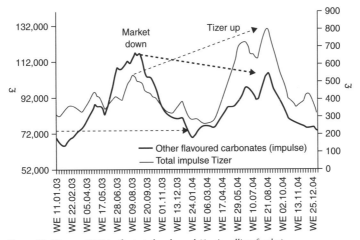

Figure 20: *Tizer vs OFC in the impulse channel (4 w/e rolling £ sales)*
Source: ACNielsen

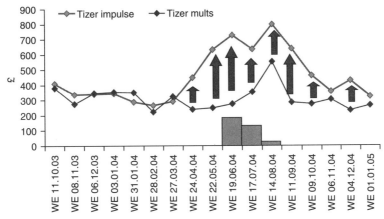

Figure 21: *Tizer sales impulse vs multiples (4 w/e)*
Source: ACNielsen

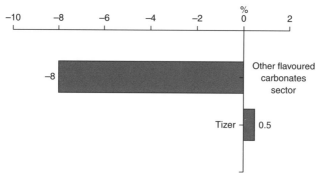

Figure 22: *£ Value growth, Tizer vs market (total GB, w/e to Jan 05)*
Source: ACNielsen

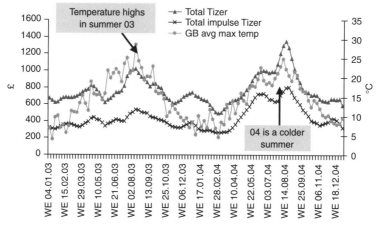

Figure 23: *Tizer sales, total and impulse vs GB average maximum temperature*
Source: ACNielsen (weekly data) and the Met Office

multiples.[5] This was a substantially better performance than the previous year, which had benefited from much better weather (Figure 23).

Also, it is worth noting that uplifts during the campaign occurred when average pricing for Tizer was 20% higher than it was during the same period the previous year. This suggests a decrease in price sensitivity that over the coming months should contribute to both higher value per unit, reduced impact from competitor promotions and thus greater profitability across the Tizer brand.

Company share price

AG Barr's company share price has also seen rapid growth in the period following this successful launch, compared to the beverage category as a whole (Figure 24). City analysts cited the Itzred launch as a critical success factor in 2004's performance versus the market.

---

5. Owing to promotional restrictions and the de-listing of Diet from Safeway and Asda.

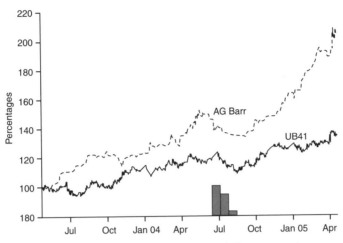

Figure 24: *Share performance (AG Barr share price vs the beverage sector)*

ISOLATION OF EFFECTS

In assessing the effectiveness of this activity it is necessary to consider and discount several factors that could otherwise explain the results outlined.

Could it have been the introduction of the new packaging?

The new identity was in fact launched in the summer of 2003, so this could not have contributed to the effects outlined.

Could it have been an unusually buoyant market performance with Tizer sales simply lifted along for the ride?

Analysis of Tizer's performance versus the carbonates market shows the category down 8% year on year and Tizer up.

Could it have been an unusually strong seasonal performance, given how sensitive the carbonates market is to summer temperature conditions?

As already shown, weekly average temperature readings for 2004 and 2003 illustrate how poor the 2004 summer was versus the previous year and its negative impact on sales of soft carbonates per se. Tizer's sales buck this trend.

Could there have been a substantial drop in competitor activity in either spend/promotions?

Year on year, competitors were spending more, not less (Figure 25).
    Average pricing analysis shows increased promotional levels among Tizer's direct competitors in the 'other flavoured carbonates' sector (Figure 26).

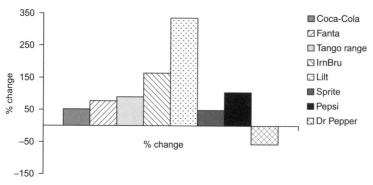

Figure 25: *% change in adspend, Tizer's key competitors (52 w/d Feb 03 vs 04)*
Source: Nielsen Media Research

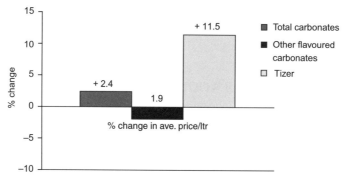

Figure 26: *% change in average price, Tizer's vs category (52 w/d Feb 03 vs 04)*
Source: ACNielsen

Could sales increases have been the sole result of an aggressive promotional strategy?

As mentioned, average pricing for Tizer was 20% higher during the campaign period versus the same period the previous year.

Could we simply explain sales gains by increases in distribution?

Although distribution played a role in the success of the launch it by no means explains the totality of the uplifts, given that distribution at the time of the campaign was no higher than it was two years previously when sales were substantially less.

CALCULATING PAYBACK

To help us understand the influence of all these factors, plus more specifically the interplay between the distribution, temperature and the campaign effects, we have constructed a detailed econometric model. This includes an innovative model of how decision-makers (in multiples and independent retailers) make decisions and act on them in anticipation of TV advertising.

The direct contribution of the TV advertising to Tizer retail sales value was £0.34m by December 2004. The total impact (including the distribution and points of distribution effects outlined above) was £0.89m retail sales by December 2004.

So with an overall marketing budget of £1.9m it seems the campaign did not pay back in this first burst alone (although this was never the intention). The available sales information means we have only been able to quantify the short-term impact of advertising, covering one summer season. We are particularly keen to observe whether the advertising impact is rejuvenated as the impulse soft drinks market moves back to its peak in the forthcoming summer. For this reason we do not yet believe we have quantified the medium-term impact.

More importantly, however, for the long term, the activity has resulted in a significant effect on price sensitivity, leading to greater resilience in the face of promotional activity and decreasing reliance on price promotions as the volume driver for the brand.

The brand is now able to charge more for its product, promote less and hold its own against competitor pricing changes. Assuming this is sustained even at a lower level, a 15% increase in the average price per litre could, over a year, equate to an additional £1.5m in sales for the brand.[6]

Furthermore, we must also consider other financial benefits. The ability to focus sales through the impulse channel will result in a reduction in overall promotional costs, thus increasing the brand's profit margins. In addition, the increase in AG Barr's share price, although by no means solely attributable to the successful launch of Itzred, suggests a business that is now considered to have two hero brands, rather than just the one.[7]

CONCLUSION

The campaign achieved all of its stated objectives.

We caused reappraisal of the brand and helped to bring it closer to the forefront of teenagers' minds despite a relatively limited budget. We generated trial among non-drinkers and occasional purchasers and, most importantly of all, have achieved a greater presence in the profitable impulse sector without alienating the interests of the core business in the multiples.

Rather than remaining a brand primarily bought by mums, this campaign has given teenagers permission to include Tizer in their portfolios, and by doing so has given this long-standing brand a whole new lease of life.

'... living proof that Tizer has indeed finally dropped its shackles.'

Clarity Research, 2004

---

6. 15% based on the midpoint between lowest and peak increases calculated using 2003 sales pattern as an 'average year'.
7. That is, Irn Bru.

11

University of Dundee
University Challenge. Serious Fun

Principal author: George Cumming, Frame C
Media agencies: MediaCom

EDITOR'S SUMMARY

Back in 2000, Dundee was a middle-ranking Scottish university, with fewer and fewer people applying every year. However, the university decided to take action. They hired Frame C to create the first of a series of campaigns extolling the virtues of student life at Dundee.

Students are looking for a good time as well as a good degree. The 'Serious Fun' campaign showed that Dundee offered both. The campaign took a provocative approach, and used a bold mix of media, from TV and radio to bus sides and beer mats.

The results were dramatic. Applications have increased by 83%. Not only that, but the quality of applicants has improved. This has allowed the university to select more able students, so that drop-out rates have fallen, degree results have improved, and graduates have found jobs more easily. These improvements have been noted by the *Times Good University Guide*, which now ranks Dundee as the top Scottish university.

The judges were impressed with the scale of these results, and how they helped to transform the university. They also liked the way Frame C organised several different campaigns and media around a single idea, for which they awarded the paper the prize for Best Integration.

INTRODUCTION

In spring 2000, Frame C picked up what appeared to be the poisoned chalice of a university in a severe downward spiral. Applications had fallen by 38% over the three years prior, and the university had turned to advertising in desperation.

Five years on, the University of Dundee is proud of its massive resurgence, its quantum leap in terms of the quality of applications coming in, and a brand identity that has commonly taken established universities centuries to grow.

'As Vice Chancellor in 2000, I was extremely concerned that I was about to inherit serious problems. I have been very impressed by the impact and results delivered by the Serious Fun campaign. It resonates with students and prospective students. The university's reputation ultimately depends on excellent staff and students, and advertising communications also play an important part in our ongoing progress.'

Sir Alan Langlands, Principal, University of Dundee

This case is unique in its sector: higher education. Not only did it break the 'rules', but it championed advertising in virgin advertising territory. Academia and advertising were close, but only in their proximity in a dictionary. In a crowded market, the first 'Serious Fun' campaign delivered sledgehammer advertising that ruffled the feathers of academia. Risky or risqué (probably both), the initial campaign provoked both broadsheets and tabloids into action, at the same time making the Dundee University Court wince at the realisation of the controversy.

SIGNIFICANCE

This is an important case study, which demonstrates the following learning.

- The value of really understanding young people (and targeting them separately).
- The value of a compelling and differentiating positioning in a crowded market.
- A creative idea that integrates across all promotional activity, affording a unique insight into the potency of brand building in an overly traditional market.

RESULTS

Resulting from the 2000–04 campaigns, demand for places has leapt by a huge 83%, school leaver entry through UCAS clearing has dropped to a nominal 3%, and 97% of graduates take up employment within three months of graduation from 65% in 1999. The university has also been voted the 2004 *Sunday Times* Scottish University of the Year, making the top five shortlist for the UK University of the Year. A return on investment of 16 times advertising spend (1596%) over the four campaigns (entry statistics for 2004 campaign not available until October 2005) has even changed the mood of the university's bean-counters from 'serious' to 'not quite so serious'.

BACKGROUND

The market

Until the early 1990s the market in Scotland consisted of the ancient and established universities such as St Andrews and Edinburgh, and the raft of universities opened under the Labour Government in the 1960s, such as Stirling, Strathclyde and Dundee. The early 1990s heralded the upgrading of many polytechnics to university status, making a university education open to a wider audience. As the 1990s and 2000s have unfolded, access to a university education has become even more available. Table 1 is a guide to market segmentation in 2001, clearly showing the strong correlation between age and reputation (rank).

TABLE 1: THE TIMES UNIVERSITY GUIDE, 2001

Established & 'Ancient'			The Middle Order			Young Upstarts		
Institution	Year formed	Times rank	Institution	Year formed	Times rank	Institution	Year formed	Times rank
Edinburgh	1583	6	Stirling	1967	41	Robert Gordon	1992	59
St Andrews	1411	10	Dundee	1967	42	Abertay	1994	68
Glasgow	1451	23	Strathclyde	1964	43	Caledonian	1991	72
Aberdeen	1495	26	Herriot-Watt	1966	49	Napier	1992	73

The model in Figure 1 highlights some of the key participants in the marketing and conversion processes, from school leaver to employed graduate. This simple overview presents the big picture of external and internal brand influencers, and the pressure points from a financial perspective.

Universities are dependent on securing government funding, and with each place short of the target quota leading to four years (average time of study), one bad year can trigger several years of potential problems.

The ideal target is to have a combination of key dynamics and standards in place: high entrance qualifications, low UCAS clearing entrants, high demand (choice of applications) and, of course, excellent conversion of applications by the university.

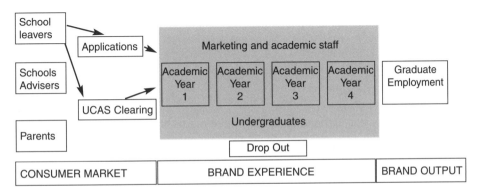

Figure 1: *Simplified university model*

THE CHALLENGE

As the advertising has progressed, the client has become more demanding of the agency; however, in 2000, the message was specific:

- arrest the decline in applications
- improve the quality of applications by reducing UCAS entrants.

By 2003, after some impressive results, the remit demanded concentration on differentiating the university from the rest of the market.

RESEARCH AND INSIGHT

A variety of research methods was adopted, none more effective than getting out and interviewing in the cinema foyers, fast-food outlets and pubs of Dundee. A team of researchers, including agency staff, interviewed around 450 school leavers and young people. This constituted around 8% of annual application numbers. Additional in-depth interviews were, and are, held with university staff, current undergraduates and schools liaison officers.

A number of insights were gained, some dispelling popular perceptions about this media-savvy, computer games-reared, generation.

- As the ABC1 consumers of the future, they do not tolerate corporate-style advertising, finding it patronising and stale.
- They hold a strong belief in 'work hard, play hard'.
- They are of the opinion that 'A serious education is as important as a good social life' and 'A good education is a platform to a fulfilling career.'

Several issues were clear.

- The market was dormant to multi-channel advertising (in 2000 no TV advertising existed in Scotland in the sector).
- The majority of the target audience (school leavers) had a totally different opinion of what communication triggers captured their attention beyond the 'flowery prospectus designers'.
- Any proposition would have to balance serious education with social and lifestyle messages.

STRATEGY

How we used our research and insight

An initial strategy was defined as having three main thrusts.

1. Engage school leavers with high-impact, innovative advertising, creating a clear differentiated position for the university.
2. A brand proposition that cuts through all communication activities and conversion points.
3. Focus communications on the 'hot' catchment areas of Tayside, Fife and Strathclyde.

Why these were important

Engaging school leavers

Speaking to the central target audience in a tone that resonates with their attitudes and values is critical. Being controversial in a sector where one century of tradition blends in with another would undoubtedly be risky. This receptive audience had been neglected.

Brand proposition

It can be said that a brand is a thousand small expressions, so the ability to maximise communications in as many spheres of our target audience's life as possible, necessitated a commanding proposition that worked outdoors, indoors and in print. The opportunity to assert a brand could never be greater, the market embraced the comfort of tradition – one free from the perceived 'contamination' of commercial advertising.

Catchment areas

The perception of Dundee being a dull and depressed area is a notion held by many people in Scotland, and one that apparently will not die easily. Dundee is, in fact, a vibrant city, in the process of dispelling the 'jam, jute and journalism' tag, and focusing on new technology and economic growth. Lying outwith the main population central belt of Glasgow and Edinburgh, it is an altogether harder call to choose to move 50 miles away to a city whose perceived stock value is low, than to settle for home life at Strathclyde, Heriot-Watt or Stirling University.

On the other hand, 64% of school leavers were leaving Tayside, going to big city universities, mainly through a lack of a viable local alternative.

CREATIVE COMMUNICATION

Original campaign

Armed with clear strategic goals, the common denominator from the research finding was the fundamental attraction of going to university:

- the *serious* side of gaining a qualification that could lead to career fulfilment
- the social aspect (*fun*) – the campus, clubs, student union – facilities fundamental to the enjoyment to be had from student life.

The proposition of 'Serious Fun' at university was then tested in Dundee, Edinburgh and Glasgow, proving its credibility with the 15–19-year-old audience.

Taking the controversial approach, the proposition was translated into four 10-second TV ads, which contrasted and compared serious with fun, using sexual and drinking innuendos, which provide both a narrative and visual illustration of the ads and the controversy, thereby generating additional (free) PR exposure.

The 2000 Serious Fun Campaign comprised four TV ads, two radio scripts, bus sides, beer mats and press ads.

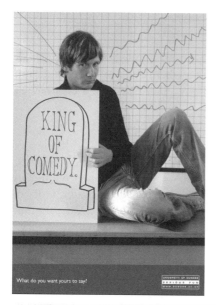 

Figure 2: *Examples of creative*

Changing creative

The 2001 campaign continued the Serious Fun proposition and its executions were significantly toned down, in part because the nut had been cracked (well, smashed to bits!) in 2000, but also in respect of the university's sense of keeping on the right side of serious and not becoming perceived as a radical establishment. 'Graphic Equalizer' was the 2001 TV execution.

In 2002, Abertay University was mimicking the graphic-type ads, so a move away from this type of execution was in keeping with the research at that time, prompting the 'Mrs Brady' campaign, which pondered the long-term benefits of education with a fun undertone. Building from additional research in 2003, conducted in and around five major universities, was the confirmation that the advertising needed to be continually refreshed. The 2003 'Epitaph' and 2004 'Discovery' campaigns have consolidated the belief in the significance education has to the success of one's career and working life (Figures 2 and 3).

Integrated communications

From a base of TV, radio and some outdoor advertising, the agency became closely involved in developing the communications content of the conversion process opportunities. Producing open-day literature and freshers' magazines became an integral part of branding and communications messages. Examples of this work can be found in Figure 3.

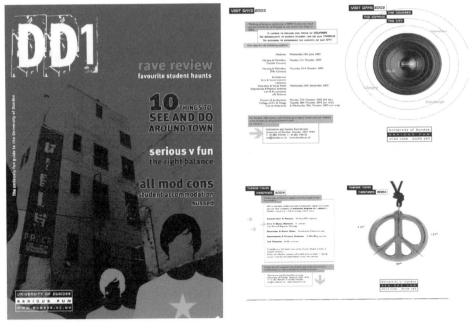

Figure 3: *Examples of communication materials*

BRAND DEVELOPMENT IDEAS

By 2003, the agency could see the possibilities of brand extension, integrating the Serious Fun proposition to make staff live the brand.

The first influence on living the brand was in the front line by ensuring that the open days and student fairs had a Serious Fun look and feel. In addition to branded promotional materials (e.g. disposable cameras on open days, gifts, takeaways, exhibition systems), academic staff were, and are, encouraged to project a balanced approach of persuasion rather than taking the all too familiar 'take it or leave it' approach. On such relationship-building, feel-good occasions, the agency encouraged the university to use staff whose presentational and relationship skills were high.

Continuing the 2003 momentum of staff immersion in the brand proposition, a 48-sheet board was hired in the vicinity of the city centre, doubling as a motivational tool, a reminder of the university's achievements (e.g. Top Scottish University in 2004 *Sunday Times* Guide). Staff could drive past this every day and feel a sense of involvement.

Bringing undergraduates into open days as student ambassadors also proved to be a worthwhile means of creating 'buzz', with closer affinity between young people in the same age group.

CAMPAIGN RESULTS

Expectations

Reflecting on the initial brief, the following outcomes were required as a minimum:

- maintenance and improvement of consumer demand (applications)
- an improvement in the quality of applications (driving UCAS clearing entry levels down)
- creating a brand identity that maximised the appeal of the university for its high-quality education, sports and social facilities.

Consumer demand

There is probably no clearer graphic than Figure 4 to communicate the arrest of the decline and the dramatic increase in demand for places. With the first campaign redressing the decline, the upside from 2001 onwards has delivered an 83% increase from the low point in 1999.

No other university in the UK can match Dundee University's growth rate in consumer demand: Figures 5 and 6 illustrate rapid growth in Scotland and the UK respectively.

Of course, distorting the St Andrews figures was the 'Prince William factor', which played a significant part in causing untold grief to many unsuccessful but optimistic young female school leavers.

Quality of applications

When looking for primary evidence of key quality indicators in this market one would turn to:

- UCAS clearing numbers
- entry level requirements.

Then, ultimately, to their effect on the longer term:

- numbers of graduates taking up full-time employment
- drop-out rates.

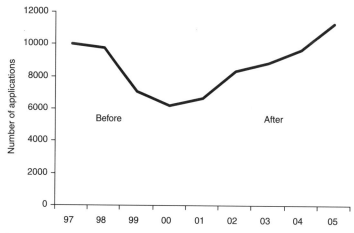

Figure 4: *Turnaround in demand*
Source: UCAS statistics

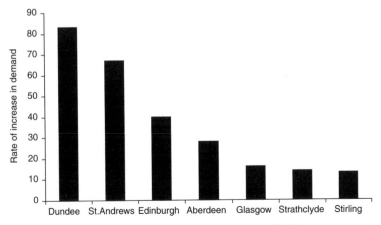

Figure 5: *Rate of increase in applications in the Scottish market, 2000–05*
Source: UCAS

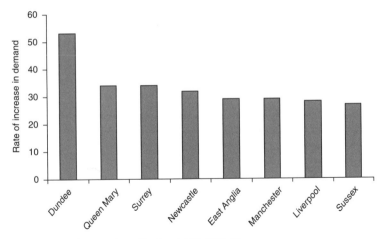

Figure 6: *Rate of increase in applications in UK, 2001–04*
Source: UCAS statistics

UCAS clearing entrants

Figure 7 quite clearly shows the dramatic drop in school leavers entering with sub-standard higher qualifications. Reducing the number of entrants who are not qualified to join the courses potentially reduces the risk of drop-outs and enhances the possibilities of improved final degree standards.

Entry requirements

Increases across the board between 2002 and 2006 reflect a marked improvement in the standards required to enter the university. The percentage change in points required per discipline are listed below:

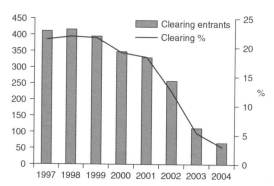

Figure 7: *Dundee University UCAS clearing entrants*
Source: UoD admissions statistics, 2004

- Arts and Social Sciences 9%
- Engineering 20%
- Law 18%
- Life Sciences 20%
- Physical Sciences 10%.

Basic economic theory dictates that, where supply is limited and demand is high, the 'price' can be driven up. This is an important point: *as Dundee is, in effect, increasing the value of its courses, while continuing to increase demand (a prime example of brand value and repositioning in the market).*

This is another good example of why the gap between the University of Dundee and the established end of the market is reducing.

Graduate employment

The graduate employment fill rate has moved from 95% to 97%, clearly showing the growing demand for a Dundee education.

Drop-out rates

The university has seen drop-out rates fall. It is unfair to directly correlate the standard of applications to drop-out rates as, often, many school leavers with good results have achieved these thanks to significant support mechanisms (small classes, extra tutors, etc.). Common sense tells us, though, that the level of entry grades must be an element of influence.

Market share

Geographical growth

While applications have predominantly originated from the Tayside and Fife regions, there is a healthy growth in demand in Strathclyde. While most outdoor and promotional activity has been locally based (Tayside), the success for Strathclyde can be wholly attributed to TV.

TABLE 2: DOMICILE AND INCOME IMPACT OF CAMPAIGNS

Region	Increased no. of entrants 1999–2004	Value of income (£m)
Tayside	441	6.2
Strathclyde	307	4.3
Fife	303	4.2
Lothian	96	1.3
Rest of Scotland	158	2.2
TOTAL	1305	18.3

Source: Client working papers

Table 2 shows the domicile and increases of entrants from each region. It reinforces the impact of the TV campaigns, as 43% of the university's increase in numbers comes from regions where TV advertising was the lead communication.

Change in profile

Table 3 shows the shift from the middle-order segment to the lower end of the established 'high end' of the market. We can see from Table 4 that the university's share has moved from 6% in 2000 to 9% in 2005, using the middle and upper market segments as a realistic base.

TABLE 3: TIMES GOOD UNIVERSITY GUIDE, MOVEMENT 2000–05

Established & 'Ancient'			The Middle Order			Young Upstarts		
Institution	2005 rank	2001 rank	Institution	2005 rank	2001 rank	Institution	2005 rank	2001 rank
St Andrews	1411	9	Aberdeen	1495	34	Rbt Gordon	1992	58
Edinburgh	1583	13	Strathclyde	1964	37	Abertay	1994	66
Glasgow	1451	22	Stirling	1964	38	Caledonian	1991	77
Dundee	1967	28	Herriot-Watt	1966	46	Napier	1992	88

TABLE 4: UPPER QUALITY SEGMENT OF SCOTTISH UNIVERSITY MARKET, APPLICATION TREND 2000–05

Established university market	Degree applications						
Institution name	2000	2001	2002	2003	2004	2005	% change 2005/2000
University of Dundee	6,190	6,653	8,360	8,847	9,638	11,302	83%
University of St Andrews	6,019	8,720	7,867	7,144	8,337	10,064	67%
University of Edinburgh	26,006	27,261	28,740	28,063	32,134	36,359	40%
University of Aberdeen	8,936	10,574	11,410	10,906	10,913	11,403	28%
University of Glasgow	20,804	21,631	23,887	23,107	22,628	24,193	16%
University of Strathclyde	14,345	15,117	15,898	16,147	16,185	16,348	14%
University of Stirling	7,998	9,059	9,134	8,908	8,335	9,045	13%
Heriot-Watt University Edinburgh	5,822	6,426	7,365	6,665	6,769	6,413	10%
Scottish degree application totals	96,120	105,441	112,661	109,787	114,939	125,127	30%
University of Dundee share	6%	6%	7%	8%	8%	9%	

Source: UCAS

Return on investment

If you consider that a Dundee student will spend four years (on average), funded at approximately £4k per annum, and that the university has finite capacity targets, it is easy to understand the importance of filling courses. Over the campaigns, a return of 16 times the advertising spend (agency and media costs) has been achieved. The incremental funding benefit is a huge £12.5m from an ad spend of £782k.

Other impediments

The university continues to rely on the advertising agency as its only source of external marketing. Any public relations benefits achieved have been driven by the effect of advertising. Double bubble, some may say.

CONCLUSION

The initial decline was immediately arrested and followed by some highly notable business results in tandem with the building of a unique brand. One whose internal essence is in harmony with the promise it makes to its existing and prospective consumers.

The commercial reality is that the university has managed to put up its price (entry requirements), drive up its sales demand (applications) and improve its quality (UCAS clearing), resulting in a more commanding market position, as reflected in Table 3. Financially supported by the fantastic return on investment over the Serious Fun campaigns, the agency and university have established sustained success.

THE FINAL WORD

'We faced a big, big challenge.'

'Student life here was second to none, but the message wasn't getting through.'

'Our relationship was based on trust. The agency understood our market and by creating every piece of literature with our message, the advertising was the catalyst to our success. The results speak for themselves.'

Gordon Craig, Director of Recruitment and Admissions

Section 3

Bronze Winners

12

Arriva Buses

Getting bums on seats

How Arriva buses bucked the trend of declining passenger numbers

Principal authors: Mike Rayner and Nicola Simpson, Cogent Elliott
Media agency: PHD Compass

EDITOR'S SUMMARY

The objective Arriva set for this campaign was a tough one: to increase the number of passenger journeys, in the face of a long-term decline in passenger numbers in the market as a whole.

Cogent Elliott's strategy was to target light-to-medium frequency bus users, who they found could be persuaded to use the bus more often if they had access to useful, relevant, up-to-date information about their local bus routes and destinations.

The result was a massive six-monthly door drop of bulletins across half of the Arriva network. The bulletins featured user-friendly route maps; destination suggestions; guides to service frequencies and money-off vouchers – each tailored to specific routes.

The judges were impressed by Arriva's 'test and control' approach. By comparing the performance of marketed and un-marketed routes, this paper shows that the campaign stimulated over a million extra journeys in the test period alone.

This is a good example of how routine evaluation can help make communications more effective, in this case leading Arriva away from an advertising-led awareness campaign towards a more tightly focused information campaign using DM.

INTRODUCTION

Buses provide a socially vital, environmentally sound, economically important service to millions. Despite this, the industry has been drastically under-promoted, and has been suffering a severe decline in passenger numbers for decades.

Our paper describes the journey Arriva and its advertising partner Cogent Elliot took in bucking this trend – undertaking the largest marketing campaign ever seen in the industry. It tells how, over the course of three years, we were able to:

- change travel behaviour patterns, leading to over a million extra journeys
- increase passenger numbers in the face of relentless market decline
- show that routes supported by marketing activity increased passenger journeys compared to those that weren't
- establish a positive return on marketing investment.

THE BUS INDUSTRY

Buses are fundamentally important to the UK's social infrastructure – carrying more passengers every year than any other form of public transport. They play a vital role in society, bringing people to town centres, boosting local economies, and providing links for education, employment, medical and social needs. Buses offer significant environmental benefits over motor cars, helping to reduce traffic congestion and vehicle emissions.

Set up in 1997, Arriva is the third largest operator in the industry, with a 14.4% market share.[1] Arriva employs 17,000 people and has a fleet of over 6000 buses.

Arriva operates across the UK, working with local authorities, employers, new home and industrial park developers, and local residents' groups to ensure services best meet local needs.

BUS USAGE

Arriva's core market is located outside London; although it does operate in the capital, it is on behalf of the 'Transport for London' organisation, which does not allow individual operators to self-promote.

This core market has seen severe decline ever since the 1950s and throughout the last decade (see Figure 1).

Passenger journeys decreased between 1993 and 2004 by 13.2%: from 3264 million journeys to 2833 million. This is underscored by the number of bus kilometres travelled, declining from 2242 to 2143 million kilometres over the same period.[2]

---

1. Source: Bus Industry Monitor.
2. Source: DFT Survey of PSV and Light Rail Operators.

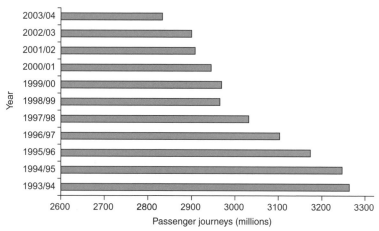

Figure 1: *Passenger journeys by bus, Great Britain (excluding London)*
Source: National Travel Survey

THE RISE OF THE CAR

The most important factor influencing this downward trend in bus usage is access to a car. The National Travel Survey (NTS) shows that people without access to a car make seven times as many bus journeys as those with access. NTS data shows that, between 1998 and 2000, households without a car travelled 632 miles a year by bus, while households with access to a car travelled just 169 miles. In 2002/03 the number of households in Great Britain without a car had fallen to just 27% (Figure 2).

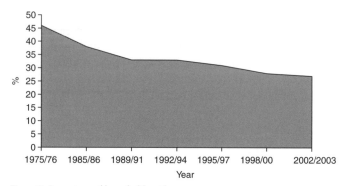

Figure 2: *Percentage of households with no car*
Source: National Travel Survey

Car ownership was increasingly affordable, and equated to status, achievement and personal wealth – decreasing bus usage seemed inevitable. This was compounded by the fact that, in relation to cars or even trains, the sector was massively under-marketed, with 600 times less share of voice than that enjoyed by car manufacturers (Figure 3). Any campaign by a bus operator had a tough market to compete in and a difficult job to do.

| Bus advertising Aug. 1999–July 2000 = £929,208 | Train advertising Aug. 1999–July 2000 = £25,174,925 | Car advertising Aug. 1999–July 2000 = £604,000,000 |

Figure 3: *Media spend comparison*
Source: ACNielsen/MMS

THE CHALLENGE

Arriva faced two sets of objectives, one internally set and the other externally.

'Primary objective: to grow patronage by 2.5% per annum over the next five years.'

Arriva Strategy Document, 2000

In addition, along with other bus operators, Arriva found itself under political pressure to increase patronage as a result of government initiatives to raise the profile and drive greater use of public transport, as it sought to:

'Improve accessibility, punctuality and reliability with an increase in patronage of more than 10% [originally set at 8%] from 2001 levels by 2010 with growth in every region.'

Public Service Agreement, 2000, amended 2004

Arriva not only had to meet its own business growth objectives but also demonstrate commitment to government targets. In the face of an ever downward trend in passenger numbers and the inexorable rise of the motor car, challenge was the word!

ALL ABOARD

Arriva realised that heightened efficiency and quality of the core service it offered was essential in achieving these targets. In response, it invested over £250m in its fleet, service and staff training. The company believed, however, that operational investment would not be enough – a marketing campaign would be required to persuade people on to its buses. Cogent Elliot was appointed to help do the persuading.

DRIVING TOWARDS A STRATEGY

We knew from public research that the main reason for people not using the bus was that they had their own mode of transport (Figure 4). Strategically Arriva wanted to get these non-users out of their cars and on to its buses.

The potential was huge: 30% of people never used the bus, equating to a potential market of 13.4 million adults.[3] Putting this into perspective, with 86% of passenger kilometres travelled by car and van,[4] a mode switch of just 1% would equate to a 4.8% increase in bus usage.

---

3. Source: TGI.
4. Source: DETR.

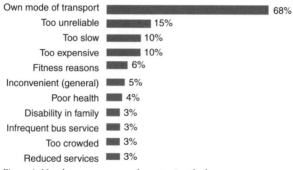

Figure 4: *Non-bus users: reasons for not using the bus*
Source: MORI, 2000

Research helped us to identify the key barriers to bus usage. An important strategic insight was that – over and above people's often negative perceptions of buses, drivers and the service itself – bus travel wasn't even on the radar for many people (Figure 5).

As if to support our ambitions, research also showed that 10 million non-users would consider using buses in the right circumstances.[5]

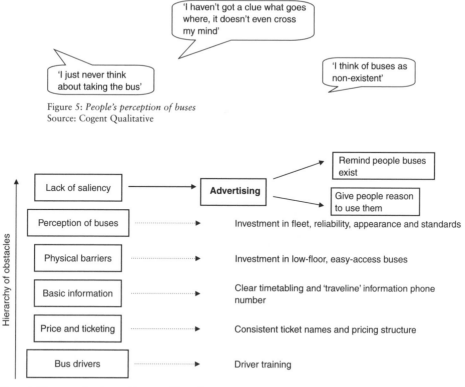

Figure 5: *People's perception of buses*
Source: Cogent Qualitative

Figure 6: *Non-users: barriers and how to address them*

5. Source: Confederation of Passenger Transport.

Other potential barriers to bus travel were already being addressed by Arriva's operational investment. Making buses salient for non-users, and giving them a reason to use, seemed to be the real task for marketing (Figure 6).

The creative insight was that although buses are a mass transport medium, every person's trip is individual. Our creative work emphasised how bus travel could very much be a part of everyday life; the strapline 'Going your way' epitomised the communication.

THE START OF THE JOURNEY

The North-East was selected as a test region.

Over the course of its first year the campaign punched hard in the cinema, in press, on the buses themselves and on radio (Figures 7–11).

ARRIVA
Going your way

North East Media 2001		Jan	Feb	March	April	May	June	July	August	Sept	Oct	Nov	Dec
Cinema 60 Seconds (49 Screens)				9th - 29th			8th-28th			21st Sept - 11th Oct			
Radio 30 Seconds				5th-16th			4th-24th						
Radio 20 Seconds				16th-25th			4th-24th			17th Sept - 17th Oct			
Local & Regional press				5th - 26th			11th-25th			17th Sept - 8th Oct			
Bus sides				1st - 31st			1st-30th			1st - 30th			
Door-to-door	502,068			12th - 26th									
	511,756						11th-25th						
	519,051									17th Sept - 1st Oct			

Figure 7: *Media schedule, 2001*

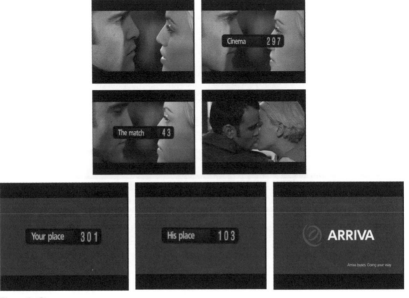

Figure 8: *Cinema*

Figure 9: *Local press*

Figure 10: *Bus sides/super sides/streetliners*

Figure 11: *Bulletins (information leaflets and discount vouchers)*

THE FIRST STOP

To evaluate the impact of the advertising-dominated campaign, Arriva commissioned a tracking study to measure awareness (Figure 12).

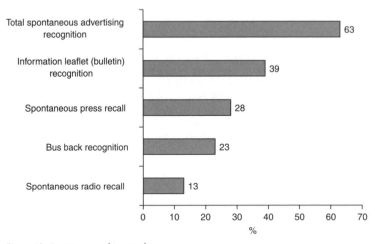

Figure 12: *Awareness tracking results*
Source: NFO Image and Awareness Tracking Study

In other words, 63% of potential bus users could spontaneously remember some aspect of the campaign: a very encouraging response. Within that, it was clear that bulletins were delivering the highest awareness levels.

None of our data seemed to suggest, however, that these enhanced levels of awareness were resulting in an observable transport mode shift among non-users.

A CHANGE OF ROUTE

Despite awareness success, our inability to prove a behavioural change among non-users meant we had to make some important strategic decisions before significant investment was undertaken in rolling the campaign out to the rest of the country.

Analysis of patronage in the above campaign suggested that it was easier to persuade medium and light bus users to make *more* journeys, than it was to convert non-users. Common sense dictated, therefore, that we change the focus of our targeting. Once again, the scale of the opportunity was enormous: if we persuaded just 10% of the country's 13.6 million medium and light bus users to make just two more journeys per year by bus, the result would be over 2.5 million incremental journeys.

Research found that as well as delivering the best awareness figures, people were very receptive to information leaflets (bulletins); 73% of users keep timetables/leaflets at home for reference and 44% of bus users would most like to find out about potential ticket offers via leaflets delivered through the door.[6] On the basis of

---

6. Source: Arriva, 'Perceptions and Expectations of Bus Services'.

BRONZE

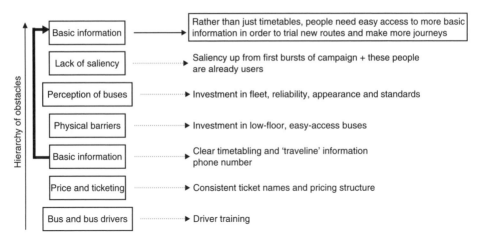

Figure 13: *Medium and light users: barriers and how to address them*

all of the above, the decision was taken to move media monies exclusively to the bulletin format.

We re-examined our model of barriers to bus travel (Figure 13). For light and medium users, lack of saliency was obviously not so much of a problem – they were more aware of the existence of buses and might well be taking one to town once a week. The problem in most cases was that this was the only journey they were familiar with – they simply didn't have the information or motivation they needed to trial new routes. Statistically we knew that 88% of these people lived six minutes away from a bus stop[7] but if, as was often the case, they didn't know where the buses went from that stop ... the likelihood that they would try a new route, making additional journeys, was small.

BACK ON THE ROAD AGAIN ...

Our new brief was to provide light and medium users with all the information and motivation they needed to trial new routes and make more journeys by bus.

Research showed that bus trips were most commonly made for shopping (17 trips per person per year), commuting (14 trips), leisure (13 trips) and education (nine trips).[8] We incorporated these reasons into the creative work by developing simple route maps, easy-to-use frequency tables, icons for landmarks and suggested destinations, and routes customers could trial, as well as discount vouchers (Figure 14). All the information people needed to try a new route and make more journeys was at their fingertips – or on their doormat.

The bulletin format provided a versatile template, with each creative variant being tailored for the relevant Arriva corridor (group of routes), allowing completely relevant, up-to-date local information to be incorporated. Between autumn 2002 and autumn 2004 a highly targeted, logistically complex door-drop

---

7. Source: National Travel Survey.
8. Source: National Travel Survey.

Traveline number   Destination icons   Frequency tables

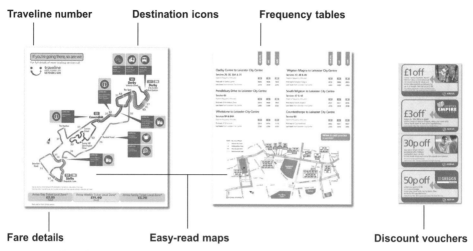

Fare details   Easy-read maps   Discount vouchers

Figure 14: *Bulletin features*

campaign was in place (see the media schedule in Table 1). At its peak, no less than 74 different bulletins were designed, produced and delivered in a single burst of activity.

Media targeting focused on people living within 10 minutes' walk of an Arriva bus stop. The bulletins were delivered by Royal Mail, Newshare, Solus and MicroSolus to get the best possible coverage along the different corridors.

TABLE 1: MEDIA SCHEDULE 2002–04

Year	Period	Corridors	Creative variants	Reach
2002	Autumn	26	2	838,139
2003	Spring	74	3	2,592,926
2003	Autumn	69	2	2,514,404
2004	Spring	68	2	2,409,557
2004	Autumn	70	1	2,446,439

THE CREATIVE

Examples of the creative are shown in Figures 15–19.

Figure 15: *Autumn bulletin, 2002*

Figure 16: *Spring bulletin, 2003*

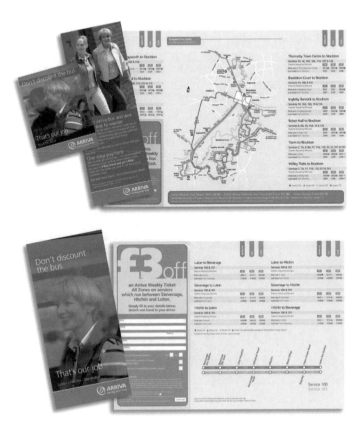

Figure 17: *Autumn bulletin, 2003*

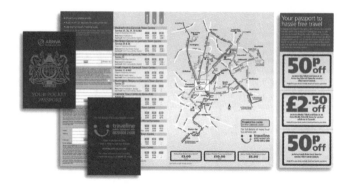

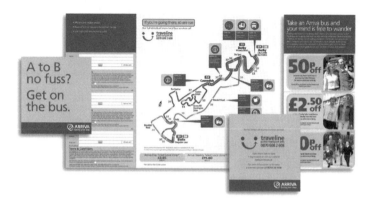

Figure 18: *Spring bulletin, 2004*

Figure 19: *Autumn bulletin, 2004*

CAMPAIGN ANALYSIS

2002: commercial results

In the autumn of 2002 Arriva ran its first test of the new strategy, albeit with a relatively small number of marketed corridors. It was obvious that the activity was having some impact. From the off, redemption levels for the discounted vouchers in the bulletins stood at 0.8%, a figure considered respectable for this and other relatively 'low-interest' categories. The $64,000 question was whether the activity was helping to generate incremental patronage and hence meeting Arriva's objectives. Data available showed a modest increase in customer journeys, and anecdotal evidence at depot and driver level was positive. On that basis, Arriva opted to extend the marketing activity to corridors representing just under half of passenger income.

2003–2004: commercial results

Measuring and ultimately proving the success of any marketing programme in the bus industry is notoriously difficult; undoubtedly this is the main reason why there has been so little of it! The biggest problem is the sheer range of factors that can affect patronage. From the everyday, such as a bad spell of weather or a price promotion from a competitor, to the unforeseen – a petrol shortage, or the death of the Queen Mother and subsequent extra bank holiday; all these will affect people's likelihood to choose the bus.

Arriva was aware of the need to construct a statistically robust 'unmarketed control' against which marketed activity could be measured. In this case, of course, after the 2002 test round of activity, marketing was to be applied to corridors that represented just under half of total Arriva passenger income. This enabled a like-for-like comparison between marketed and unmarketed corridors, eliminating the effect of external environment factors, predictable or otherwise. Ultimately it allowed a hugely reliable statistical analysis – key for evaluating the campaign.

Patronage numbers for the composite marketed and unmarketed routes were tracked for six weeks immediately prior to each burst of activity, and for six weeks immediately afterwards. Because patronage numbers in each case were so vast, (c.45 million journeys for each six-week period!), we could be confident that direct comparison between the marketed and unmarketed sets of patronage numbers would be reliable and relatively small differences statistically significant.

The results of this comparison were conclusive (see Table 2).

Those corridors exposed to marketing showed an increase in patronage between the 'pre-' and 'post-'periods, while corridors that weren't showed a decrease in passenger numbers – essentially the campaign seemed to be stemming the relentless loss of passenger journeys that the whole market was suffering.

To interrogate further, we investigated the relative performance of marketed vs unmarketed corridors on a rolling 12-month basis. We looked at year-on-year figures for the 'pre' activity periods, and then compared the relative improvement or decline in performance in the 'post' period to give us a feel for the impact the activity had had on the underlying rate of decline or growth over the course of a year.

TABLE 2: MARKETED VS UNMARKETED CORRIDOR PATRONAGE

2003

Unmarketed corridors

Total patronage: six weeks pre-campaign (spring) plus six weeks pre-campaign (autumn)	72,058,546
Total patronage: six weeks post-campaign (spring) plus six weeks post-campaign (autumn)	61,491,416
Difference	**–14.7%**

Marketed corridors

Total patronage: six weeks pre-campaign (spring) plus six weeks pre-campaign (autumn)	32,544,264
Total patronage: six weeks post-campaign (spring) plus six weeks post-campaign (autumn)	33,189,058
Difference	**+2.0%**

2004

Unmarketed corridors

Total patronage: six weeks pre-campaign (spring) plus six weeks pre-campaign (autumn)	78,874,597
Total patronage: six weeks post-campaign (spring) plus six weeks post-campaign (autumn)	77,897,445
Difference	**–1.2%**

Marketed corridors

Total patronage: six weeks pre-campaign (spring) plus six weeks pre-campaign (autumn)	28,499,574
Total patronage: six weeks post-campaign (spring) plus six weeks post-campaign (autumn)	29,772,441
Difference	**+4.5%**

For example, if a data point showed a decline of –2% for the 12 months to the 'pre' period, and a +2% increase in the 12 months to the 'post' period, then the incremental change could be measured as a +4% percentage shift in performance.

In every case, the unmarketed corridors showed year-on-year decline in both the pre and post periods. By contrast, the marketed corridors showed a positive shift in performance in every post-period (Figure 20).

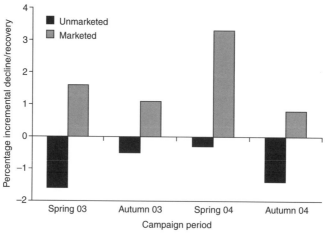

Figure 20: *Year-on-year variance: marketed vs unmarketed corridors*

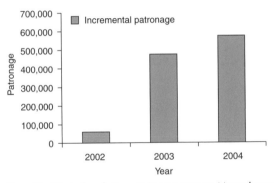

Figure 21: *Effect of marketing activity on patronage (six weeks post-activity)*

The reversal of the decline in the marketed corridors represented more than a million incremental journeys as a direct result of marketing activity (Figure 21). Given that we have only tracked incremental journeys in the six weeks following marketing activity, the actual number is likely to be even greater over the longer term.

The campaign cost of generating each of these incremental journeys worked out at £1.04 in 2003 and £0.80 in 2004. Comparing that to an average Arriva ticket cost of £1.12, the campaign has more than paid for itself in each of the six-week post-activity periods in question. With further incremental journeys generated beyond the six-week analysis periods, Arriva is convinced that the longer-term return on investment has been substantial.

'NON-COMMERCIAL' RESULTS

Bus travel is a people business. The motivation of the whole team, especially at depot and driver level, impacts upon the quality of the service the customer receives, and hence their attitude towards bus travel in general.

Arriva was not alone among bus companies in the marked absence of historical marketing activity; the campaign when it began in 2001 was seen as an exciting step forward and proved very popular among staff and customers alike. Certainly it provided a very visible connection between Arriva head office and its 17,000 staff across the country.

Equally importantly, the groundbreaking and demonstratively successful campaign raised the profile of the company with other important stakeholders – including members of local and national government, who could hardly miss Arriva's highly visible and committed start to meeting the ten-year plan targets set by the Government in its Public Service Agreement.

'The campaign we ran through the first half of the decade has proved to be a great catalyst for stronger internal communications, which in turn contributed to the excellent levels of customer satisfaction we continually achieve. It would also be true to say that the campaign has contributed to the recognition of Arriva as a real industry leader in this sector.'

Catherine Mason, Managing Director, Arriva Midlands

CONCLUSION

The objective Arriva set for this campaign was very clear: to increase patronage. This in the face of a long-term decline in passenger numbers in the market as a whole, and a seductive, heavily promoted and increasingly powerful competitor: the motor car.

Ultimately, it succeeded in generating more than a million incremental journeys by giving light and medium users the relevant and accurate local information they needed to extend their existing usage of buses.

In doing so it has demonstrated the value of marketing investment in a sector that has always been notoriously suspicious of it, and has set a model and platform for a campaign that continues today to improve the company's patronage.

13

ATS Euromaster

A *new paradigm for tactical retailer advertising*

Principal authors: Steve McCarron and Peter Harris, BDH\TBWA
Contributing author: Kate Murphy, BDH\TBWA

EDITOR'S SUMMARY

This paper illustrates one of the golden rules of retailing: 'retail is detail'.

Rather than using a 'one size fits all' approach, BDH\TBWA devised a framework for highly localised tactical advertising that could be fine-tuned to the needs of individual car repair centres.

By focusing expenditure on those stores that needed it most, and tailoring messages to local consumers, the agency were able to use funds more efficiently. This enabled them to tackle the decline in ATS's sales without actually spending any more money.

The judges were impressed with the forensic detail of the agency's thinking. Did you know that the salty sea air means that drivers in coastal towns need to get their brakes done more often? We felt that other retailers could learn from this kind of micro-analysis, and hence awarded this paper the prize for Best New Learning.

We also liked the way the agency took advantage of their localised approach to demonstrate effectiveness, showing how sales grew in advertised stores, even though they declined elsewhere.

INTRODUCTION

Plenty of ink has been spilt on demonstrating how 'brand building' campaigns have supported positive sales uplifts for retailer brands, often to the neglect of 'harder nosed' tactical advertising, designed to drive immediate sales. However, as we all know, immediate sales are the life blood of all retailers and a key benchmark of corporate health.

This is why anyone who is in control of a retailer's advertising budget will dedicate an enormous percentage of it towards tactical activity. And this is why it is a serious business to ensure that the tactical budget is used in a way that will generate the best return possible.

This paper tells the story of how we changed ATS Euromaster's (ATSE's) approach to using tactical advertising, in order to transform the effect it would have on generating sales.

Our approach was based on that golden rule of retail: 'retail is detail' – that is, great retailing is about directing intellectual energy towards the micro level, in order to fine-tune individual centre offers, so that as much value is extracted out of the individual customer as possible.

We took the view that great tactical advertising is simply an extension of this. If the tactical advertising strategy could be 'fine-tuned' in order to accommodate the idiosyncrasies of the retail estate, then surely this would deliver more efficiency.

We demonstrate how, by rejecting a 'one size fits all' approach and through getting to know the retail estate, we transformed the way tactical advertising delivered a return to the business.

First, we show that we achieved more with less and, second, that we created longer-term sales effects as well as the more familiar short-term uplifts.

Furthermore, we go on to show a four-fold payback from the advertising in terms of new sales, and that this yielded a more efficient return on investment vs the 'one size fits all approach' of previous years.

BACKGROUND

ATSE is the UK's number two 'fast-fit' operator in the UK. It sells tyres, exhausts, batteries, shock absorbers, brakes, oil and MOTs for motor vehicles, through its 533 centres across the UK. While B2B trade had performed well in recent years, the 'consumer' trade was in year-on-year decline. In summer 2004, ATSE came to us with a brief to start reversing this decline.

THE TASK

As shown in Table 1, market share was in decline year on year, driven by the growth of 'independents'.

This was reflected in sales, which were accelerating in their year-on-year decline. Figure 1 illustrates this trend, and also projects what might have happened in the second half of 2004, had this trend been left to continue.

TABLE 1: ATSE CONSUMER MARKET SHARE

Company	2003	2004
ATSE	7%	6%
Local independent	38%	40%
Kwik Fit	16%	16%
National Tyres & Autocare	3%	3%
Others	36%	35%

Source: GfK

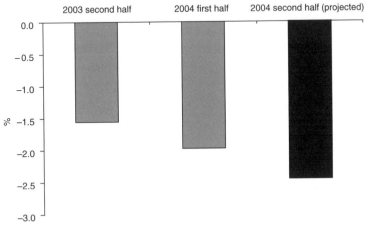

Figure 1: *Year-on-year sales decline for ATSE's consumer business*

The marketing objective was to halt this accelerating year-on-year decline (and so prevent the scenario projected above). The onus, however, would fall entirely on the effectiveness of the advertising approach. All the other key market dynamics, prior to the September–November campaign period were working against us, as outlined below.

- *Media budget*, as defined in terms of spend/month, would be one-third of that in previous years (Table 2).

TABLE 2: ATSE AVERAGE MEDIA SPEND PER MONTH

2004 campaign	£83k
2001–2003 average	£254k

- *A lapse in recent activity*: for the first time in recent history the estate had received negligible support in the six-month period prior to the Autumn activity (Table 3).

TABLE 3: ATSE FIRST-HALF MEDIA SPEND

Year	ATSE first half media spend
2001	£2392k
2002	£1498k
2003	£1886k
2004	£69k

- *The quality of our lead promotion* would be no stronger than in previous years (Table 4).

TABLE 4: SUMMARY OF ATSE'S LEAD PRICE/SALES PROMOTIONS SINCE 2002

2002	Promotion
January	Four tyres for £59.99
February	Buy one get one half price, tyres
March	Buy one get one half price, tyres
April	Buy one get one half price, tyres
May	Up to 1/3 off tyres
July	Up to 25% off tyres
2003	**Promotion**
February	Four tyres for £59.99
March	Buy one get one half price, tyres
April	Save up to 25% on tyres
May	Save up to 20% when you buy four tyres
July	Buy one get one half price, tyres
August	Save up to 25% on tyres
November	Save up to 25% on tyres
December	Exhaust sale, 30% off
2004	**Promotion**
August	£10 off any new Michelin tyre

We knew that tactical advertising could be a key driver of sales. However, given these countervailing market dynamics, and the reduced media budget, we knew that a radical new approach would be required.

THE APPROACH

We therefore set out to challenge the way things had previously been done.

The conventional advertising approach for retailers with a national retail presence was to run a national advertising campaign across the entire estate, carrying a homogeneous creative message. Indeed this had been the approach of ATSE in previous years (Table 5).

TABLE 5: SUMMARY OF ATSE HISTORICAL MEDIA ACTIVITY

Year	Media	Total spend
2001	National TV	£3.4m
2002	National press	£2.8m
2003	National press	£3.0m

We used an internal planning tool called 'Conventions Planets' in order to elicit the assumptions underlying this approach (Figure 2).

We identified the underlying assumption responsible for driving this system as being 'Efficiency = taking a "mass approach" to communications'.

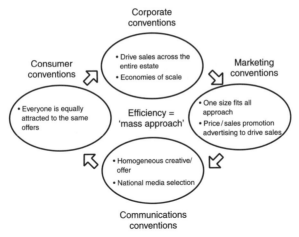

Figure 2: *Summary of 'Conventions Planets' analysis of national retailer tactical advertising behaviour*

Given that our strategy would depend on being able to 'deliver more for less', the idea of efficiency was a critical one for us. We therefore challenged this definition, and generated a new set of Corporate and Consumer assumptions, as detailed below.

- *The retail estate is not equal.* That is, some areas of the retail estate will benefit from advertising more than others. If we could target activity around those centres that could deliver a proportionately higher return in sales, that would give us more efficiency.
- *The customer profile is not equal.* That is, not all customers have the same levels of demand for fast-fit products and services. If we could identify how levels of demand differ between different areas, then we could tailor our creative to carry the right messages to unlock the potential demand. Once again, we believed that if this could be achieved, then the activity would be made to work that bit more efficiently.

In summary, this approach would have massive implications for our marketing and communications strategy in terms of:

- determining which centres to support, and
- determining which creative messages to run in each area.

PUTTING THE APPROACH INTO ACTION

We created a local media campaign, which featured advertising and leaflets in local press (see Figure 3), and local radio advertising.

Regional press would be our focal point, providing the flexibility to target individual centre catchment areas, as well as providing the space to feature a number of offers in a single execution. Furthermore, research indicated that 'in the market' consumers would use this media to actively seek offers.[1]

---

1. The Conversion Study, 2004, Millward Brown (available from the Newspaper Society).

Figure 3: *Local press insert*

We ran our activity over three months, during September, October and November 2004.

Choosing which centres to support

We segmented the centres in order to understand which could really benefit from a fresh injection of customer demand. We looked for centres with the potential to convert leads effectively today, as well as generating business tomorrow through delivering an impressive customer experience.

This would enable us to generate an efficient short-term return on our investment, as well as some more long-term effects through recommendations and repeat business.

Our segments were as follows.

- **The top performers:** 44 centres selected on the basis of strong performance over the previous 24 months. We wanted to select a group of well-tuned retail machines, which we believed could convert leads effectively and generate additional business.

- **Underperformers with potential:** 21 centres, which had underperformed over the previous 24 months in terms of sales. Those with operational shortcomings (e.g. stock/service levels/centre condition) were stripped out in order to create a group that could really benefit from a fresh injection of customer demand.

- **Refurbs:** 22 centres that had recently been refurbished and renovated. We believed that an improved centre offer and in-centre morale would put them in

ATS EUROMASTER

an excellent position to capitalise on fresh demand, and generate future business through repeat visits and recommendations.

In a departure from the historical blanket approach, we had identified 87 centres for special attention.

Furthermore, when we analysed the recent sales performance of these centres, it became apparent that because of the high percentage of underperformers within this group, the negative year-on-year sales performance of the overall business was actually even more exaggerated (Table 6).

TABLE 6: YEAR-ON-YEAR SALES PERFORMANCE OF CAMPAIGN
CENTRES VS THE OVERALL CONSUMER BUSINESS

Centres	Year-on-year performance: pre (April–July)
Campaign group of centres	–7.4%
Total ATSE	–2.3%

We realised that unlocking the potential of these centres would be critical to turning around the overall performance of the business.

Choosing which creative messages to run

We knew that the best way to drive demand among 'in the market' customers would be to target relevant offers to them. Therefore, we designed a template that would enable us to clearly communicate five offers simultaneously, without compromising clarity (see Figure 4).

Figure 4: *Ad targeting relevant offers*

Each ad would run with the lead price promotion in the main headline (which, as explained earlier was '£10 off any new tyre'), supported by four secondary offers in the body of the ad.

Given that, at any one time, ATSE had around 10 secondary offers (Table 7) that it could potentially communicate, we had to decide which ones to feature in our advertising.

TABLE 7: THE OFFERS

Primary message
£10 off any new tyre

Secondary messages
1. Michelin tyres from £31.99 (awareness message)
2. Free 10-point safety check
3. 20% off brake pads
4. Oil and filter change from £15.99
5. Free mobile tyre fitting
6. 15% off any batteries
7. 15% off a complete exhaust system
8. Club Sixty – over 60s get 10% off every Thursday
9. MOTs available (awareness message)
10. Free battery testing and fitting

As described earlier, our hypothesis was that demand for specific fast-fit services would vary depending on the relevant catchment area. We wanted to determine where the demand for product/service areas existed, and make sure we communicated the right offer in the right place.

We therefore worked with Experian to divide the UK into geodemographic clusters. We then crossed these clusters with our sales data, in order to understand which type of fast-fit service each group would be more likely to 'buy in' to. Table 8 shows the eventual cluster groups that our centres fitted into.

TABLE 8: GEODEMOGRAPHIC CLUSTERS

Geodemographic cluster group	% of estate
Northern city industrial	5.2
Coastal retirement	8.9
Isolated rural	2.5
Central London	1.4
New southern suburbs	1.4
Wealthy commuters	11.5
Market towns	7.2
Affluent suburbs	3.7
Manufacturing heartlands	10.5
Middle England	15.0
Local communities	17.7
Poor remote towns	5.4
Truck centres	9.7

The results transformed the way in which we viewed each centre. For instance, coastal locations over-indexed on brakes – most likely down to corrosion caused by sea air – whereas rural areas over-indexed for batteries – most likely down to prolonged periods of downtime associated with vehicles in these areas.

This determined which combination of offers we ran in each area. Each area ran a different combination designed to extract maximum value from that marketplace.

RESULTS AND PAYBACK

Our approach

We have compared our campaign centres with centres that received no advertising support (our control group), in order to remove underlying changes happening irrespective of the advertising.

We have used year-on-year comparisons in order to remove the influence of seasonality.

Furthermore, the comparison with a control group of centres removes subtler degrees of seasonality. Regional, year-on-year changes in seasonality are not significant because both the campaign and control groups are composed of centres from across several regions and the evaluation spans several months.

Furthermore, by using a 'control group', the effect of competitor advertising has also been screened out. Competitor advertising would affect the campaign and control groups in a similar way.

A significant improvement in sales

Table 9 indicates how we succeeded in reversing the high year-on-year decline that our campaign centres were suffering from.

TABLE 9: CAMPAIGN CENTRES – YEAR-ON-YEAR SALES SHIFTS

Year	Pre (April–July)	During (Sept.–Nov.)	Post (Dec.)
2003	5,246,383	4,818,645	4,237,178
2004	4,858,818	4,765,445	4,189,042
Campaign yr on yr	–7.4	–1.1%	–1.1%

This left us with an overall improvement of 6.3% across those centres vs the pre-period, with this improvement persisting into the post-period.

We then looked for the same shifts among our control group centres. However, in contrast to the campaign centres, we found very little change (Table 10).

TABLE 10: CONTROL CENTRES – YEAR-ON-YEAR SALES SHIFTS

Year	Pre (April–July)	During (Sept.–Nov.)	Post (Dec.)
2003	25,086,564	24,320,633	20,311,127
2004	24,790,479	24,336,812	20,134,741
Control yr on yr	–1.2%	+0.07%	–0.87%

Whereas there was a 6.3% improvement among the campaign centres, there was only a marginal improvement in sales in our control group. In effect, the campaign centres outperformed the control group by 5% during the campaign, and by 5.9% during the post-period. This 'over-performance' is summarised in Figure 5.

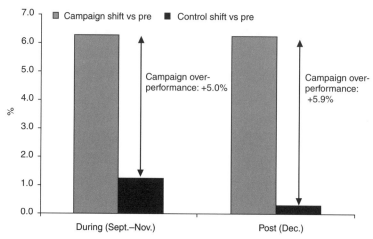

Figure 5: *How the control group over-performed the overall business*

The results indicate that our strategy of targeting centres in order to unlock a relatively large potential was paying off. Furthermore, our hypothesis that those centres would also start to generate future business also appeared to be borne out by the impressive post-campaign results.

How the product/service offers we prioritised drove those results

The following analysis demonstrates how sales of the products and services, which we prioritised, were responsible for the overall sales improvements (Table 11).

TABLE 11: KEY PRODUCT CATEGORIES – CAMPAIGN GROUP OVER-
PERFORMANCE VS CONTROL GROUP CENTRES

Product	During (Sept.–Nov.)	Post (Dec.)
New car tyres	+2.6%	+3.0%
MOT	+3.5%	+26.7%
Brake pads	+13.4%	+9.7%
Exhausts	−3.1%	+10.1%

The main product categories featured in the campaign all demonstrate significant over-performance compared to the control group.

Furthermore, in most cases these product areas saw positive year-on-year growth (Table 12).

TABLE 12: KEY PRODUCT CATEGORIES – CAMPAIGN GROUP YEAR-
ON-YEAR PERFORMANCE

Product	Pre (April–July)	During (Sept.–Nov.)	Post (Dec.)
New car tyres	−5.7%	+2.4%	−2.3%
MOT	−11.0%	−6.3%	+10.0%
Brake pads	−8.5%	+4.3%	+0.5%
Exhausts	−1.1%	+4.0%	+5.7%

A significant payback to the business

We have calculated that the 5.0% over-performance during the campaign period was worth £0.53m, and that the 5.9% over-performance in the post period was worth £0.25m, making a total incremental £0.78m retail sales during September–December 2004.

However, it was our hypothesis that these centres had the potential to generate future business through repeat visits and recommendations; we have therefore projected a longer-term payback occurring into 2005. The sales data for early 2005 indicate that although the performance differential enjoyed by the 'campaign centres' had begun to decline, it still remained. The differential performance is now 5.4% (down from 5.9% in December).

We have projected a decay rate for this performance differential (Figure 6). The rate is based on that observed in the first months of 2005.

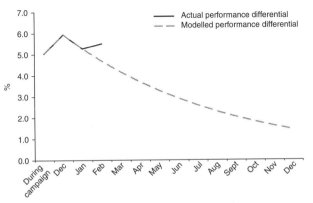

Figure 6: *Projected 'over-performance' of control centres for 2005*

This is a deliberately conservative projection, using a slightly faster decay rate than the one actually observed in early 2005.

The analysis suggests that the extra sales revenue within campaign centres during 2005 will be £1.7m (Figure 7). When combined with the £0.78m figure for 2004, this gives us a total figure of £2.48m.

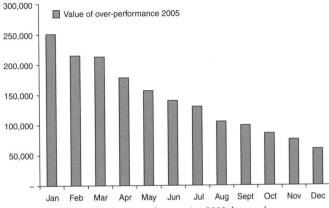

Figure 7: *Value of projected 'over-performance' in 2005, by month*

Based on a total spend of £566,000 for 2004, this would translate to a return of £4.38 of new sales generated for every £ of advertising money spent. Based on ATSE standard product margins these incremental retail sales were more than enough to cover the cost of the advertising.

We achieved our objectives

As described at the beginning of this paper, our overall objective was to halt the year-on-year increasing sales decline against all the odds. Figure 8 illustrates that this was achieved. It also projects what the decline would have been had the activity not occurred, based on the £0.78m of performance increased as calculated above.

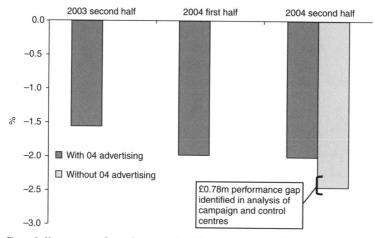

Figure 8: *Year-on-year sales performance of total business vs projected*

A new definition of efficiency

Finally, we can demonstrate that not only did our approach deliver short- and longer-term payback effects, but vs our historical approach it was a much more efficient way to plan the activity.

It is difficult to draw comparisons between the new approach of 2004 and the historical approach of previous years because the activity ran for only three months, rather than all year round as in previous years.

We have therefore taken our payback definition of '£4.38 of new sales generated from every £1 of advertising money invested' and calculated what we would have achieved in 2004 had our budget been comparable with that of previous years.

We have increased our total payback three-fold on the basis that, in previous years, around three times as much advertising money would have been invested in media during this period.

Figure 9 illustrates that, on this basis, where media spend is equal, the 2004 activity would have performed much more strongly than in previous years, through considerably slowing down the decline in year-on-year sales for the first time.

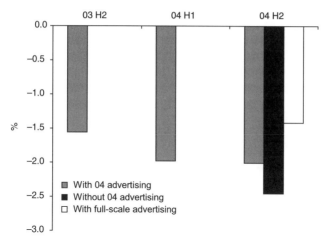

Figure 9: *Comparison of year-on-year sales looking at actual and projected scenarios*

CONCLUSION

This paper has demonstrated how a different way of approaching tactical advertising for a national retailer allowed us to deliver significant payback, while achieving our objectives against the odds.

By challenging the conventions of how national retailers approach tactical advertising, we believe that we have created a new paradigm for approaching this sort of activity.

We believe that the assumption of 'efficiency' that underlies the 'mass approach' is actually a myth. The better paradigm involves getting right up close to the client estate, and applying retail's golden rule: 'retail is detail'.

It will be through deepening their understanding of the retail estate that advertising agencies in the future will discover how best to unlock sales for the client, and ultimately achieve more with less.

14

Blood Donation

New strategy, new blood

*How a new strategy made a difference
to levels of blood donation in Scotland*

Principal author: David Watson, The Bridge
Media agency: MediaCom

EDITOR'S SUMMARY

When new rules, intended to tackle the problem of new variant CJD, restricted the supply of blood donors in 2004, it looked as if the Scottish Health Service faced a crisis. Unless they could recruit enough extra donors to offset the restrictions, there would be a blood shortage. Advertising was going to have to work harder than ever.

The Bridge met the challenge with a new strategy that focused on making a personal connection with the donor. Research showed that the biggest single reason people didn't give blood was that they didn't feel they had been personally asked. By making people feel that the ads were talking to them individually, response rates were significantly increased, and targets for donations were exceeded. All of this was achieved efficiently, with cost per response falling by half.

The judges particularly liked the way radio was used to fine-tune the supply of donors to meet short-term variations in demand.

BACKGROUND

On 16 March 2004, the Health Secretary John Reid announced that all those people who had had blood transfusions since 1980 would be excluded from future blood donation. This policy was introduced as a measure to reduce the possible risk of vCJD (new variant Creutzfeldt-Jakob disease) transmission by blood transfusion. People who have been the recipients of blood transfusions tend to be more likely to become blood donors themselves. These previously transfused donors (PTDs) made up a significant proportion of existing blood donors. To exclude them from the donor base in Scotland would have a major impact on the blood supply.

In addition, the extent of the problem did not extend only to PTDs. Previous experience had shown that adverse publicity (such as that in connection with the HIV virus in the 1980s) would have a considerable secondary impact on blood donor recruitment. It was estimated that the issue of vCJD transmission in blood would lead to a loss of up to 10% of the Scottish donor base.

The immediate effects of this crisis were serious enough. However, it occurred at a time when the donor base had been declining for broader social and demographic reasons. In 1991, donors aged 17–24 accounted for 26% of the donor base, but by 2001 accounted for only 20%. At the same time, an ageing population required more operations and hospital care. In addition, trends such as exotic travel, body-piercing and tattooing had also affected donor numbers (deferral periods can be up to 12 months following any of these activities). Deferral rates among new donors had more than doubled since 1993 and currently nearly one-third of all new donors are turned away at their first session.

Therefore the vCJD crisis took place at a time when there had been an overall decline in the level of blood donations in Scotland over many years. The crisis in blood stocks was alleviated only in 2003/04 with an emergency appeal. This drastic and unusual step was taken because donor attendances were expected to be only 300,000 (see Figure 1). Yet, this was something undertaken as a last resort and could not be repeated every year. The long-term future of blood stocks needed to be placed on a more secure footing.

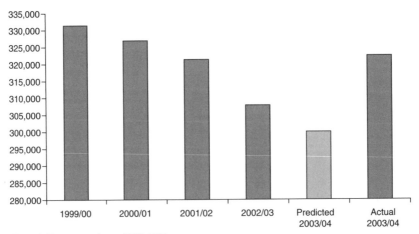

Figure 1: *Donor attendance, 1999–2004*

The combination of the deferral of PTDs and long-term erosion of the donor base meant that there were no longer enough blood donors to reliably support Scottish healthcare. The Scottish National Blood Transfusion Service (SNBTS) had to recruit donors, and quickly developed an integrated marketing strategy to stimulate the recovery of the Scottish blood donor base.

THE NEW STRATEGY

SNBTS estimated that it needed to attract 58,000 new and returning/lapsed donors in order to repair the donor base and to offset the effects of the vCJD crisis. (Returning/lapsed donors are those who haven't given for more than two years.)

However, as Figure 2 makes clear, this was a massive task. Over the last 15 years, the annual number of new and returning donors has fluctuated only slightly and was part of a longer-term decline. Between 1989/90 and 1999/2000, new donor levels averaged 42,994. By 2003/4, this figure was only 38,381.

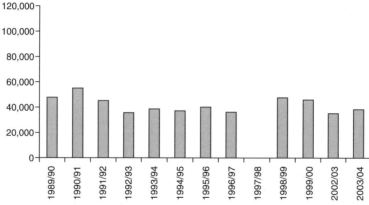

Figure 2: *New and returning donor attendances, 1989–2004*

Put into this historical context, the target of 58,000 new and returning donor attendances was incredibly challenging. It meant delivering over 50% more new and returning donors than had been achieved in 2003/04. It was clear that in order to affect such a step-change in donor numbers, a step-change in strategy was required.

The first task of The Bridge's marketing strategy was to separate out a clear role for the advertising (to ask people to register to become a blood donor) and a clear role for the below-the-line activity (to manage the database) (see Figure 3).

At the heart of the strategy was the idea of personal relevance. Extensive desk research of blood collection campaigns around the world revealed a common theme: the importance of making a personal connection with the (potential) donor.

Only 6% of the Scottish population are blood donors. Blood donation just isn't at the top of people's minds. Most people in Scotland agree that giving blood is a good thing. They also understand the need for blood donors, yet for 94% of the population the concept of blood donation is clearly not something they are actively

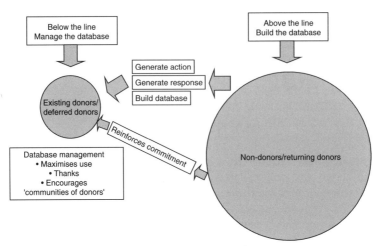

Figure 3: *A model of how The Bridge's strategy would work*

engaged in. It was crucial that the advertising engaged with people and made them think that their contribution would be important. The strategy needed to make the issue of blood donation personally relevant.

Research from worldwide donor recruitment campaigns revealed a stunning insight: when questioned, the biggest single reason non-donors gave for not giving blood was that they felt they had never been asked. Although people were aware of a general request or 'asking' for blood donors, they didn't feel it was actually directed at them. They felt the advertising was asking someone else. Clearly, success in reaching the new donor targets would depend on making it obvious to the viewer that it was they who were being asked to donate blood. It needed to feel like a personal request. This would give blood donation a personal relevance that it previously didn't have.

EXECUTING THE STRATEGY: THE CREATIVE WORK

For the new strategy to deliver results, there were four fundamental issues that the creative work needed to address. First, it needed to leave the viewer in no doubt that it was they who were being asked to register to become blood donors. Second, it needed to do this in an emotive and engaging manner. Third, in order to deliver the stiff response targets, it was crucial that the direct response element of the commercial didn't feel tagged on. It needed to be integral to the creative idea. Finally, it was vital that the message was delivered without causing anxiety. Any tone of crisis would only lead to donor fatigue.

Although it was important for the new commercial to generate as many blood donations as possible, donor attendances (and consequently blood stocks) needed to be manageable. Blood has a limited shelf life of only a few days and collecting too much blood would mean that the SNBTS would be faced with higher than acceptable levels of wastage. Therefore the strategy needed to work like a tap – able to turn the donor supply on and off, and airing the commercial only when there was a need for blood.

Nurse: I'm sure they'll call

Dad: She's bound to call soon son

Doctor: Don't worry, he'll call in a while

VO: It's not someone else they're looking for.
It's you. Scotland needs you to give blood.
Whether you've never given before or just
haven't given for a while, call 0845 90 90 999.

Figure 4: *'Call'*

Following qualitative research, 'Call' was identified as the television script that resonated most with new and lapsed donors. The campaign was launched on 2 August 2004 and ran until 31 August at a weight of 500 TVRs across Scotland (see Figure 4). Blood supplies were healthy until later in the year, when two radio commercials, 'Your Call' and 'Accident' ran in November and December. The TV commercial 'Call' was broadcast again in January 2005.

THE RESULTS

Prior to developing the new creative work, the SNBTS had been using a rebranded version of a National Blood Service (NBS) commercial, featuring Gary Lineker and other celebrities. The effectiveness of the new strategy will be measured against the effectiveness of the Lineker commercial and also against targets set by SNBTS.

The new strategy was an immediate success. A pre and post test using the TNS Omnibus reported that the commercial was demonstrating considerable cut-through. Between the pre and post test, unprompted awareness of advertising for blood donors rose from 62% to 73%. Furthermore, the new commercial hit a prompted awareness level of 57% after just one month of advertising. This is compared to prompted awareness of the Lineker commercial of 54%, after three years of airtime and thousands of ratings.

RESPONSE DATA

Television activity: August 2004

The NBS commercial last ran in July 2004, the month before 'Call' was launched. Therefore a direct comparison of effectiveness can be made between the two. Figure 5 illustrates the comparative spend and Figure 6 the level of response for each commercial.

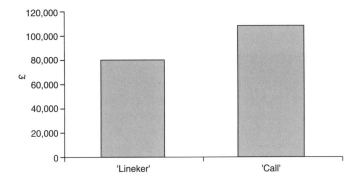

Figure 5: *Comparative spend between 'Lineker' (July) and 'Call' (August)*

Figures 5 and 6 offer clear evidence of the increased effectiveness of 'Call' in generating response: a 35% increase in media spend between the two commercials resulted in nearly a 300% increase in responses. Yet the success of the new commercial wasn't just measured in terms of increased response – it was also far more efficient, as a comparison of cost-per-response data makes clear (see Figure 7).

Furthermore, in-depth analysis of the response data shows that the new commercial was more than four times as effective in recruiting the key target of new donors (see Figure 8). Significantly, 'Call' also proved twice as effective in motivating returning donors to register.

The new commercial played the major role in motivating people to call the donor line: 74% of new donors cited it as their reason for calling. The success the

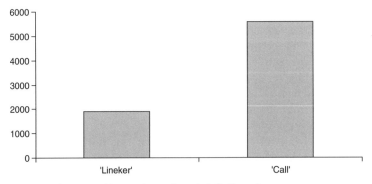

Figure 6: *Calls generated by 'Lineker' (July) and 'Call' (August)*

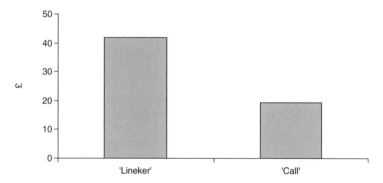

Figure 7: *Cost-per-response comparison between 'Lineker' (July) and 'Call' (August)*

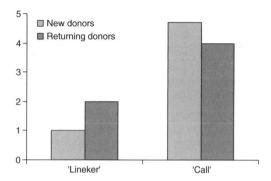

Figure 8: *Comparison of responses per TVR between 'Lineker' (July) and 'Call' (August)*

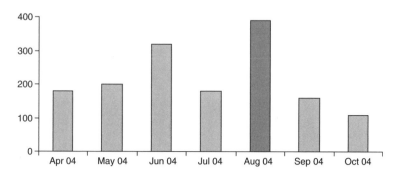

Figure 9: *Website registrations per month, 2004*

new commercial had in attracting calls to 0845 90 90 999 was mirrored in the success it had in generating registrations on the website (see Figure 9).

Radio advertising: November and December 2004

Evidence of the success of the new strategy was reinforced by the responses generated by the new radio commercials. Their launch in November saw the highest call numbers since August (see Figure 10).

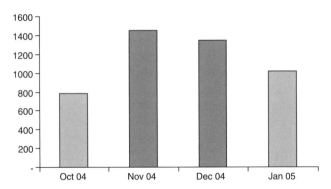

Figure 10: *Calls to 0845 90 90 999 (by month), October 2004–January 2005*

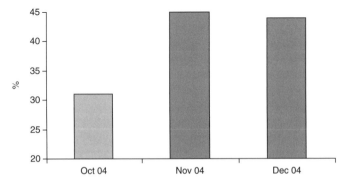

Figure 11: *Percentage of new donors calling 0845 90 90 999*

The new radio commercials also proved effective in recruiting those all-important new donors (see Figure 11).

Just like the new television commercial, the cost per response of the new radio commercials was proving the efficiency of the new strategy against the old one (see Figure 12).

The effectiveness of the new strategy in generating calls was further underlined by the response data for January 2005, which showed that 'Call' was continuing to deliver over three times the number of calls per TVR than the Lineker commercial.

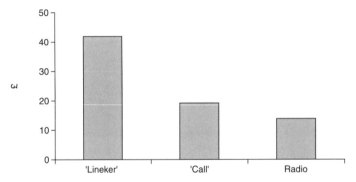

Figure 12: *Cost-per-response comparison between 'Lineker', 'Call' and new radio commercials*

Donor attendances and blood collection

Responses data such as this was very encouraging, but what was really important was increasing blood donations. The new strategy was equally effective in motivating people to become blood donors. It had an immediate impact on donor attendances – bearing out the 'tap on, tap off' strategy – and it helped the SNBTS surpass its exacting targets for August (see Figure 13).

This upturn in donor numbers in August is in comparison to the figures for July 2004 when the NBS commercial was running. It delivered only 96% of the month's overall target (see Figure 14).

The SNBTS had hoped that the new strategy would have a significant effect on donor numbers and had expected an upturn. However, the success of 'Call' was beyond its expectations, delivering 23% over the projected target for the week following the launch of the commercial and 15% over the projected target across the whole month (see Figure 15).

Furthermore, a profile of donor attendance shows that the new strategy was also working in terms of attracting increased numbers of returning donors as well as the all-important new donors (see Figure 16).

And it wasn't just new and returning donors that were motivated to action by the new commercial. It also appears to have helped build donor loyalty by persuading regular donors to give more often (see Figure 17).

This resulted in a considerable increase in the number of donations (see Figure 18).

The success of the television advertising in increasing donor attendances was matched by the radio advertising in November (see Figure 19).

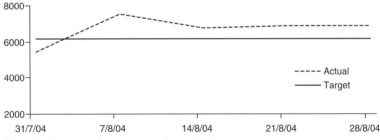

Figure 13: *Donor attendances vs target, August 2004*

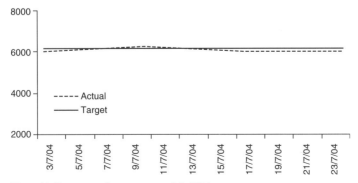

Figure 14: *Donor attendances vs target, July 2004*

213

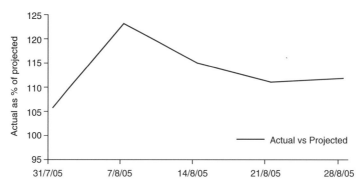

Figure 15: *Donor attendances, actual vs projected, August 2004*

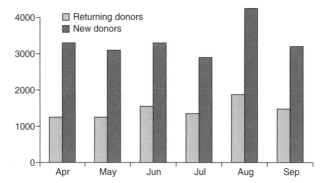

Figure 16: *New and returning donor attendances, April–September 2004*

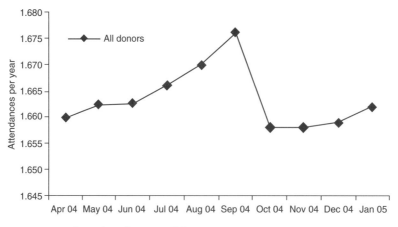

Figure 17: *Annual attendance frequency (all donors)*

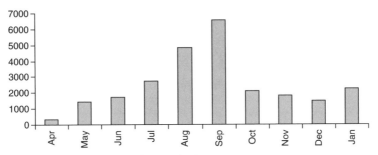

Figure 18: *Additional donations from regular donors*

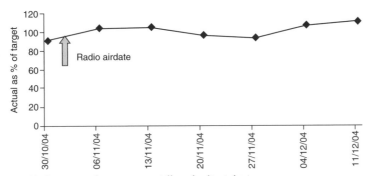

Figure 19: *Donor attendances vs target (effect of radio airdate)*

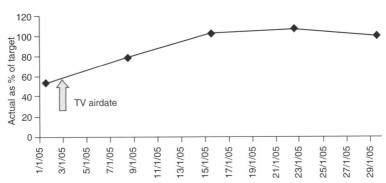

Figure 20: *Donor attendances vs target (effect of TV airdate)*

A further burst of television in January also boosted donor numbers from the traditional New Year low (see Figure 20).

By 31 January 2005, the SNBTS was well on its way to reaching its targets. Year-to-date figures show that donor attendances were on target for the year and up 2% from 2003/04, and that the number of new donors was up 9% on the previous year. The number of new and returning/lapsed donors currently stands at 46,527, an average of 5170 per month. Taken over a 12-month period, this equates to 62,040 new and lapsed donors for the year – some 7% over the target of 58,000 that was required in order to repair the donor base and offset the effects of the vCJD crisis.

Other factors

Holiday periods and major sporting events are detrimental to blood donation. Anything, in fact, that disrupts people's routine will affect blood-donation levels. The new campaign was launched on 2 August 2004, 11 days before the start of the largest sporting event in the world: the Olympic Games. The Games ran until the end of the month. Not only that, but August is a significant holiday period with one bank holiday at the end of the month. Despite these obstacles, the new strategy delivered responses, donors and attendances well over target.

There is also evidence to show that in May (when there was no advertising, but there was a bank holiday as in August) blood donations failed to meet the target for most weeks (see Figure 21).

Likewise, in October, when there was no advertising, calls and donor numbers were down and below target (see Figures 22 and 23).

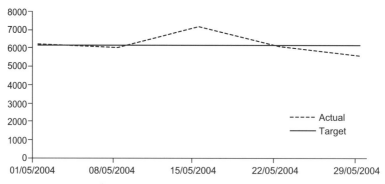

Figure 21: *Donor attendances vs target, May 2004*

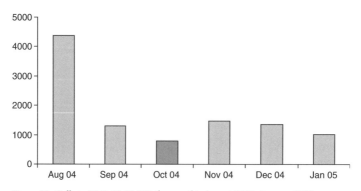

Figure 22: *Calls to 0845 90 90 999 (by month), August 2004–January 2005*

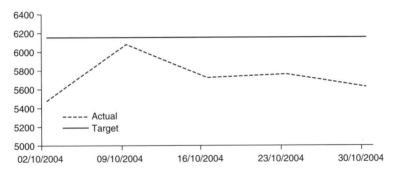

Figure 23: *Donor attendances, October 2004*

RETURN ON INVESTMENT

The maintenance of blood stocks is vital to Scottish healthcare. They are used in all aspects of the health service – from operations such as hip replacements to treatment for leukaemia to accident and emergency units. All depend on having blood stocks available. This paper demonstrates what a clear and unambiguous role advertising has played in ensuring healthy blood stocks in Scotland. The new advertising strategy has proved extremely effective and, without it, there is no doubt that the SNBTS would have had to issue an emergency appeal for donors (as it did in October 2003). In this context, the return on investment cannot be quantified in monetary terms, but in far more significant terms: without it, the health service in Scotland may well have ground to a halt.

15

Children's Hearings

Panel membership

Principal author: Michael Kemsley, Barkers
Contributing author: Emma Taylor, Consultant
Media agency: Feather Brooksbank

EDITOR'S SUMMARY

Scotland's Children's Hearings system works with young people who may have offended, or have been neglected or abused. It concentrates on the welfare of the child and puts decisions into the hands of a Panel of everyday people.

However, Panel members are exposed to highly traumatic cases, and are expected to sacrifice their free time without pay. Not surprisingly, applications to the Panel have been in decline for some time. Barkers' task was to reverse the decline in respondents and attract a broader cross-section of the community.

Previous campaigns had unintentionally stressed the negative aspects of the work, but research revealed that there were many positive aspects to Panel membership, which Barkers emphasised in a new campaign, aimed at a wider audience.

The effect on response rates was dramatic – applications almost quadrupled, and cost per response fell. As a result, a uniquely Scottish system of justice was saved from extinction.

BACKGROUND

This paper explains how Scotland's Children's Hearings system has used advertising to inspire and motivate local people in local communities. The Children's Hearings system works not only with offenders but with children who have been neglected or abused.

For several years the number of people applying to join Panels had been in desperate decline. The future of the system hung in the balance and morale among those in the field was low. An urgent call to action was required that would strike a chord with people from all walks of life.

This paper will demonstrate how a change in advertising led to a dramatic turnaround in fortune for the Children's Hearings system. We will prove that advertising became the driving force for recruitment. We will show how an advertising strategy with a positive rather than negative focus effected a massive shift in the entire culture and philosophy of the Hearings system.

THE PROBLEM

Supporting, and where necessary reprimanding, children who become involved in crime or public misbehaviour is by its nature a very sensitive issue.

What makes the Children's Hearings system so unique is that each case is heard before a Children's Panel. The Reporter, an official employed by the Scottish Children's Reporter Administration, oversees the hearing but it is the Panel members that discuss the case and make recommendations for the future of the child.

Every Children's Panel includes three members of the local community. The aim is that these are three people who represent the local area and who each bring experience and fresh thinking on how the needs of the child can best be met. Their decision is informed through discussion with the child and those with parental responsibilities, with social workers and through reports from other appropriate parties. The Children's Panel is about finding the best outcome for each child that comes before it.

Panel members have to be committed to their role. Although full training and support is given, the demands placed upon each member should not be underestimated. The role entails exposure to highly traumatic cases, weekend work, time away from work for training courses and a general demand on free time. It is also unpaid. There are some 30 Children's Panel groups operating throughout Scotland, each one dependent on the cooperation of local volunteers for its ability to function and its very existence.

MARKETING OBJECTIVES

The initial objective was to reverse the decline in respondents, which threatened to bring about the demise of the Children's Hearings system.

A secondary objective was to bring together a broad cross-section of the community on the Panel. In general, would-be Panel members consisted of a high percentage of women, older people and people from higher socio-economic groups. This left a large part of the community under-represented, going against the whole ethos of the system.

Applications for the Panel could be made by telephone through a response-handling centre or the campaign website.

THE TASK

Attracting new blood to the Panel is crucial, and this has taken place annually with a recruitment campaign for Panel members every September throughout Scotland. A small media campaign including national and local press and radio had, for a while, been performing adequately. However, from 1998 onwards, the response level declined until it reached the point where the number of applicants became so low that the minimum Panel membership was in direct jeopardy. Among authorities it had been agreed that, in general, at least 4000 applicants per annum were required to generate sufficient numbers to maintain Panel membership.

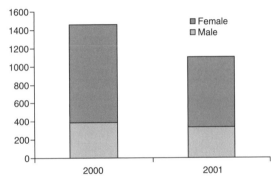

Figure 1: *Campaign response rate for 2000 and 2001*

As shown in Figure 1, the total responses to the handling centre for the 2000 campaign were 1460, falling further to 1105 in 2001. Of these, in 2000 only 8% came from C2DE groups, while in 2001 this dropped even further, to 6%.

Clearly the decline was dangerously close to profoundly damaging Scotland's unique system. The challenge was set.

THE STRATEGIC SOLUTION

With applicants at such a low level and a massive increase in budget out of the question, a new creative brief was developed for the 2002 campaign.

It was recognised that the role of research in developing this brief should be an important one. A qualitative programme was conducted among seven groups in the primary target: 25–45 BC1C2D. Given the desire to boost applications from those under-represented on the Panel, the ratio of groups was weighted towards men and lower socio-economic groupings.

To enhance understanding of the motivations to join the Panel, groups of Panel members who joined in 2001 were also consulted. A substantial stakeholder consultation was under way that encouraged blue-sky thinking. What could we do better? Where did we need to be giving our messages? Was advertising failing? Perhaps it wasn't a job for advertising after all? These questions and more were thrown open to discussion, leaving no stone unturned. Local Children's Panel Advisory Committees (CPACs) were a key focus and their extensive knowledge of the subject matter was probed deeply.

Researchers and advertising planners worked tirelessly to tease out the issues, in particular the negative associations people had with the Panel. It seemed that to study the negatives would be crucial in finding a long-term solution to the recruitment problem.

In developing the new brief, a massive number of stimuli were tested at research and in stakeholder consultation. A vast range of ideas featured, including those the agency felt to be uninspiring, so we could truly get behind the reasons why they were rejected. The creative from earlier years was also redrafted and resubmitted as a concept for testing. The following points summarise the outcome.

- We found a lack of awareness that the Children's Hearings system was unique to Scotland. Once this was explained, there was a real feeling of national pride that Scotland was at the cutting edge in this field.
- People were far more likely to apply to join their local Panel than they would be to apply for a national Panel. It was less intimidating and more relevant.
- The perceived amount of time that would have to be allocated to Panel duties was a major barrier to applying. There was extremely low awareness of what this would amount to in reality – people didn't really know if it would be 10 minutes a week or 6 hours.
- Most people perceived Panel members to be educated, middle-class and slightly elitist, which discouraged those in lower socio-economic groups from applying. They felt that anything they would have to say would have less value than those from higher socio-economic groups and that it generally wasn't a role for people like them.
- The concept of 'policing' young criminals was thought to be frightening and problematic, and there was a lack of awareness about the caring and positive side of the Panel work.

We discovered that the main motivations to join the Panel were clear and very strong, very personal drivers. People wanted to help children – especially those local to their area. They wanted to make a difference, to give something back to society. There was a thirst for knowledge about the system, its successes and what it could do. More generally there were a substantial number who wanted to use membership as an opportunity for personal development and lifelong learning, particularly to develop an existing interest such as childcare or social work.

It became clear that previous creative work had done nothing to address these issues. The use of black-and-white images, as shown in Figure 2, had actually put across a message of depression and helplessness rather than that of a caring and inspirational role. The use of vocabulary such as 'trouble' and 'challenge' reaffirmed the more confrontational aspects and said nothing of the help that members give to young people. The advertising had, correctly, sought to advise of the serious and important nature of the role but had inadvertently created a new barrier to applicants.

It was also apparent that we needed to produce less of what would be considered a traditional recruitment campaign and more of a product-based advertising campaign. New thinking and research showed that a recruitment-led format was in fact counterproductive.

A new strategy was required that would engender wider appeal for the Panels. We had to make the broadest audience possible interested in the system and its

Figure 2: 'Alone'

work, emphasising the positives of the Panel rather than the negatives. We had to associate a new set of brand values with Children's Hearings.

We had to deliver this locally and we had to speak to people about their community. Above all, we had to show that it was a worthwhile journey to go on, and we had to take into account that each individual has a different idea of what constitutes worthwhile. The new brief was an extremely difficult one: to turn current perceptions upside down. We had to appeal to new people and we had to engage them in a deeply emotive, positive way.

THE IDEA

A more open, caring and accessible approach needed to be taken towards the creative. We needed to encourage people to do their bit for their local community, for young people from their own part of town. As such it had to become less intimidating and more inspirational.

The new Children's Hearings had to stand for 'my local area and the kids that live here', it had to be 'for people like me' and it had to show the philanthropic value. What was needed was optimism, and all advertising and marketing collateral would need to be reframed as such.

Consultation work was again under way. It was imperative that those involved in the management of the Panels, in particular CPACs, bought into, and more importantly understood, the new focus.

It went deeper than advertising. CPACs were guided through the process of preparing more positive and welcoming packs. The new optimistic essence of the work cascaded down to all levels. Expertise was shared on engaging elected officials and local media, and on developing public information points such as libraries and supermarkets. The new optimism about Children's Hearings would permeate at all levels and create a new wave of applicants, vying for recognition as one of society's enablers.

As a result of all this work, the ads shown in Figures 3–6 were developed for the 2002 campaign.

THE COMMUNICATION ACTIVITY

2002

For 2002 the advertising activity was split into two parts, to allow for both an awareness and a recruitment campaign. The awareness campaign used national and regional titles for one week commencing 26 August, while the recruitment campaign took advantage of local and national press and 16 Scottish radio stations.

The agency negotiated a supplement in the *Sun* to support the advertising. Every effort was made to ensure that the *Sun* grasped the philosophy of the campaign, and case studies were produced that highlighted individuals and how the role had enriched their lives.

Figure 3: *'Lauren'*

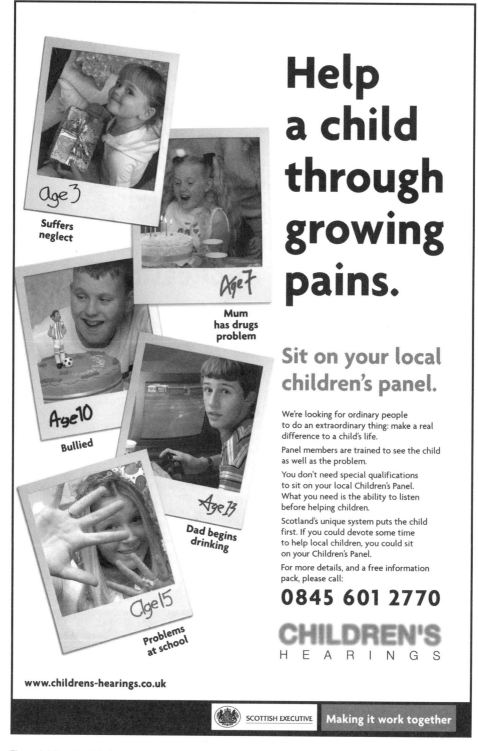

Figure 4: 'Growing pains'

Figure 5: 'Priceless'

Figure 6: 'What kind of ...'

Campaign guides were distributed across all local authority areas and included an overview of the campaign, artwork that could be tailored for local use and tips on making the campaign successful at a local level.

The awareness campaign achieved coverage among all adults of 67.4% at 2.1 OTS. The recruitment strand of the campaign achieved 78% at 5.8 OTS among all adults for press and 68% cover at 8.5 OTH for radio. The total media budget was

£178,196 (excluding VAT, ASBOF and agency fees) and the paid-for media activity lasted for a total of five weeks.

2003

In 2003 the campaign received a cut in overall budget while still requiring high response rates to ensure the Panel's success. An extra creative execution was added to those used in 2002. This execution was produced with the specific aim of halting the decline in male applicants and appeared within the sports pages of press titles.

National and local press were used, plus local radio for the general campaign. From a total media budget of £148,730 the campaign achieved 68% at 8.5 OTH among all adults on radio and 67% at 2.1 OTS. Paid-for media activity lasted for a total of three weeks.

THE RESULTS

According to the data presented in Figure 7:

- in 2000 a total of 1460, 27% male (390) and 73% female (1070), respondents were logged;
- in 2001 a total of 1105, 30% male (334) and 70% female (771), respondents were logged;
- in 2002 a total of 4133, 23% male (938) and 77% female (3195), respondents were logged;
- in 2003 a total of 3816, 30% male (1118) and 70% female (2698), respondents were logged.

An overall increase in respondents of 374% was achieved from 2001 to 2002.
According to the data presented in Figure 8:

- in 2000 the breakdown of respondents by age can be shown as 18–30 23% (343), 31–40 35% (519), 41–50 26% (378) and 51+ 16% (220);
- in 2001 the breakdown of respondents by age can be shown as 18–30 27% (293), 31–40 37% (403), 41–50 25% (272) and 51+ 12% (137);

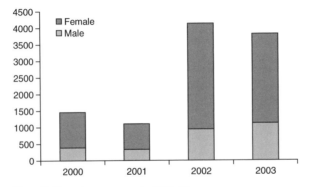

Figure 7: *Campaign response rates 2000–03*

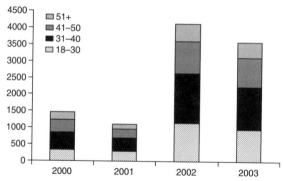

Figure 8: *Responses by age*

- in 2002 the breakdown of respondents by age can be shown as 18–30 28% (1146), 31–40 36% (1492), 41–50 23% (954) and 51+ 13% (541);
- in 2003 the breakdown of respondents by age can be shown as 18–30 25% (954), 31–40 34% (1297), 41–50 23% (878) and 51+ 12% (458) and unknown 6% (229).

According to the data presented in Figure 9:

- in 2000 the breakdown of respondents by socio-economic group can be shown as AB 32% (465), C1 34% (506), C2 4% (52), DE 4% (58) and F 26% (379);
- in 2001 the breakdown of respondents by socio-economic group can be shown as AB 53% (587), C1 15% (161), C2 4% (47), DE 2% (27) and F 26% (283);
- in 2002 the breakdown of respondents by socio-economic group can be shown as AB 30% (1246), C1 32% (1315), C2 5% (208), DE 6% (257) and F 27% (1107).

Please note that there is no comparable socio-economic information available for 2003 due to a change in classification used for that year's figures.

These figures demonstrate the actual level and type of respondents contacting the response centre. Although local authorities were encouraged to build upon the success of the advertising campaign through localised promotion using campaign creative work, there has been no other promotional work to which we could attribute such a massive increase in response levels.

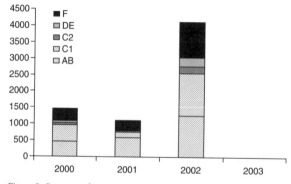

Figure 9: *Responses by socio-economic group*

No significant change to length or composition of media was observed throughout the four-year period, which suggests that it is the creative execution that has brought about such an upturn, rather than a change in media strategy.

In 2002, national press advertising reaped dividends with as many as 508 people citing the *Daily Record*, and 363 people the *Sunday Mail* as their reason for calling. The special *Sun* supplement performed extremely well, with the number of respondents driven by the *Sun* totalling 239. Local press yielded over 171 respondents from the *Glasgow Evening Times* and 158 from the *Edinburgh Evening News*. Radio also performed extremely successfully, with 346 respondents who had heard advertising on Radio Clyde, 330 on Real Radio and 209 on Radio Forth.

To put this in context, only 44 people contacted the response centre as a result of word of mouth.

PAYBACK/RETURN ON INVESTMENT

For this we can simply presume that the total amount of budget spent on media advertising can be divided by the number of respondents to the handling centre. This gives us a straightforward cost per respondent. The breakdown for this year on year is shown in Table 1.

TABLE 1: COST PER RESPONDENT CALCULATIONS

Year	Total respondents	Total budget	Cost per respondent
2000	1460	£89,629	£61.39
2001	1105	£99,375	£89.93
2002	4133	£178,197	£43.12
2003	3816	£148,730	£38.98

CONCLUSION

Getting people to sacrifice their free time and expose themselves to potentially upsetting situations without pay is no mean feat. We have proven that small budget doesn't equate to small campaign, and the magnitude of the work required us to reach out throughout Scotland. Response growth from 2001 to 2002 was 374%.

It's a simple campaign, the results are straightforward and it's extremely effective. We can clearly show how advertising achieved goals and revolutionised recruitment to the Children's Hearings system.

16

First Choice

Get Me Out Of Here!

How sponsorship cuts through the jungle and onto the high street

Principal authors: Phil Georgiadis, Marie Robinson and
Shabaz Shariff, Walker Media
Contributing author: Oliver Croom-Johnson, SPP

EDITOR'S SUMMARY

This is an excellent example of how to use TV sponsorship well.

Back in 2003, First Choice was a relatively new brand. To put their brand name firmly at the forefront of consumers' minds for the 2004 holiday-booking season, First Choice decided to sponsor *I'm a Celebrity... Get Me Out Of Here!*

This illustrates one of the golden rules of sponsorship: make sure that the sponsorship fits the brand. Set in the Australian jungle, 'I'm a Celebrity...' had a natural appeal to people who love travel.

Not content with that, First Choice actively exploited the sponsorship through many channels, including online, SMS, promotional DVDs and competitions tied in to the programme.

The judges were also impressed by the way First Choice took the sponsorship theme into their organisation, with 'Bush Tucker Trials' taking place in their stores. Not only did this raise staff morale, but it also differentiated First Choice from other high street chains, and generated valuable press coverage.

The result was an improved brand image, increased sales and a 13% increase in pre-tax profits.

INTRODUCTION

This paper is designed to show how broadcast sponsorship can be genuinely taken through the line and onto the high street in a manner that is preached, but seldom practised, leading to a significant raising of the bar both in terms of recognition and appreciation for the sponsor and a quantifiable commercial benefit.

BACKGROUND

In 2002/03, the First Choice group consisted of a number of individual travel and holiday businesses – Bakers Dolphin, Holiday Hypermarkets, Travel Choice and Air 2000 being the principal ones. With the unification of the group under the single banner of First Choice, and the creation of 325 First Choice-branded retail outlets, there was a requirement to provide a cohesive and identifiable brand proposition (i.e. that consumers could be provided with their first choice whatever their holiday requirements).

DIFFERENTIATION WITHIN A COMPETITIVE MARKET

Until very recently the retail travel market had been dominated by the traditional players – Thomas Cook, Thomson and MyTravel in their different guises. Over the preceding decade, the market had been developing within increasingly vertical lines, with the owned retail divisions being increasingly incentivised to sell house product.

Into this mix has come the burgeoning use of the internet, encouraging an increasingly sophisticated consumer not only to research his or her options via the web, but also inviting the new breed of online agencies such as Expedia and Travelocity to market their wares directly and aggressively to the consumer.

Previously, the retail arms were able to establish recognisable advertising properties – 'I want to run away' and 'Don't just book it – Thomas Cook it' from Thomas Cook, and the unforgettable 'Getaway' from Lunn Poly. It is difficult to recall any similarly powerful identities in recent times.

The 'safety in numbers' mentality predicates that the three main offline retailers all concentrate their outlets within a few hundred yards of each other in the high street, the discounts in the windows are the same, the shopping experiences in the stores are similar, and this is all supported by familiar styles of advertising at the same time of year (Figure 1).

A proposition that could provide a genuine point of difference to the consumer, whether through advertising or in the high street, would surely reap significant benefits.

FIRST CHOICE'S OBJECTIVES

Much of the discussions with First Choice, in planning the activity for 2003/04 and beyond, revolved around the question of establishing the First Choice name and providing it with standout in the traditional clutter of the market. In fact, it was the

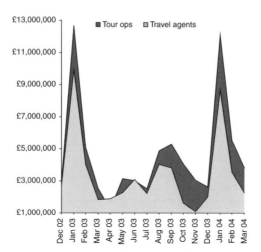

Figure 1: *Tour operator and travel agent advertising spend trends*
Source: Nielsen Media Research

very first question Sam Turnbull, Marketing Director of First Choice, asked: 'Are we going to just do what everyone else does?'

The set objectives were:

- establish the First Choice name
- create brand fame (in that old advertising adage, make First Choice 'famous'), but also make it a brand of choice
- drive business
- provide an online route and establish the online proposition.

There was one other thought we held to in setting objectives. Whatever route we decided to take, we wanted ideally to exploit for the long term. This would both take First Choice out of the short-term 'whatever-discount-it-is-this-year' generality of the market and enable us to establish a brand personality.

THE SOLUTION

Broadcast sponsorship was an area of the communications pantheon that had been discussed over the planning period with more than cursory interest. It was attractive due to its ability to create immediate awareness and impact and almost instant popularity. We knew that it would satisfy the requirements of establishing the First Choice name and, assuming the correct property was identified, the creation of brand fame. Via the option of putting the URL on the sponsor credits, it would also establish an online proposition alongside the main brand and, again subject to selection of the correct property, a route through to a sponsor website.

One other advantage to broadcast sponsorship is that of longevity. The sponsor has first option on future series of a sponsored show, and hence it would satisfy our requirement of subscribing to a long-term marketing property.

I'm A Celebrity … Get Me Out Of Here! (IACGMOOH!) is simply the biggest event show on British television, and when we learned that V Energy Drink, sponsor of series two, was not going to renew its sponsorship, we knew we had to be a contender for the property. Hosted by the talented and popular TV duo Ant and Dec, it had already created national stars out of Phil Tufnell and Linda Barker, resurrected Tony Blackburn's career, and attracted average audiences of over nine million for series two. It had an audience that not only matched First Choice's ambitions for size and stature, but was also in the top four programmes[1] for all First Choice's key target audiences:

- adults 25–34
- adults 35–44 with children
- adults ABC1 25–34
- adults ABC1 35–44.

It is one of those extraordinary programmes that appeals to all sectors of the population, and when those who 'specially choose to watch' the programme are matched on TGI with those who take package holidays, the crossover is compelling, especially so for families with children.

Additionally, the programme was to be transmitted over a period of 16 days from 25 January to 9 February, covering the critical booking period for the holiday market, and with on-air First Choice-branded promotional trailers for the programme running for the two weeks from 10 January to the programme launch.

THE DEVELOPMENT

A large part of the attraction for us was what was available to us outside the programme. Unlike most other entertainment programmes, *IACGMOOH!* has a multi-layered involvement with its audience. It attracts a huge online community, allows promotional offers of DVDs of the show, and encourages the usual plethora of competition entrants when major prizes are offered. Hence, quite apart from the on-air sponsor credits on ITV1 and ITV2, the agreed package included:

- on-air promotional trailers
- full sponsorship of the *IACGMOOH!* website clicking through to the First Choice website
- branding on all online games, video downloads and the newsletter
- branding on all SMS applications
- First Choice competitions to win money-can't-buy holidays (to Australia, for both staff and consumers, with a visit to the set on the final day of the show)
- joint DVD promotion in the *Sun*.

Lip-service is often paid to the notion of taking a sponsorship property into the high street, but it is not necessarily followed by action. However, First Choice embraced the concept immediately and wholeheartedly. All 325 shops were to be dressed with jungle foliage, there were to be jungle noises on a tape loop in-store, and the windows were to be fitted out with references to both jungle and programme.

---

1. Source: BARB Top Programme Report.

THE CREATIVE

All received wisdom from historical research into broadcast sponsorships will tell you that the concept is well received by audiences. The only area where you will attract negatives is where either the viewers do not see the sponsor as a natural 'fit' with the programme, or if they do not like the sponsor idents.

As far as 'fit' was concerned, we were absolutely confident that it would be seen as 'a natural'. As far as the ident content goes, the key is to ensure that there is a clear link between sponsor and programme. Two extra considerations for First Choice were:

1. to inform people of the different First Choice businesses involved (Travel Shops, Holidays and Holiday Hypermarkets)
2. to demonstrate range of offering.

The idents, conceived by Phoenix plc, First Choice's integrated agency, took three families of animals, each of them to act as spokespersons for different elements of the business – short haul, long haul and cruises. They were then placed inside a representation of the Bush Telegraph hut from the show, from where they could expound on their favourite holidays. They were animated, charming and amusing by turns, and there were a total of 33 executions to ensure against any wearout in a series of such concentration.

Figure 2: *TV idents*

THE SHOW AND ITS VALUE

The show was arguably *the* television hit of 2004. The chemistry among a cast that included Lord Brockett, John Lydon (aka Johnny Rotten) and Jennie Bond exceeded all expectations, with the added and ongoing bonus of the relationship between Jordan and Peter Andre. A summary of the show's achievements would include:[2]

- the highest audience ever for a reality programme
- reached 75% of the UK population across the 16 days
- averaged 11.1 million and a 43% share across the series
- an audience of 15.0 million and a 56% share to the finale.

The fledgling ITV2's extensions to the show also garnered record-breaking audiences, with four shows attracting over one million viewers and the final night taking 2.9 million.[3]

---

2. Source: BARB/TNS.
3. *Ibid.*

In terms of value for money when compared to advertising, the airtime alone on ITV1 and ITV2 was calculated conservatively at £3.6m, well over double the investment, excluding the branded on-air trailers promoting the programme prior to launch.

THE OFF-AIR EXPLOITATION

The success of the off-air extensions to the sponsorship matched that of the on-air activity.[4] There were:

- 9.1 million page impressions to the *IACGMOOH!* website
- 1.2 million unique users
- 10.1 million total votes (by phone, SMS, interactive)
- 29,000 people entering the First Choice competition to win a holiday
- 1.5 million video downloads
- newsletter to 482k registered users
- referrals from itv.com/celebrity, which accounted for 15% of the traffic to the First Choice website.

The above additional elements provided in excess of over £400,000 worth of impact, giving a total commercial value of over £4m to the property.

IN-STORE

Uniquely, the Consumer and Trade Marketing Departments of First Choice joined together in creating a complete in-store experience, with all store managers around the country organising their own Bushtucker Trials, replicating some of the esoteric jungle life eaten by the celebs in confectionery form for customers (Figures 3 and 4). Australia Day was similarly something to be dressed up for and celebrated. The result was that the First Choice shops genuinely created a point of difference in the high street, providing a fun, enjoyable element to the holiday-purchasing experience.

This was the first time that a sponsorship of a television programme had been integrated so completely into an in-store environment, and it proved to be a huge motivator for the staff. Their instruction was loud and clear: 'We *must* continue this sponsorship – it's the best thing we do!'

THE PUBLICITY

The interest and publicity that surrounds this show is phenomenal. It is front-page news for all the red-tops and many of the qualities over the duration of the show: 83 front covers in the national press and 54 front covers on magazines (see the examples in Figure 5).

---

4. Source: BARB/TNS.

Figure 3: *'Bush Tucker Trial' at First Choice Holiday Hypermarket, Staines*

Figure 4: *'Bush Tucker Trial' at First Choice Holiday Hypermarket, Basildon*

Figure 5: *Front-page news in the UK*

On a more parochial note, it was remarked upon favourably in the travel trade press ('Whoever thought this up was a genius', *Travel Trade Gazette*) and the marketing press ('First Choice is this year's sponsor ... the synergy with the programme and its audience should deliver significant benefits to the advertiser', *Media Week* 'Pick of the Week').

Sponsorship News also picked up on the deal. According to its editor, Jonathan Gee, 'First Choice Holidays ... must be laughing all the way to the bank, and I would be surprised if they don't have an option at least on the next series.'

Finally, it was voted number two in *Campaign* magazine's Top Ten Sponsorships of 2004.

THE RESEARCH

There were two research studies covering the sponsorship of *IACGMOOH!*. One was that undertaken by IPSOS-RSL as part of ITV's sponsorship offering, the other was First Choice's own on-going study from Hall & Partners. All the research results proved to be outstandingly positive, but for the sake of brevity, we will quote just a small selection of the findings here:

- total spontaneous recall among regular viewers 74%[5]
- credit recognition 93%[6]
- appropriateness of sponsor 72% vs average of 62%[7]
- liked the sponsor credits 78% vs V Energy Drink at 76%[8]

---

5. Source: IPSOS-RSL.
6. *Ibid.*
7. *Ibid.*
8. *Ibid.*

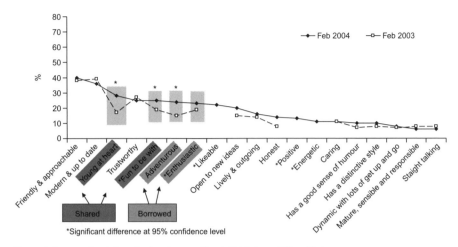

Figure 6: *Borrowed and shared values between I'm A Celebrity and First Choice*

- 'The 2004 campaign has cut through well – far better than any previous campaign, TV or press'[9]
- 'The strong levels of sponsorship cut-through means that the majority of press and poster recognisers are also sponsorship recognisers'[10]
- sponsorship recognition highest when benchmarked against other sponsorships, and second only to Cadbury's and its sponsorship of *Coronation Street* for spontaneous linkage to programme[11]
- 'Repertoire consideration for First Choice has dramatically increased and is now at best ever levels'[12]
- 'The sponsorship's effect upon the brand's saliency is one of the strongest we have ever seen'[13]
- First Choice was described as being friendly and approachable, modern and up to date, young at heart and trustworthy.[14] (See Figure 6.)

BUSINESS RESULTS

No matter how positive the out-take of the sponsorship by the above methods, it is how the business is driven that is by far the most important benchmark. Indeed, this was one of the objectives of the sponsorship.

Precise numbers and profit-per-booking figures are of course commercially sensitive. However, trading figures show that the value of bookings across the immediate sponsorship period when compared to the previous year was +17%, equating to an incremental profit figure of just over £2m (Figure 7).

9. Source: Hall & Partners Europe Ltd.
10. *Ibid.*
11. Source: Hall & Partners Europe Ltd, BARB/DDS, Network, ITV1 only, 19 January–15 February 2004.
12. Source: Hall & Partners Europe Ltd.
13. *Ibid.*
14. *Ibid.*

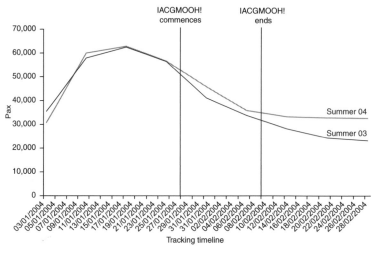

Figure 7: *Year-on-year sales before, during and after sponsorship*

In December 2004, the company unveiled a 13% rise in pre-tax profits to £98.3m for the year to 31 October.[15] Whereas, as with all marketing activity, one could not possibly ascribe this exclusively to the sponsorship of *IACGMOOH!*, it was by far the most important and visible part of the marketing effort, and without doubt was a major contributor to what was an excellent achievement in a tough, commodity-driven, low-margin market.

CONCLUSION

In conclusion, all the set objectives were achieved, probably by more than we anticipated. In addition, it is gratifying to report that:

- all research findings and any empirical comment was extremely positive
- we attained well over double the commercial impact for First Choice compared to the investment
- First Choice's annual figures demonstrated significant growth in a difficult market.

It is not surprising therefore that the decision to undertake the sponsorship of series four was not long debated, even though the scheduling of the series was moved forward from January 2005 to November/December 2004. If the timing was not quite as ideal for the holiday market as that of series three, the scheduling provided us with other benefits.

In terms of branding, it allowed us to establish First Choice's credentials at a time of low clutter while continuing the association with a property of the calibre of *I'm A Celebrity*. It enabled us to set up the sponsorship as a platform from which the turn-of-year activity could be launched and, with the animated animal characters from series three having been updated and made a tad more

---

15. Source: www.bbc.co.uk.

sophisticated, we could carry this creative treatment through to the turn-of-year advertising.

Crucially, it gave us the opportunity to fulfil the original aim of identifying a strategy that would provide longer legs than the traditional short-term discount offers. We do not believe it is compromising confidentialities to indicate that discussions for the sponsorship of series five, planned for autumn 2005, are well advanced.

17

Fox's Rocky

Halting plummeting sales in a declining market

How rap helped Rocky sell with more of a crunch

Principal author: Paul Stallard, PWLC
Media agency: Equinox

EDITOR'S SUMMARY

Back in 2003, the future looked bleak for Fox's Rocky. Sales of chocolate biscuit bars as a whole were in decline, and sales of Rocky were declining in line with the market.

In October 2003, Fox's launched a new campaign intended to increase sales among young children. The new ads featured Rocky, an animated rap artist who would make the brand cool among young kids, without alienating their Mums.

The results show all the signs of effective fmcg advertising. Brand awareness increased, as did propensity to buy, and hence penetration. Market share increased, and the decline in sales was reversed, even though the rest of the market continued to suffer.

The judges felt that this case was proved very thoroughly. The timing of the sales increases clearly matched the timing of the campaign, and advertised areas significantly outperformed non-advertised ones.

The judges also felt that there were indications of broader effects beyond sales uplifts. The brand seems to have become less dependent on promotions, and the ads also seemed to have helped gain some distribution. Both effects augur well for the long-term health of the brand.

INTRODUCTION

The scene: a high-level business conference populated by smart executives. The chairperson takes the stage ...

'Welcome to the 2005 inspirational business seminar. It's a pleasure to introduce our keynote speaker. He's a rap star and a successful entrepreneur. He's here to talk about how he transformed the fortunes of his brand by making it more relevant to kids, without alienating their parents. Ladies and gentlemen, I give you ... Rocky R.'

The lights go down. The PA blasts out a funky hip-hop backbeat. Rocky and his entourage enter the room in a dazzling haze of designer suits and sparkling bling. Rocky takes the stage as the beats fade ...

Figure 1: *Rocky R takes centre stage*

'Yo. How ya doin' my business homies. It's a blast to be here. I'm more used to takin' the stage to perform my rhymes but I got some learning to share about making brands work harder. A few years ago my chocolate biscuit bar brand was struggling. I was even thinking about quitting the business.

'There were two sides to the problem. The A side was the chocolate biscuit industry as a whole. People just ain't eating so many. Everyone's eating healthier. And there's just more and more snack options to choose from. A few years ago any self-respecting kid was guaranteed a chocolate biscuit in their lunchbox. Now it ain't so simple.

'On the B side, when we had spent on ads we hadn't been cool. You can spend as much money as you like talking to the kids, but if you ain't cool they won't listen. It was time for me to get more involved with the brand. To make it rock again. Now it just ain't cool to talk about being cool like this, and this ain't just my story. So I'm gonna let the smart guys in my agency crew explain how we made Rocky a cool brand for kids, a smart brand for parents and made sales rise again in a sector that's declining. Check it out now.'

THE MARKETING AND COMMUNICATIONS SOLUTION

To restore Rocky's fortunes in the declining chocolate biscuit bars (CBB) category we set ourselves three key objectives:

1. increase market share
2. increase audience penetration
3. halt sales decline and drive long-term uplift in base rate of sales.

TARGET AUDIENCE

To achieve these goals we knew we needed to appeal to two audiences.

First, we needed to engage with opinion-forming 8–11 year olds. These pre-teenagers, or 'tweenagers', are at a stage when they're just starting to flex their independence from their parents. They are at the top of the ladder at school and realise they're on the verge of teenage liberation. Going out and dating isn't part of their world quite yet, but being in with the right set of peers at school is. It's a time when they need to be seen doing, saying and using the right things to attain playground kudos. And kudos is crucial.

Our aim was to make Rocky a brand that delivers this kudos. Qualitative research told us that Penguins and other chocolate biscuits are for kids – they're the things your younger siblings get fed. But Rocky has got more attitude – when you eat one your mouth is filled with crunch and chocolate – it's substantial. By eating a Rocky instead of a Penguin in front of your peers you're signalling that you're not a kid any more.

Research groups revealed that kids' music tastes were increasingly driven by hip-hop artists such as Eminem and P Diddy. The term 'funky' kept recurring in groups to describe why they found this genre cool. So we developed a new Rocky proposition of 'A funky mouthful of crunch' and set out to deliver this proposition in a way that reflected teenage liberation as seen through the eyes of a pre-teenager. That was when we picked up the phone to Rocky R. He was perfect for delivering the kind of aspirational teenage kudos we were after. He raps the language of teenagers but is warm, accessible and humorous enough to engage in the pre-teenage world.

And he was ideal to help us engage with our secondary audience. We needed to give Rocky playground kudos, but we also needed to make sure mums were happy to put it in their weekly shopping basket. Research with mums showed that we should avoid a brand spokesperson who was too edgy, who would make mums feel like they were being pestered by their kids to buy a brand that wasn't 'good for them'. We wanted mum to smile with recognition at a character her kids loved, be reassured about the product quality and even enjoy the occasional Rocky herself as a result. Ultimately mum was always the gatekeeper, buying more than 85% of Rocky bars. She needed to be clearly targeted.

THE CAMPAIGN: REACHING KIDS AND MUMS

This dual audience informed our media strategy. We wanted Rocky R to make his appearances in media where mum and kids were both present. This led us by a process of deduction to a TV campaign focused on dual viewing occasions.

The campaign ran on terrestrial channels. The campaign excluded London, Southern and Anglia regions to provide an opportunity to test media performance by region. The bulk of the campaign was delivered in peak-time, centre-break, family viewing spots like *Coronation Street* and *Stars in their Eyes*. There were two bursts of activity (Table 1) with an overall media spend of £1.2m.

TABLE 1: ACTIVITY BURSTS

Launch phase	1–28 October 2003
Follow-up phase	19 April–16 May 2004

We ran one 30″ execution across both phases. 'Paparazzi' featured Rocky R arriving at a poolside party in his limo and rapping his way through the ad. The ad promotes all Rocky products including Rocky Rounds, which had been launched some time before, and Rocky Bars. Rocky R references these products throughout to grab attention. He outwits his paparazzi follower to ensure he ends up falling in the pool and by demonstrating the 'crunch moment' everyone gets when they bite into a Rocky.

Figure 2: *'Paparazzi' TV ad*

RESULTS OF THE ADVERTISING

Chocolate biscuit bars: a sector in decline

Trends around healthy eating, concerns around obesity and spiralling choice in the snack sector mean that decline within the CBB sector is consistent and increasing.

In 2002, total sector sales stood at £422m. By 2004, this had declined by 9.2% to £383m, a loss of £38.7m of sales. And this decline was accelerating: 5.8% of the overall 9.2% occurred 2003–04 (Figure 3).[1]

---

1. Where data allows we have broken the year in October so that the third period of 52 w/e 02/10/04 coincides precisely with our advertising campaign, which launched at the beginning of this period on 01/10/03. Where data reporting periods vary from this we have used a year end as close as possible to our advertising period.

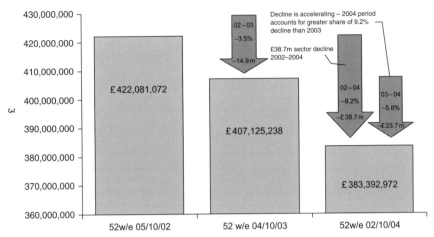

Figure 3: *Annual market trends in all CBB brands 2002–04*
Source: IRI, total GB

Rocky decline above market trend

Until our advertising ran, Rocky's fortunes were similar to other leading CBB brands. Decline in the CBB sector between 2002 and 2003 was –3.5% (Figure 3). Rocky value sales declined by –12% over the same period (Figure 4). This equates to a loss in sales value of £3.6m, considerably more than the sector average of 3.5%.

Advertising reverses Rocky sales decline

The new Rocky campaign reversed this sales decline. Following the launch of advertising in October 2003, sales were up by £765,000 relative to the previous year, an *increase* of 2.9%.

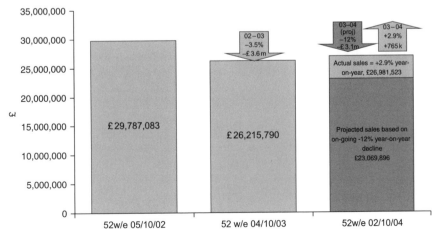

Figure 4: *Annual market trends in all Rocky brands 2002–04*
Source: IRI, total GB

Had Rocky sales reflected the sector trend of −5.8%, sales loss would have stood at £1.5m. Had they continued to reflect Rocky's downward trajectory of 12%, losses would have stood at £3.1m (Table 2).

TABLE 2: ROCKY SALES

Rocky sales increase 2003–04	Lost Rocky sales at sector trend of −5.8%	Lost Rocky sales at year-on-year Rocky trend of −12.0%	Incremental sales value
£765k	£1.5m	£3.1m	£2.3m–£3.9m

Rocky sales therefore increased by between £2.3m and £3.9m during the campaign period. In the next main section ('Isolating the advertising effect') we will demonstrate that the advertising drove these sales independently of any other variables. We will first demonstrate that the advertising period also coincided with an increase in audience penetration, market share, spontaneous awareness and propensity to purchase.

Increase in audience penetration

Another aim of the advertising was to generate trial among new users of the Rocky brand. In the year prior to the advertising, audience penetration was 22.7% (Figure 5). In the year following the advertising, it increased by 2.5% to 25.2%. In a marketplace of 24.5 million, this equates to an additional 612,500 UK households becoming purchasers of the brand.

Increase in market share

The period of the advertising also tallies with an overall increase in market share for Rocky brands of 0.59% to 7.04% (Figure 6). In a market worth £383m, this

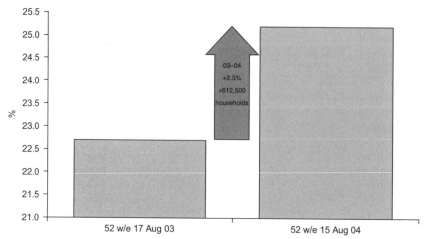

Figure 5: *Annual penetration pre- and post-campaign*
Source: TNS

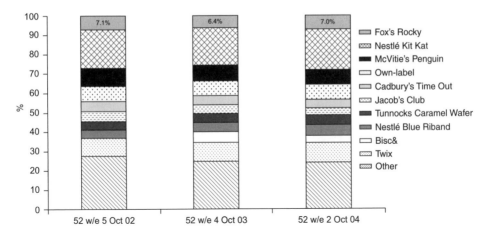

Figure 6: *Annual market share pre- and post-campaign*
Source: IRI, total GB

translates to £2.26m additional sales. This matches our previous estimation of £2.3m incremental sales value achieved by the advertising, assuming lost Rocky sales at sector trend of –5.8%. During much of 2004 Rocky overtook Twix as number three in the CBB sector.

Increase in spontaneous awareness and propensity to purchase

Pre- and post-advertising quantitative research was conducted by an independent research company.[2] This showed an increase in spontaneous awareness of all Rocky brands from 23% to 28%. Consumers 'likely to purchase' Rocky rose from 30% to 38%. Consumers who were aware of the advertising ranked Rocky higher on brand descriptors around 'cool' and 'crunch' than consumers not aware of the advertising.

ISOLATING THE ADVERTISING EFFECT

Sales uplift during campaign bursts

We can first demonstrate the effect of the advertising by demonstrating sales effect during specific periods of campaign activity against sales vs the preceding month for all Rocky brands and all CBB brands (Figure 7). During the first burst of activity Rocky sales increased 15.2% over sector trends. In the second burst they increased by 29.1%.

Possible influencing factors

Sales increase could be driven by other variables. We can demonstrate that the advertising was the key variable responsible for halting the decline in Rocky sales.

---

2. Research conducted among 644 mums and kids aged 8–11 by SPA Research, September and November 2003.

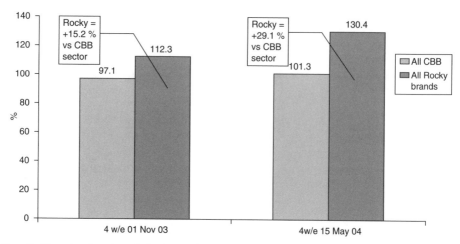

Figure 7: *Change in sales volume during four-week campaign bursts vs previous four weeks*
Source: IRI, total GB

Other possible influences include those shown below.

- Changes to product, packaging or price
- Competitor activity
- Changes in distribution
- Sales promotion activity
- Regional variations affecting sales patterns
- Seasonality

We will consider each of these in turn in order to isolate the effect of the advertising in driving sales improvement.

Changes to product, packaging or price

No changes took place to any of these variables either during the period of our advertising or in the preceding two-year period.

Competitor activity

Our advertising coincided with a period of increased competitor spend (Figure 8). The launch of Bisc& in 2003 was supported by high levels of media investment. This investment continued into our advertising period, although at lower levels than in 2003. Media spend on Twix and Kit Kat, however, increased significantly during the period of our advertising. Kit Kat is known to have spent £10m in total marketing budget on the launch of Kit Kat Kubes during the same month our campaign launched.

Changes in distribution

There were no changes to listing of Rocky in major multiples until after our second, follow-up, burst of advertising. Advertising spend and proven advertising effectiveness led to post-campaign expansion of Rocky listings in Tesco, extending listings into non-advertised regions in the south-east.

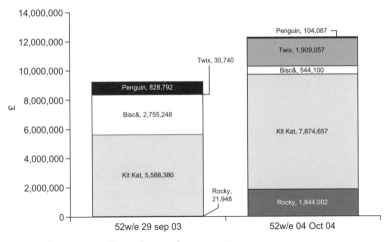

Figure 8: *Competitor media spend pre- and post-campaign*
Source: Nielsen Media Research

Sales promotion activity

We can demonstrate that Fox's reliance on sales promotions reduced relative to the wider CBB market during our advertised period. Base sales in the CBB sector declined steadily 2002–04 (Figure 9) and promotional sales increased, as CBB brands increasingly relied on sales promotion to steady sales decline.

Rocky bucked this trend (Figure 10). Following the launch of the advertising at the beginning of the year, base sales ran counter to market trends by outperforming the previous year. Rather than a repeat of the massive drop in base sales 2002–03, 2004 sales remain comparable with 2003 levels. Fox's was thus able to reduce its reliance on promotional sales relative to the wider market. Promotional sales for Rocky are in decline vs the steady increase occurring in the CBB sector.

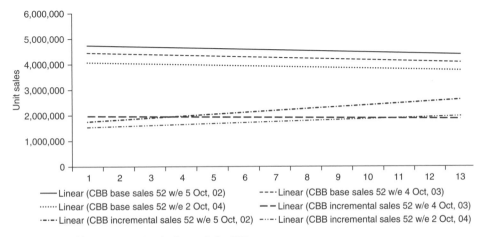

Figure 9: *Annual basic vs promotional sales trends for CBB sector*
Source: IRI, all GB

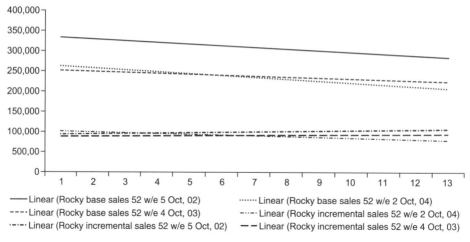

Figure 10: *Annual basic vs promotional trends for Rocky*
Source: IRI, all GB

We can also demonstrate the effect of the advertising independently of sales promotion. In Tesco, one promotional period overlapped with our first advertising period, with a BOGOF offer on Rocky bars coinciding with the final week of our advertising, running for two weeks from 21 October 2003. Of the 14.4% of total sales uplift, 11% was driven by the advertising during the first three weeks of activity (Figure 11).

Regional uplift
Sales uplift was greater in regions with TV advertising vs regions with no TV advertising (Figure 12). Improvement in Rocky sales over the previous month in each campaign burst was 13.6% and 12.4% greater in TV regions vs non-TV regions. It was 6% and 18.8% higher than the market trend.

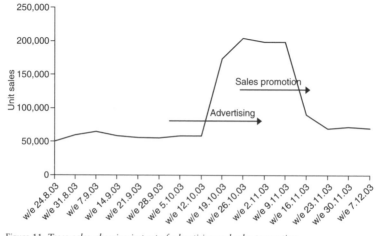

Figure 11: *Tesco sales, showing impact of advertising and sales promotion*
Source: Tesco EPOS data

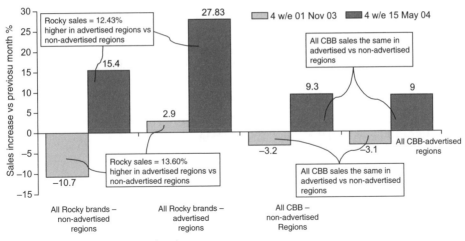

Figure 12: *Regional variations in Rocky sales*
Source: IRI, all GB

Seasonality

Figures 4, 8 and 9 above are based on monthly data over a three-year period. They all demonstrate that increases in Rocky sales occur year on year. Sales improvements cannot therefore be driven by naturally occurring seasonal variations.

Summary: no other variables account for sales improvement

TABLE 3: INFLUENCES ON SALES

Variable	Effect
1. Changes to product, packaging or price	No change before or during campaign
2. Competitor activity	Increased competitor media spend during advertising period
3. Changes in distribution	No change until after campaign
4. Sales promotion activity	Increased sales volume from base sales, decreased reliance on promotional sales vs CBB market
5. Regional variations affecting sales patterns	Uplift in TV advertised regions vs non-TV advertised regions
6. Seasonal variations affecting sales patterns	Sales improvement demonstrable year on year

CONCLUSION

The campaign objective was to:

- increase market share
- increase audience penetration
- halt sales decline and drive long-term uplift in base rate of sales.

In the first year of the campaign we achieved:

- 0.8% increase in market share
- 612,500 new households purchasing Rocky
- reduction in increase of promotional sales vs base sales relative to CBB sector
- overall sales increase of between £2.3m (over year-on-year market trend) and £3.9m (over year-on-year Rocky trend).

With an overall media spend of £1.2m the advertising achieved a return on investment of between 1:1.91 and 1:3.25 (Table 4).

TABLE 4: RETURN ON INVESTMENT

Sales increase	Media spend	ROI
£2.3m	£1.2m	2:1
£3.9m	£1.2m	3:1

We have shown a demonstrable cause and effect between a campaign designed to engage with mums and 8–11-year-old kids, a rise in brand awareness and propensity to purchase in that audience segment, and a growth in audience penetration and market share. This has resulted in a halt in decline of base sales for Rocky, a reduced reliance on promotional activity and an increase in sales worth between £2.3m and £3.9m in a declining sector. We believe we have isolated the Rocky R advertising effect by removing all other possible reasons for the success of Rocky in the sales period analysed. Rocky R will be playing an on-going role in driving the commercial success of Fox's Rocky in an increasingly competitive environment.

18

Lancashire Short Breaks Campaign

The Midas touch

Turning a box of old coupons into £8,267m

Principal authors: Claire Longfield and Catherine Warrington,
Radford Advertising Marketing and Tony Openshaw,
Lancashire Tourism Partnership (LTP)

EDITOR'S SUMMARY

Prior to 1999, Lancashire had done very little marketing activity. However, in September of that year, the Lancashire Tourism Partnership approached Radford with a very simple brief: to 'do something' with their existing customer database, which at that time was little more than a box of old coupons and spreadsheets.

The outcome was a long-term campaign using direct mail, specialist press and door drops that has evolved over several years.

Careful targeting has been crucial to the success of the campaign. Analysis of the data revealed that people likely to visit Lancashire were older than expected, and also more downmarket and more local. Refining the targeting to reach these people helped Radford to achieve impressive response and conversion rates.

As a result, the customer database has doubled in size, and it is estimated that an extra £8m worth of tourist revenue was generated – 39 times more than was spent on marketing.

This is a good example of how evaluation research can shape and improve a campaign. The judges were impressed at the way Radford learned from the data, and developed the campaign over time.

INTRODUCTION

The Lancashire Tourism Partnership (LTP) was set up in 1997 to address a seven-year project named 'Raising the Profile'. The task was to develop a marketing strategy to raise the profile of Lancashire and to develop key market sectors. 'Short breaks' was identified as one such market.

Prior to 1999, Lancashire had done very little tourism marketing activity. Each of the district partners and numerous private-sector suppliers had placed a few local ads and mailed several newsletters and flyers to people on their 'databases' – nothing centrally coordinated or, more importantly, monitored.

Ironically it took an office refurbishment to discover the Aladdin's cave that would become the now valuable Lancashire Short Breaks database. Boxes of old coupons and print-outs of Excel spreadsheets destined for the skip were rescued by the new LTP Marketing Manager from under a soon-to-be-discarded old desk. These boxes landed on our desk in September 1999 with the brief: 'Let's do something with these!'

The outcome of that brief, along with subsequent strategy brainstorms, was a long-term, targeted and integrated campaign incorporating direct mail supported by specialist press and door-drops promoting Lancashire as a short-break destination. The subsequent campaign success will be discussed throughout this paper.

Working closely with Radford, LTP identified the key objectives as:

- to grow the LTP database as a valuable marketing tool accessible to all partners
- to increase the volume and value of short-break visitors between 1999 and 2004
- to increase the average length of stay to four nights.

However, before these objectives could be tackled, the key issue of weak brand identity had to be addressed. Subsequently, the starting point for the project was to create a new brand identity for Lancashire to ensure consistency of image and messages across all communications.

BACKGROUND

It was recognised that any marketing activity aimed at the short break market needed to address the fundamental issue of the lack of brand identity for Lancashire, which prior to 1999 had not been marketed as a discrete county. Lancashire was perceived to be a wet, grey destination with the lasting impression being at best the over dominance of Blackpool and at worst flat caps and whippets!

The re-launch budget was set at £40,000 and private sector and district partners needed to see tangible results from their investment in any marketing activity.

Target market

The first step was to go back to basics and ask ourselves 'Who is the customer?' Following a marketing planning seminar with district and private-sector partners, this is who the key participants believed their target audience to be:

- SKI brogues 55+ – 'Spending the Kids Inheritance', liking the good things in life, likely to be National Trust members
- new empty nesters – 45–60, AB – those with increased time and money since the kids have gone
- 35+, BC1 – likely to have longer holidays, may be into walking, countryside and outdoor pursuits.

Understanding and redefining the target audience

The first step for the project was to test some assumptions regarding the identified target audience for short breaks. The 20,000 coupons from people who had previously requested information on Lancashire were profiled by Claritas.

The profile report made interesting reading. The assumption of upmarket over-50s couples visiting art galleries and National Trust properties in green wellies was fundamentally wrong!

So who were they? First, two-thirds of the enquirers were women. More importantly, however, was the fact that the database was:

- of a lower socio-economic grouping than anticipated (C1, C2, D)
- with a subsequent lower household income than expected
- mainly aged over 55.

Also surprising was the fact that almost 20% of enquiries came from Yorkshire, which had previously been assumed to be too close for promoting short breaks in Lancashire.

The findings were used to refine the choice of media used for the short-breaks campaign and also to purchase cold data.

All this information was used to direct the creative brief in terms of photography style, colour palette, tone of voice and even a new logo and strapline. A set of brand guidelines was produced for all partners to ensure that the Lancashire tourism brand continued to be promoted in a consistent manner across all material.

THE SHORT BREAKS MARKETING SOLUTION

Timing

Spring and autumn were identified as the key periods for short-breaks marketing activity.

Media selection

Given the limited budget and regionally/socio-demographically focused target audience, direct mail was identified as the key enabler to all recruitment and customer communication activity. This also allowed us to avoid the wastage inherent in committing huge budget allocation to above-the-line advertising.

The purpose of using direct mail was three-fold:

1. to maintain regular contact with existing customers in order to keep them up to date with special offers, etc.

2. to generate new leads in order to grow the database
3. to keep the database 'clean' and up to date, and to gather useful lifestyle data.

Building on the profiling of the original database of 19,584, an additional 20,000 names were purchased from list brokers to match the identified profile (i.e. women aged 50–65, C1, C2 and D socio-economic groups). Half of these were in the Yorkshire TV region and half in Central, which were the top two regions from the original data.

A solus mailing was sent to these two databases in autumn 2000, comprising a welcome letter, leaflet and outer, with an option to request one of three packs: coast; countryside; short-break packages (Figure 1). This was incentivised with a wordsearch to win a weekend in Lancashire, as the profile indicated that crosswords and other puzzles were very popular with the target audience. The completed coupon was to be sent to a freepost address in Lancashire in order to capture names and distribute fulfilment packs.

Two further direct mail campaigns were undertaken in 2001 with a very different, yet very focused, message. Hit hard by the foot-and-mouth crisis, Lancashire had to communicate that the countryside was back open for business. Just under 30,000 packs were sent to a bought list of the target audience, encouraging them to take a short break in Lancashire. Responders were sent a destination guide along with a special offers leaflet. This pack was also incentivised with a weekend break free prize draw to uplift response and be used as a valuable data capture tool.

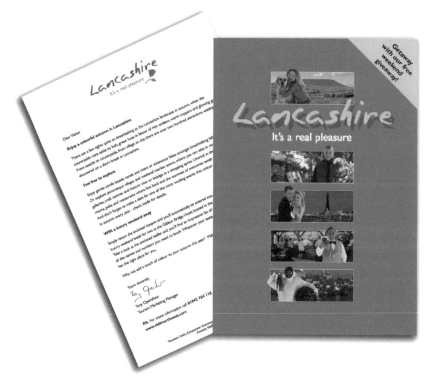

Figure 1: *Solus mailing, autumn 2000*

At the same time, the existing database was also sent details of special accommodation and attraction offers from around the region to generate visits during this difficult period.

In spring 2002, the focus of the direct mail campaign changed slightly. Lancashire wanted to communicate its involvement in the Commonwealth Games and also promote accommodation special offers and key events in the area. Again, just under 20,000 names were bought and sent an incentivised pack, and the existing database was also mailed with the same information.

In spring 2003 Lancashire wanted to promote the special events happening around the area to its existing database and test a 'recommend a friend' promotion. A concertina postcard mailing was developed to communicate these key messages and capture RAF details. This was updated for autumn 2004 and also mailed to a bought list of 20,000.

In autumn 2004, a theme-led rather than partner-led approach to the creative was used (Figure 2). The theme for 2004 was 'Country Escapes'. An innovative one-piece mailer was developed to communicate the value of Lancashire as a countryside destination and also to promote some special offers on accommodation and attractions.

Figure 2: *The autumn 2004 theme-led approach*

Door-drops

To communicate the new branding and raise the profile of Lancashire to as wide an audience as possible, the direct mail leaflet was adapted for use as a door-drop in autumn 2000 and spring 2001 (Figure 3). Royal Mail was used as the door-drop provider, as it was felt that arriving with the mail would create more impact. Royal Mail's 'Scenario' profiling was used to match the target audience as closely as

Figure 3: *Door-drop*

possible to the profile already identified and the top postcode areas were selected, again within Yorkshire and Central TV regions. A total of 241,000 door-drops were distributed in autumn 2000 and 150,000 in spring 2001. Although both campaigns enjoyed good response rates, by autumn 2001 it was felt that press and direct mail were more appropriate and cost-effective methods of communicating Lancashire's key messages following the foot-and-mouth crisis.

Advertising

TGI data was used to identify key titles that had a high proportion of readers who provided a synergy with our target audience. Only titles where it was possible to insert regionally (in Yorkshire and Central TV regions) were selected, in order to avoid wasted coverage. The core titles were *Woman's Own*, *Woman's Weekly* and *Prima* for inserts, and off-the-page ads were placed in *Reader's Digest* and *Golden Years* (a 16-page door-drop that targets 50+ households) to support each campaign (Figure 4).

BIG RESULTS DON'T NEED BIG BUDGETS

The results achieved from both the existing and bought-list direct mail exceeded expectations, producing response rates of up to 22.4% (existing) and 11.58% (cold) (Figures 5 and 6). Meanwhile door-drops were enjoying response rates of up to 1.73% against a target of 0.5%, press inserts 1.53% and off-the-page advertising 0.68%. Impressive results by industry standards and all the more so given that Lancashire was starting with a low base with major challenges in changing perceptions of the region.

Figure 4: *Magazine advertising,* Golden Years

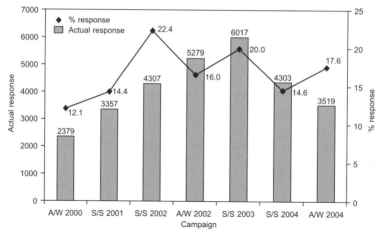

Figure 5: *Direct mail response rates (existing)*
Prior to each campaign, the database is analysed to establish the most responsive leads – by postcode, by source of enquiry and by recency of enquiry. This has allowed LTP to enjoy a consistently high response rate – year after year.

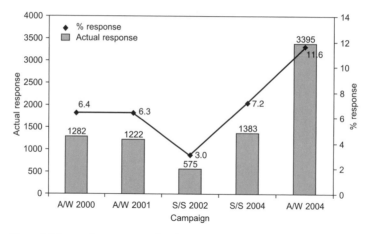

Figure 6: *Direct mail response rates (bought)*
In 2002, the buying criteria for the cold list was changed to be more upmarket, younger and from geographically further afield to capitalise on The Commonwealth Games. Unfortunately these people did not respond as well to the Lancashire offer.

Big revenue

Response rates mean nothing if they don't generate revenue. In this case they did. Lancashire Tourism commissioned an independent research company, Questions Answered, to conduct in-depth converter research at the end of each campaign. This research looked into customer perceptions of the material received and of Lancashire as a region, its attractions and accommodation. However, pertinent to this paper were the findings on conversion from enquiry (i.e. people actually visiting after requesting information), spend per visit, average length of stay and subsequent ROI (Figures 7, 8 and 9).

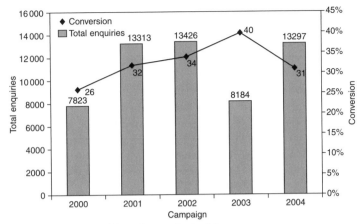

Figure 7: *Campaign enquiries and conversion to visit*
Since 2001, LTP have used special offers on attractions and accommodation to ensure that conversion to visit remains high.

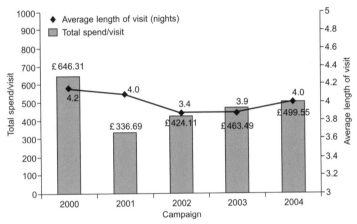

Figure 8: *Average length of stay and spend per visit*
During the Foot and Mouth Crisis of 2001, the spend per visit dropped considerably as many attractions were closed. However, LTP have still achieved the desired average length of stay of 4 nights per visit.

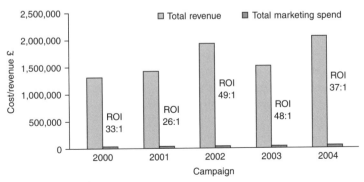

Figure 9: *Return on investment*
The lower ROI in 2001 can be explained by the Foot and Moth Crisis. However, the overall average ROI is a very healthy 39.1.

CAMPAIGN HIGHLIGHTS

- Overall performance of DM activity exceeded the anticipated response levels: up to 22.4% from the existing enquirer database against a target of 8% and 11.58% from cold list against a target of 5%.
- The Lancashire database has more than doubled to almost 45,000 profiled and clean records from a box of 19,584 coupons in just four years.
- By autumn 2004 short-break visits had increased to 4.01 nights' average length of stay with a total revenue of £8.267m and an average annual ROI of 39:1.

CONCLUSION

Having never undertaken any coordinated marketing activity prior to 1999, the Lancashire Short Breaks campaign has exceeded expectations in terms of response, cost-effectiveness and ROI. The marketing plan has evolved season after season, as each campaign has provided a learning curve and a guide for future planning and how best to spend the limited marketing budget.

The database is now held in a central location, allowing all partners to access this invaluable 'warm' data for their own campaigns without incurring the high costs associated with cold list purchase.

A further testimonial to the success of the project is that all material produced by Lancashire partners now boasts a strong, consistent look. From district brochures to promotional flyers, each piece is instantly recognisable as being part of the Lancashire family – certainly a claim that could not have been made four years ago.

To summarise, developed from a discarded box of coupons, Lancashire now looks like a focused brand, has a loyal database of customers and enjoys a healthy profit from its short-breaks campaigns … year after year.

19

Noise Awareness
Too Loud

Principal authors: David Lyle, Julie Anne Bailie, Andrea Carrigan and Dawn Reid, LyleBailie International

EDITOR'S SUMMARY

In this case, the job for advertising was relatively simple: to make people in Northern Ireland aware that help exists for victims of noise, and to tell them exactly who to contact.

However, evaluating the effects of such a campaign is not necessarily straightforward, especially on a limited budget. LyleBailie's paper impressed the judges with its thoroughness. Research showed clearly how the ads cut through, made people take noise more seriously, made them more likely to complain about it, and made them aware of precisely who they should call.

The net result was a 44% increase in the number of people reporting noise problems to their local councils, proof that advertising can help tackle a difficult social problem, even on a small budget.

INTRODUCTION

Noise is something we are all subject to, that we all create and contribute to. In conversation, music, laughter, in the workplace and at the shops, it's difficult to imagine going about our lives in complete silence. But for many people in Northern Ireland (NI), the noise levels they are subject to are unbearable. Indeed, the noise levels they have to live with are so extreme that they have become 'nuisance noise'; an anti-social pollutant that causes severe anxiety and depression.

The 'Too Loud' campaign devised by LyleBailie had to create a lot of advertising noise – with a relatively reserved budget – to communicate that help existed for victims of nuisance noise, and empower them in seeking that help.

It succeeded.

NI's first province-wide noise awareness campaign has delivered exceptional results. Awareness, influence and action have been proven to be linked directly to the campaign performance as the following results demonstrate:

- a 29% increase in the likelihood of complaining about noise
- a 100% increase in the amount of the people saying they would contact their council if they had a problem with nuisance noise
- 56% awareness levels of the campaign
- 77% of respondents said the campaign influenced them
- 80% of respondents said the campaign made them think about the seriousness of nuisance noise.

These reported behaviours are underscored by the increase in actual complaints received by the district councils, which show an overall increase in complaints received over the campaign period of 44% against the same period in 2004.

Running for only four weeks, the results show an exceptional return for a relatively limited marketing investment – proving the considered media placement and insightful creative thought and execution have created the right kind of noise with our target audience.

BACKGROUND

The Noise Awareness campaign came about through a need to communicate the issue of noise and nuisance noise. It was found that there was no clear understanding of who the public should contact for help with nuisance noise issues, therefore the primary focus of the campaign was to raise awareness of local councils as the public body responsible for addressing nuisance noise.

MARKETING OBJECTIVES

The campaign aim was to make the Northern Ireland public aware of what they can do and who they can contact, if they believe themselves to be noise sufferers, by way of a media campaign covering NI's 26 council areas over a four-week period.

The campaign was tasked with communicating that:

- it is all right to complain
- nuisance noise is a serious issue
- sufferers are not alone
- local councils are able to help and solve the problem

and had to deliver a measured improvement in the public usage of district council noise services.

THE STRATEGIC SOLUTION

The problem of noise and what constitutes nuisance noise is at the heart of our creative approach. Nuisance noise is difficult to define for both victims and perpetrators, which culminates in the further isolation of the sufferer and leads to uncomfortable misunderstandings between neighbours. Indeed, the campaign essentially has two broad audiences: the victim and the noise maker. One's home is one's refuge and for this to be challenged by the interruption of unwelcome noise or, indeed, unwelcome complaints, could result in a highly pressurised situation. This understanding was critical to the development of this campaign.

Nevertheless, the essential focus of the noise awareness campaign was in communicating to *victims* – reassuring them that their feelings of despair, anger or isolation are valid and that there is a real solution available.

THE IDEA

While the victim is the primary focus, by including examples of nuisance noise the creative also works on a secondary level – that is, the creative solution helps to universally establish the parameters for noise management, demonstrating what constitutes unacceptable social behaviour, and consequently creating a shared basis for future discussion and mediation.

Figure 1: *The campaign's striking visual approach aimed to empower victims of nuisance noise*

The animated visual approach (Figures 1 and 2) is striking; it pictorially conveys the idea of unacceptable noise in depicting a throbbing house, thumping stereo, barking dog – all examples of the most complained-about nuisance noise. It is empathetic, demonstrating the anguish sufferers endure. It is empowering – reassuring worried sufferers that they are allowed to address anti-social behaviour. Indeed, for a victim who is anxious at the thought of confrontation, who feels they are being unneighbourly or that they may be judged by others, it gives permission to their emotions and encourages their action.

Figure 2: *Press ad visual*

THE COMMUNICATION ACTIVITY

The media plan was designed to deliver ubiquity, breakthrough and value for money for the client.

In planning the noise awareness campaign there was an appreciation that different councils receive different levels of complaints. Nevertheless it was recommended that the media mix did not narrow the focus of the campaign to this level; the number of complaints received per district council is not necessarily a reflection of the extent of the noise problem. Therefore, the campaign's target audience was agreed as 'all adults' throughout Northern Ireland.

Based on an analysis of all available media, the communication objectives, the available budget and the relevance to the message, the final media plan recommended a TV campaign commencing the week of 24 January 2005 and continuing for four weeks. To complement this there were two distinct bursts of press coverage in week commencing 1 February and week commencing 15 February to cover NI Sunday and daily papers, along with some 42 provincial weekly titles.

The total media spend was £49,950.

THE RESULTS

Overall the campaign aims outlined below have each been met, and indeed exceeded in the level of improvement achieved:

- communicating that it is all right to complain
- communicating that nuisance noise is a serious issue
- communicating that those who suffer are not alone
- communicating that local councils are able to help and solve the problem
- delivering a measured improvement in the public usage of district council noise services.

The media campaign delivered audiences, frequency and reach as planned, at the same time delivering exceptional value for money – this is borne out in the following tracking research results and district council responses.

Figure 3 shows an increase across both men and women, all ages, demographics, areas and types of household in those acknowledging that they know someone who has been disturbed by noisy neighbours (the only exception being a slight decrease in ages 16–24 and 50–64). This could indicate a number of shifts:

- an increase in nuisance noise as a social issue in that it is more top of mind for the public following the campaign
- an increase in the awareness of what constitutes nuisance noise and therefore an increase in the number of people complaining (this is supported by the actual number of complaints received at district council level).

Figure 4 clearly demonstrates the success of the campaign in communicating who to contact in the event of a nuisance noise issue, and consequently achieving one of its key aims – that is, *a 100% increase in the number of respondents saying they would contact their district council.*

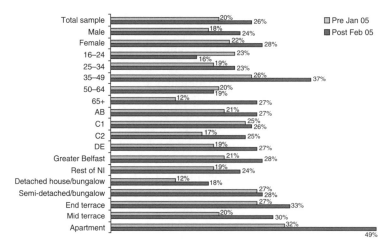

Figure 3: *Do you know anyone who is or has been disturbed by noisy neighbours? (YES)*
Base: pre Jan 05 – 500 respondents/post Feb 05 – 603 respondents
Source: Millward Brown Ulster Telephone Survey

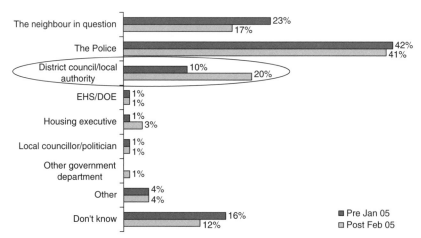

Figure 4: *Who would you be most likely to contact if disturbed by noisy neighbours?*
Base: pre Jan 05 – 500 respondents/post Feb 05 – 603 respondents
Source: Millward Brown Ulster Telephone Survey

Again, in Figure 5, we see an increase in respondents' reported behaviour with increases in those likely to complain about noisy neighbours and a decrease in people saying they would be unlikely to complain. This demonstrates that the awareness campaign is empowering people to recognise and address nuisance noise, and may also be demonstrative of an increase in understanding of what to do if faced with a nuisance noise problem.

These results show a positive move towards the public feeling that noisy neighbours are a 'very serious' issue; 48% of respondents agree that the issue is very serious, up from 33% before the campaign. This is an interesting result, which could be attributed to the themes shown in the advertising and the empathy the creative execution communicated for the noise victim (Figure 6).

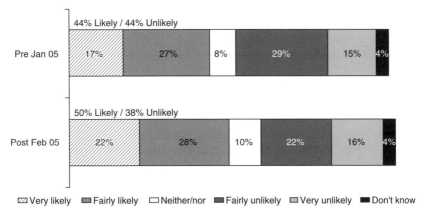

Figure 5: *How likely or unlikely would you be to complain about being disturbed by noisy neighbours?*
Base: pre Jan 05 – 500 respondents / post Feb 05 – 603 respondents
Source: Millward Brown Ulster Telephone Survey

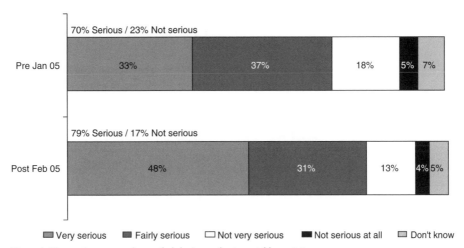

Figure 6: *How serious or not do you feel the issue of noisy neighbours is?*
Base: pre Jan 05 – 500 respondents / post Feb 05 – 603 respondents
Source: Millward Brown Ulster Telephone Survey

Prompted awareness of the campaign was significant (Figure 7), with 56% of all respondents aware of the advertising. This was higher among women, the 25 to 39 age groups and the C2 demographic. Geographical area and house types achieved around the same amount of awareness; indeed awareness levels across the sample were consistently high.

A total of 80% of respondents agreed the advertising made them think about the seriousness of noisy neighbours (Figure 8), rising to a massive 93% of respondents who had seen the ad and knew someone affected by the issue. This demonstrates the effectiveness of the campaign in engaging the audience with the message and content.

Again, influence scores for the campaign demonstrate an engaging and well-targeted message: 77% of respondents say they were influenced by the campaign.

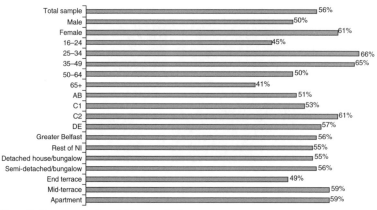

Figure 7: *Have you seen/heard this campaign?*
Base: Post Feb 05 – 603 respondents
Source: Millward Brown Ulster Telephone Survey, February 2005

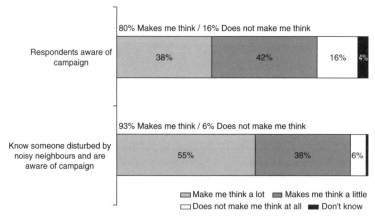

Figure 8: *To what extent does this campaign make you think about the seriousness of noisy neighbours?*
Base: Post Feb 05 aware of campaign – 344 respondents / 106 who know someone disturbed by noisy neighbours
Source: Millward Brown Ulster Telephone Survey, February 2005

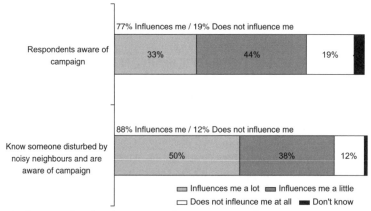

Figure 9: *To what extent does this advertisement influence you or not influence you?*
Base: Post Feb 05 aware of campaign – 344 respondents / 106 who know someone disturbed by noisy neighbours
Source: Millward Brown Ulster Telephone Survey, February 2005

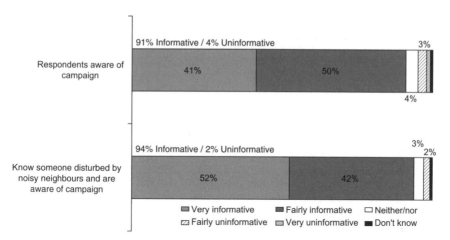

Figure 10: *To what extent did you find this advertisement informative or uninformative?*
Base: Post Feb 05 aware of campaign – 344 respondents / 106 who know someone disturbed by noisy neighbours
Source: Millward Brown Ulster Telephone Survey, February 2005

This is borne out in the statistics garnered by the district councils, which show actual behaviour change (Figure 9).

By proving that the campaign influenced over three-quarters of adults who were aware of it, the advertising effect can be isolated and thus directly connected to the resultant behavioural changes.

Our final scores show how informative the campaign was perceived to be (Figure 10). This was a 20-second TV execution that had to quickly engage the audience while at the same time communicating information about the nature of nuisance noise – a challenging brief from the outset. A total of 91% of respondents agreed that the campaign was informative, thus confirming the success of the creative approach.

As well as conducting the above research into attitudes and behaviour, each of the district councils in Northern Ireland was tasked with measuring complaint

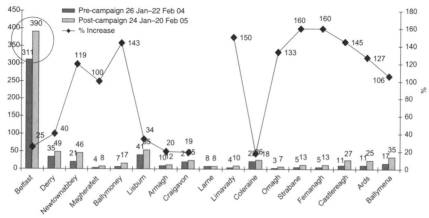

Figure 11: *Complaint levels pre- vs post-campaign, by DCA*
Note: Newtownabbey/Magherafelt/Ballymoney pre-campaign dates = 24 Jan–20 Feb 2004
Source: Environmental Officers from each DCA

levels received throughout the period of the campaign, to assess these against the same period in 2004. From the results returned by the district councils, the actual number of complaints received during the campaign increased overall by 44% – proving that the campaign impacted on actual, as well as reported, behaviours. Figure 11 shows the different complaint levels observed for those District Councils that provided the information.

The levels of complaints received during the campaign are striking. Belfast District Council, with the highest base level of complaints from 2004 and therefore perhaps the most robust example of the campaign effectiveness, shows a 25% increase in complaints received. Other areas have smaller samples to compare, but nevertheless show the impressive impact of the campaign across all district councils. Interestingly, this includes the more rural council areas, with Fermanagh showing an increase from five complaints in 2004 to 13 in 2005, and Ballymena increasing from 17 in 2004 to 35 in 2005 – increases of 160% and 106%, respectively.

PAYBACK OR RETURN ON INVESTMENT

The objective of this campaign was to generate calls to local councils. This would demonstrate that the message was getting through and that noise victims felt empowered by the campaign, which was the ultimate payback for the client. It was understood that this would create a cost implication for local councils, rather than a saving.

However, it is possible to assess the payback from the campaign in terms of preventing health problems. Nuisance noise can cause annoyance and fatigue, interfere with communication and sleep, reduce efficiency and damage hearing. The World Health Organization recommends a guideline level of 30dB LA_{eq} for undisturbed sleep, and a daytime level for outdoor sound of 50dB to prevent people from becoming 'moderately annoyed'. Physiological effects of exposure to noise include constriction of bloody vessels, tightening of muscles, increased heart rate and blood pressure, and changes in stomach and abdomen movement. These effects have cost implications in terms of the workplace, benefits and healthcare. In the long term, providing a solution to noise victims and creating awareness of what noise is nuisance noise will go some way to addressing the wider cost implications.

CONCLUSION

The 'Too Loud' campaign, through an innovative creative approach based on sound research findings and psychological insights, along with intelligent media planning, has without question delivered across all audiences with an engaging, entertaining and empowering message about nuisance noise. This is clear from independently conducted research, which confirms striking results in reported behaviour:

- 29% increase in likelihood of complaining
- 100% increase in the amount of the people saying they would contact their council if they had a problem with nuisance noise

- 56% awareness of the campaign
- 77% of respondents saying the campaign had influenced them
- 80% of respondents saying the campaign made them think about the seriousness of nuisance noise.

The campaign's impact is also reflected in observed behaviour through the council reporting on noise complaints received throughout the duration of the campaign, which showed a 44% increase. These results demonstrate a direct correlation between the awareness campaign and changes in attitude and behaviour.

20

ScottishPower
Energising The Energy People

Principal author: Alan Clarke, The Bridge
Contributing author: Brian Crook, The Bridge
Media agency: Feather Brooksbank

EDITOR'S SUMMARY

Building a brand in the energy sector is not an easy business. Gas and electricity are true commodities, and people aren't very interested in them, except when they go wrong. People only tend to switch suppliers when someone knocks on the door and offers them a cheap deal.

ScottishPower, traditionally a regional supplier north of the border, faced a strong national competitor, British Gas, and was losing customers. To ensure the future of the company, customer losses needed to be reversed, and customer numbers built up to the point where economies of scale allowed the company to compete efficiently.

The 'Energy People' campaign did just that. Customer churn was reduced, customer acquisitions increased, and overall customer numbers increased by 11%. As a result, total customer numbers reached the critical five million mark, helping to ensure the future prosperity of the company.

The judges were interested in the role that economies of scale played in this case, and the way the campaign helped internally within the company.

INTRODUCTION

In 2003 The Bridge and ScottishPower entered an IPA Advertising Effectiveness paper identifying that, to ensure the future prosperity of the latter's UK customer supply business, two challenges had to be addressed.

1. Losses among existing customers needed to be stopped quickly (success in this was detailed in the 2003 paper).
2. There was a need to establish a clear positioning for ScottishPower that would provide a platform on which it could build the business.

This year's paper addresses the second challenge and demonstrates how advertising played a crucial role in helping ScottishPower become one of the UK's leading energy supply companies. It played an internal role in helping align ScottishPower's various departments. And it played an external role in re-establishing ScottishPower as the key player (in its homeland) and helping ScottishPower 'own' the critical territory of value for money.

The result was that losses fell, acquisitions improved and overall customer numbers in Scotland grew by 11%, a return on the advertising investment of 1600%.

On a UK-wide basis customers have increased from four million to five million and, critically, the UK customer supply business has begun to offer the plc the kind of critical mass that it enjoys in other aspects of its portfolio.

THE CHALLENGE

The challenge ScottishPower faced in its customer supply and service business was both internal and external.

The internal challenge stemmed from the legacy of the various strategies that the company had followed over the previous five years. Brand extensions into and subsequent exits from areas such as telecoms and financial services had left a lack of internal focus. There was also a lack of certainty as to what the business stood for and where it was headed. This is particularly dangerous in a business where customer service and customer interaction is a fundamental part of the offering. The management knew that it was critical that this was addressed.

The external challenge had some similarities. Customers were unclear as to what ScottishPower's offering was. This was exacerbated by some of the market's basic characteristics. Energy supply is about as low-interest, low-involvement a sector as one can find. The basic product is fundamentally undifferentiated (it doesn't matter who supplies your gas and electricity, the same 'product' comes out of the pipe and through the wire). Research consistently reported that, provided they felt they were getting a good deal on price and continuity of supply, consumers were happy. This inertia was only overcome when someone literally knocked on consumers' doors offering them a 'cheaper' deal. In the chaotic market that had followed deregulation, acquisition success across the industry was driven by the promise of a substantially better price and the convenience of signing up on the spot, with around three-quarters of all 'switches' made face to face. Advertising (and branding for that matter) played little role.

ScottishPower had to re-engage with its audiences. Internal and external.

BECOMING 'THE ENERGY PEOPLE'

ScottishPower established a multi-departmental working party for Project Nirvana – a project that would define both the positioning of the company and the executional manifestation of that positioning. The Bridge was appointed to help facilitate the project and to execute the creative work – advertising and design.

In 2001 ScottishPower enjoyed brand values similar to the other energy suppliers who had retained their pre-deregulation brands – trust, heritage, size and respect – but the company was also considered to be cold and faceless.

Desk research provided an understanding of the essential role competitive prices and continuity of supply played. It also provided an insight into how an energy company could differentiate by delivering a more proactive, customer-focused approach.

Following a stage of exploratory field research, a range of broad positioning areas was identified. Each was investigated to see how it stacked up against ScottishPower's values and a range of customer touchpoints (see Figures 1 and 2).

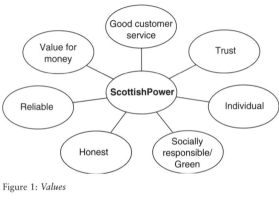

Figure 1: *Values*

Figure 2: *Touchpoints*

A series of internal workshops was followed by more consumer and B2B research, exploring different positioning statements and what they meant in practice for how the business delivered its products and service. Further research validated a refined positioning and sanity checked it against both consumer and business customers. From that came the finalised positioning statement:

'We specialise in gas and electricity so we can do more for you
and your environment.'

What was critical was the recognition that this would come to life only from the
bottom up – through the different touchpoints. It had to be brought to life via
demonstrating the 'more for you' in each of the touchpoint areas. And a critical one
in the medium term was the area of price. Consumers needed reassurance about
ScottishPower's price competitiveness. (Effectively 'doing more for you on price'
could be being competitive versus the 'gold standard' in the market at the time –
British Gas – or it could be in new and more imaginative payment methods, e.g.
'capped' or 'online'.) Beyond that we would eventually extend into other
manifestations of 'doing more for you' that customers valued (e.g. Green products
or more accurate, more user-friendly bills). A whole internal multi-departmental
project looking at the implications of 'doing more for you' was implemented.

DEVELOPING THE CREATIVE

Executing a fully integrated campaign required a communications idea that could
work across all communication channels, so it had to be much more than just an
advertising idea – it had to be flexible enough to work across all the touchpoint
areas of price, product and service. It had to be an idea where different specific
propositions could still be held together with strong branding running throughout
the commercial (even more important than usual in this low-interest market).

Four routes were developed and researched with consumers and business
audiences. The Energy People route emerged as the strongest.

BRINGING THE CAMPAIGN TO LIFE

The communications idea uses simple, distinctive animation and illustration with a
light, refreshing tone of voice to demonstrate the benefit of being a ScottishPower
customer. The simplicity of the style is meant to help underline the simplicity and
focus of ScottishPower's offering. The executions acknowledge that the consumer
may find the whole subject dull but they emphasise that, among that dullness, there
is important information (see Figure 3).

Learnings from the losses reduction campaign meant the roles for advertising,
direct marketing and direct selling were well understood.

The advertising was tasked with the context-setting role of bringing the new
positioning to life, building brand awareness and improving brand perceptions. It
would also play an important role internally by communicating the business's new
confidence and step-change in approach in the most public of environments.

Direct marketing would continue its role in delivering tightly targeted messages
that sold higher-value, 'stickier' products to existing customers either through a
direct response or in conjunction with direct selling.

Direct selling would continue to be the key channel for actually signing up new
customers.

VO: Ways to keep your energy bills down, number 6

SFX: Parade noises growing louder

VO: Now please pay attention, because some people still seem to be missing the point

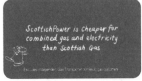

VO: For the average customer ScottishPower is cheaper for combined gas and electricity than Scottish Gas

VO: So to save money switch to us

ScottishPower
gas and electricity
0800 027 9018
The energy people

VO: Another great way to keep your energy bills down from the energy people. ScottishPower

Figure 3: *Examples of the creative work*

MEDIA

The media strategy was also driven by the learnings from the losses reduction campaign, which had validated TV's awareness-building and attitude-changing strengths in such a low-interest, low-involvement market. It also validated the strategy of making sure that whenever the advertising ran it did so at a sufficiently heavy weight. The rule of thumb established was that the effective weight for this type of message in this type of market was as high as 8 OTS.

Posters were used to up-weight certain messages locally. The media lay-down in Scotland during 2003 and 2004 involved a total spend of £1.6 million.

The advertising that ran

Consumer research during the development of 'The Energy People' positioning reinforced the critical role competitive price (not necessarily cheapest) played in acquiring and retaining customers. Consequently, the communications plan was developed to lead with advertising demonstrating that ScottishPower offered customers a range of ways to keep their energy bills down and a core price proposition that ScottishPower was cheaper than British Gas, the biggest player in the market (and the company that was taking 75% of ScottishPower's customer losses).

WHAT HAPPENED?

Internal success

The internal success of the campaign can be observed in the revised structures within the business; in the project teams that were developed to address the different touchpoints; in the number of new (focused) products that were developed and launched; and in the business's growing confidence in the role for advertising and subsequent increase in investment. The internal success can also be witnessed in the atmosphere within customer supply and service.

External success

To be deemed a success the advertising would need to achieve the following:

- show that it was cutting through in a low-interest market
- demonstrate that it was changing perceptions – and, critically, winning the battle with British Gas
- show that it was establishing ScottishPower as a value-for-money supplier
- show that it was establishing ScottishPower as a preferred supplier.

Evidence comes from three main sources:

1. Advertising tracking in the Scottish TV region
2. 'voice of the Customer', ScottishPower's principal barometer of customer satisfaction
3. Internal customer numbers and lifetime value data.

The advertising successfully cut through in a low-interest,
low-involvement market

Although spontaneous advertising awareness is low when compared to some fmcg brands, it is ScottishPower's relative position that matters. It has risen from 12% to 22% and ScottishPower's is consistently the highest in the sector, higher than Powergen and dramatically overtaking British Gas, despite British Gas having higher TV and total media spends (see Figure 4).

Prompted advertising awareness has more than doubled from 18% to 41% (see Figure 5).

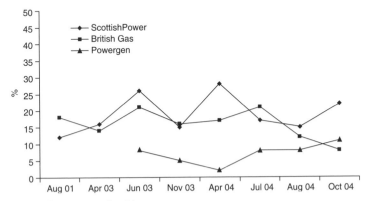

Figure 4: *Spontaneous advertising awareness*
Source: advertising tracking

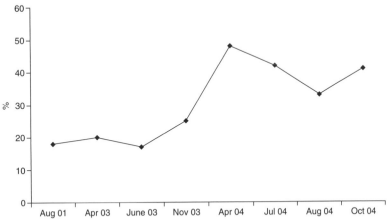

Figure 5: *ScottishPower prompted advertising awareness*
Source: advertising tracking

Not only did it cut through, it communicated the desired
'competitive prices' message …

'Attributable recall' grew during the campaign, reaching 83%. 'Attributable recall' records very specific ad message codes such as 'ScottishPower is cheaper for gas and

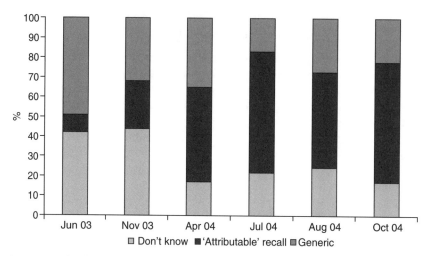

Figure 6: *Attributable recall*
Base: respondents who recalled ScottishPower advertising
Source: advertising tracking

electricity', 'cheaper than British Gas' and 'keeping bills down'. Generic recall records codes such as 'cheaper' and 'switch to ScottishPower' (see Figure 6).

... which has driven forward price perceptions

'Voice of the Customer' reports ratings on five out of seven value-for-money measures improved among those aware of the advertising. All seven fell among those not aware of the advertising.

This positive movement is supported by the advertising tracking, which reports that the period of heaviest advertising coincided with peak agreement that 'ScottishPower is cheaper than British Gas for ...

- both gas and electricity'
- gas only'
- electricity only'.

Similar findings were reported for 'Offers competitive prices', 'Reassures you on competitiveness' and 'Willing to help reduce bill'.

The advertising also had a positive impact on brand perceptions ...

While brand measures on 'Voice of the Customer' go up and down over time (reflecting the broader profile of the company in the media) the difference in ratings between those aware of the advertising and those not aware of the advertising has widened on the key measures 'ScottishPower is the best supplier of gas and electricity' and 'Overall, how satisfied are you with ScottishPower?'

The advertising tracking reports every brand attitude statement improving, with peak levels again coinciding with the period of heaviest advertising.

... with The Energy People positioning becoming increasingly established among those aware of the advertising (see Figure 7)

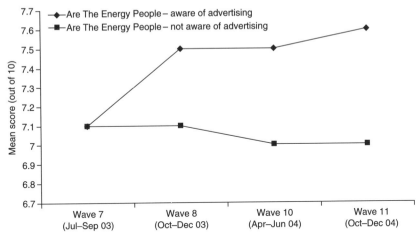

Figure 7: *'ScottishPower are The Energy People'*
Source: Voice of the Customer

The outcome was that ScottishPower has become established as the consumer's front-of-mind supplier ...

First-mention brand awareness of ScottishPower has risen from 20% to 69%, while British Gas has fallen from 53% to 26% (see Figure 8).

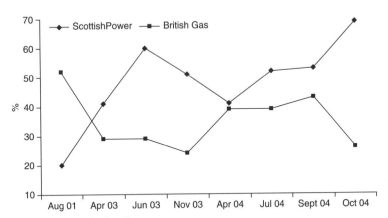

Figure 8: *First-mention brand awareness*
Source: advertising tracking

Spontaneous brand awareness has reached almost saturation point and leads British Gas (see Figure 9).

The brand is almost as high profile among non-customers (i.e. those ScottishPower could hope to recruit), spontaneous brand awareness having grown by half to reach 90% (see Figure 10).

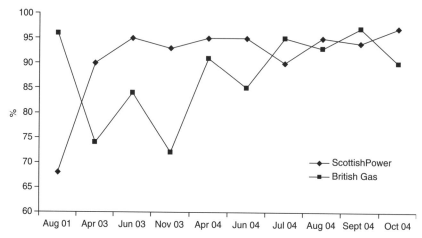

Figure 9: *Spontaneous brand awareness*
Source: advertising tracking

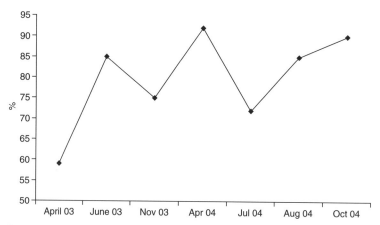

Figure 10: *ScottishPower spontaneous brand awareness (non-customers)*
Source: advertising tracking

... and as the market's preferred supplier

When asked who they would choose if they could choose only one company to supply all their energy needs, twice as many consumers picked ScottishPower than picked British Gas (see Table 1).

TABLE 1: FAVOURED ENERGY SUPPLIER

	November 2004
ScottishPower	51%
British Gas	26%

Source: advertising tracking

This has resulted in a reduction in customer losses and growth in the total customer base

ScottishPower's customer number data report that the customer base has grown every month since the advertising launched to sit at an all-time high. Churn (ScottishPower's measurement of customer turnover) among core customers has fallen during the campaign.

DISCOUNTING OTHER FACTORS

It wasn't because ScottishPower's relative price position changed

ScottishPower's core products maintained their position as competitive on price but not cheapest on the market.

It wasn't because we had the advertising market to ourselves

British Gas outspent ScottishPower each year (see Figure 11).

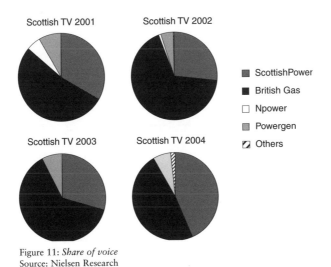

Figure 11: *Share of voice*
Source: Nielsen Research

It wasn't because of additional investment in other communications activity

ScottishPower didn't significantly increase spend in other communications channels.

MANIFOLD EFFECTS

ScottishPower is the only big winner in the customer numbers game

In a nil sum game, ScottishPower is the only major player to have significantly increased its net customer base over the last two years. British Gas has been a major net loser; all the others have held pretty steady.

The impact in Manweb

While this paper focuses on the impact in the Scottish market, the advertising also ran on Granada TV to support the ScottishPower Manweb region (ScottishPower bought the local electricity company Manweb shortly after deregulation and has taken on the role of 'legacy' supplier). The marketing environment means the advertising worked differently and it would need another paper to describe it; however, the bottom-line result has seen ScottishPower grow its customer base by more than 20,000 during the last two years, which generated an additional £5 million in lifetime value, a 223% return on the media investment.

The impact nationally

The scale considered necessary by the industry to compete effectively is five million customer accounts. When this activity was conceived, ScottishPower had just 3.5 million. The Energy People positioning strategy has driven all ScottishPower's marketing activity over the last two years, during which time it has become the UK's fastest-growing energy company, with more than one million new customers in the last 12 months. In January 2005 ScottishPower broke through the five million customer barrier.

Marketing communications resource

Recognising the success of the campaign and the important role it now has in the success of its business, the resource allocated to marketing communications within the marketing team at ScottishPower has grown from two to a team of five, headed by the newly created position of Head of Campaigns.

PAYBACK

Between May 2003 and November 2004 ScottishPower's customer base in central Scotland grew by 146,563, an increase of 11.1%. The cost of advertising (including all TV production) was £2.3 million. Customer lifetime value varies and is confidential; however, we can say that it typically averages in the mid-£hundreds. Even based on an average lifetime value of £250 (which would be at the bottom end of the spectrum), that would equate to a return on the advertising investment of nearly £16 for every £1 spent. And while we accept that advertising can't claim to have been directly responsible for every acquisition made or retention saved, there is no doubt that the new brand positioning and advertising have been fundamental to the success of ScottishPower.

21

Silentnight – My First Bed

A media strategy you can trust

Principal author: Gary Wise, Feather Brooksbank
Creative agency: MWO

EDITOR'S SUMMARY

This is a good example of a thoughtful and well-integrated campaign. To support the launch of their new My First Bed range of beds for children, Silentnight ran a multi-channel campaign designed to stimulate sales through 'pester power'. Ads in TV and cinema got kids excited in the product, while ads in magazines like *Practical Parenting* reassured their mums about quality. An interactive web site allowed parents and kids to explore the product together, and thus converted interest into sales.

The result was increased awareness of the brand and the new product, leading to an increase in sales and market share.

The judges were impressed by the co-ordinated way different media were used in this case. In particular, they thought that putting the product into cinema foyers so that children could experience them immediately after seeing the ads was a very clever idea.

I'm going to explain the media strategy devised by Feather Brooksbank to launch Silentnight's My First Bed range. To do this, I won't be using any jargon or marketing clichés. Instead, I'll be explaining the impact of the campaign through the eyes of our core consumers, parents and children, and highlighting how trust was the key to our success. The My First Bed product was launched two years ago. This paper tells the story of its success from launch to present day.

My First Bed was a new direction for Silentnight. The core strength of the brand prior to the launch was among older purchasers who bought in to the brand attributes of comfort, support, relaxation and home. Silentnight recognised that younger consumers were beginning to favour more fashion-orientated purchases – particularly bedsteads – largely as a result of the interior-design boom with TV programmes like *Property Ladder*, *DIY SOS* and *Changing Rooms*. It decided that it would need to innovate in order to remain the leading player in the bed market.

An in-depth research programme was undertaken among mothers of children aged one to eight, and the My First Bed product was created.

My First Bed is a unique product, with a unique mix-and-match concept (explained later). The challenge for the advertising was to introduce this unique product to a long-established bed marketing environment where the traditional values of support, relaxation, and so on, had always been prominent, and media strategies had focused on direct response (daytime TV/national press). The media for this project would need to be innovative and exciting to reflect the nature of the product, but would also need to tap in to the key motivators for parents to go out and buy a new bed for their children. We needed to launch this product and to lay the foundations for future growth within a new lifestyle, branded bed market. We also needed to make sure that the shift of budget towards this new product would not be to the detriment of the core Silentnight brand.

The objectives of the advertising were as follows.

- Generate awareness of My First Bed as a Silentnight product.
- Maintain core brand awareness, even though budget would now be shifted to the My First Bed product.
- Drive sales of My First Bed.

Our consumers will now take over ...

Simon, aged 7 and a ¼

'Someone asked me to rite, about why I love My First Bed so much wich is weerd coz I'm not that good at riting. Anyway my first bed is harry hippo. He has a hippo head, and hippo feet and its made by Silentnight and he looks like this (I look much oalder now!) [see Figure 1].

The reeson why I love my hippo bed much is coz I got to choose every bit of him. I chose the colour of my headboard I chose the colour of the base I chose the stripey matress I chose the hippo head (and I could have chose a duck or football or heart and other stuff) and I chose the hippo feet (coz it would be stewpid for a hippo to have duck feet or something) and I chose all of it on the intrenet where I put all the bits together myself. I also love my hippo bed coz, its got a secret storage bit and im not telling you where it is

Before I got my hippo bed I had a boring bed that had horrybal springs that stuck in my back. then me and my mum went to the cinema and saw a duck bed in the entrence and I got to play with it and my mum rote on a booklet and sent it off and entered a competishen. She said that it ment that they would be able to have our details and then ring us to ask questons about advatising and stuff. Then we went in the cinema and saw Shrek. which was reelly funny and before it came on there was a advert for My First Bed wich was a cartoon with hippos in it and it made me want one more so I said to my mum that I reelly wanted one and we should buy the one in the entrence but she said that she had picked up a brosher and it would be ok and I might be able to get one one day.'

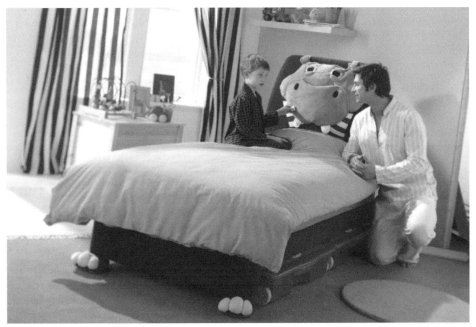

Figure 1: *Simon and his 'Harry Hippo' bed*

Simon's mum, Lorraine

'When choosing a bed for my kids, I need to choose a brand that I can trust. Being an ever-worrying parent, I have read all sorts of things about the importance of kids' sleep and how moving them from a cot to their first bed can have disruptive effects. The fact that Silentnight consulted a child psychologist (Dr Dorothy Einon) to examine its My First Bed product was certainly encouraging. The psychologist said that the Hippo and Duck Play Pals would be almost 'guardian-like', watching over children as they fall asleep or wake up. She also noted that the secret storage pockets were ideal for children, who crave places to keep their belongings and like to keep 'secrets' away from siblings (like Simon hiding his Lego Knights from his little sister!). It is also encouraging that Silentnight has its beds tested to British Standards (passing the threshold for domestic flammability risk etc.), it has consulted back-care experts and uses a Miracoil spring system to guarantee support during growing years.

Silentnight has asked me to write a bit on the advertising for My First Bed. I don't know a great deal about advertising, but I do know what works for me and what doesn't! As Simon has already told you, we saw the bed in the foyer of a cinema, which sparked Simon's interest (even though it wasn't actually his 'first' bed!). We love going to the cinema together to see the latest kids' films and it was a bit of fun for the kids to play with the different characters and things that you can choose when putting the bed together.

Before that, I had already seen the advert in my favourite magazine (they tell me it was called a bound-in insert!). I really trust *Living etc* to choose advertisers who sell products that will be good quality and that I can trust for my family. The way the leaflet stood out from the rest of the magazine also grabbed my attention and suggested that this was a quality product. The leaflet showed all of the benefits of the product and the range of options for the beds, which was interesting. Then, when I saw the same leaflet in *Practical Parenting* (I told you I was ever-worrying – I'm always looking in there for tips!), I definitely began to think that this must be a decent product, because I know they wouldn't allow anything but the best kids' products in the magazine.

After all this and the cinema experience, we saw My First Bed advertising on TV. The kids loved the ad because it included the same Hippo and Duck characters that they'd seen before. It also made me think that they must have invested in the beds a lot to be able to put them on TV. Simon was obviously very excited, as he'll tell you now ...'

'I saw My First Bed on the televishen and got reely exited becoz it ment that mum and dad mite buy me one becoz when people go on televishen it means that they are good. So when I saw it I told my dad about when me and mum had seen it in the cinema and that it looked reely good and was reely comfotabal, and that I reely reely wanted one. and I had done for ages.

So then me and my dad went on to the intrenet and went to see the bit about beds where they had the Hippo bed an the Duck bed and all the other beds on there. It was reely cool coz I got to put all the bits together and …'

'He's really cute when he's excited, but he does tend to repeat himself! Pete (my husband) is pretty cynical when it comes to advertising, but he does trust me when I've done my research and is a bit of a sucker for the kids' excitement. So, when Pete and Simon had finished creating the Hippo on the internet and given him a name, it seemed like Harry would soon become part of the family.'

And now back to us …

We came to the conclusion that we would need to have fun with the brand in order to excite kids and showcase the unique aspects of the product. The mix-and-match feature led us to think about the product as a toy, so we knew that interactivity would be important. We also needed national coverage to lay solid foundations for the product. However, none of this would be successful if we couldn't persuade our key purchasing audience (parents) to trust the brand.

The theme of trust was utilised throughout the media schedule, both in terms of media selection (magazines that are trusted, TV that gives status and 'big brand' values) and timing (bound-in inserts followed by cinema and then TV). This timing strategy was designed to grow trust in a very specific way; the bound-in inserts would act as a catalogue to show range and product benefits, the cinema would add a fun element and excite kids, then the TV would reinforce brand equity and provide the necessary brand status that is important for building trust. It was vitally important in this trust-building operation that parents were reached both on their own in a trusted environment (magazines) and together with their kids (cinema) – the former to generate interest in the product and the latter to exploit pester power. The interactivity of the cinema foyer display would be invaluable in openly displaying the product to our audience and letting them test it for themselves without the pressured sales environment of a showroom.

RESULTS

Did we achieve our first objective: to raise awareness of My First Bed?

As highlighted above, we handed out competition leaflets in the cinema foyers where the bed display stunts were happening, so that we could call our audience and ask them what they thought. A total of 194 five-minute interviews took place in September 2003 (Solihull and Huddersfield). The results were undeniably encouraging. Here are some findings:

- Silentnight top in unprompted brand awareness of bed manufacturers with 51%
- Silentnight top for bed manufacturers who make beds for children at 50% vs nearest competitor Slumberland at 8% (see Figure 2)
- 70% of interviewees had heard of My First Bed (see Figure 3)
- 78% recalled seeing the cinema advertising
- Silentnight top for unprompted cinema advertising recall (followed by Peugeot, Frosties and Vauxhall)
- 85% thought that cinema was the right environment for the My First Bed message (see Figure 4)

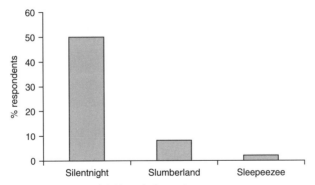

Figure 2: *Awareness of children's bed manufacturers*
Source: Dipsticks Research, September 2003

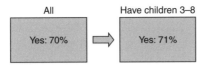

Figure 3: *How many had heard of My First Bed?*
Source: Dipsticks Research, September 2003

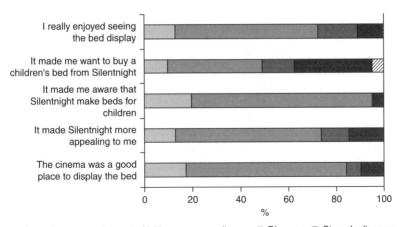

Figure 4: *Attitudes to cinema advertising*
Source: Dipsticks Research, September 2003

- it did the job very well and evoked trust – it was 'for' our target audience, they 'enjoyed watching it' and it made Silentnight 'more appealing' to them; creative work, from MWO, had engaged well with the audience through continued use of the popular Hippo and Duck cartoon characters
- 87% of respondents with kids aged three to eight remembered seeing the foyer stunt (84% of all interviewed)
- the foyer stunt did the job very well and evoked *trust* – over 50% agreed that it made them want to buy a children's bed from Silentnight (see Figure 5)

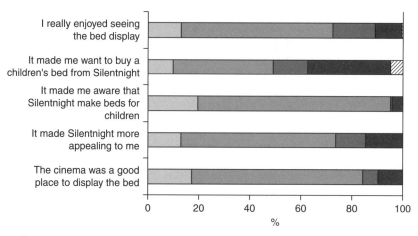

Figure 5: *Attitudes to bed display*
Source: Dipsticks Research, September 2003

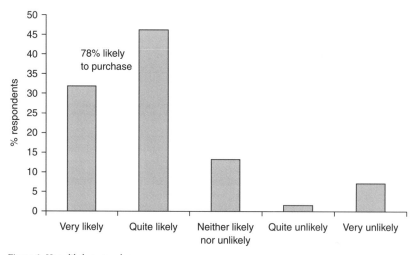

Figure 6: *How likely to purchase*
Source: Dipsticks Research, September 2003

- 75% felt more favourably towards the brand after seeing the display
- 78% said that, if they were going to purchase a children's bed, they would be likely to choose Silentnight (see Figure 6).

In addition to this research, a BMRB access study has been used from launch to the present day. Figure 7 clearly shows the effect of advertising – with an uplift of 22 percentage points.

Did we achieve our second objective: to maintain awareness of the main Silentnight brand, even though budget was shifted to the My First Bed product? Yes. Overall brand recall is higher now than it was in January 2003 (see Figure 8).

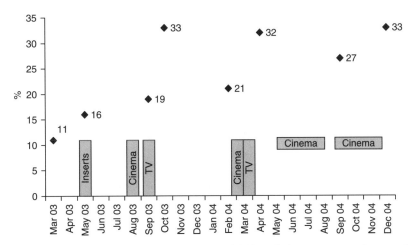

Figure 7: *Awareness of Silentnight as a manufacturer of children's beds (spontaneous and prompted)*
Base: 1000 women
Source: BMRB Access

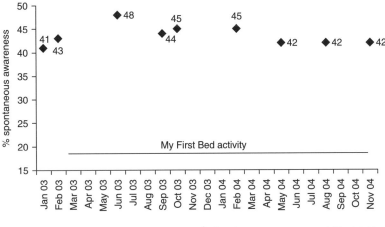

Figure 8: *Spontaneous recall for Silentnight*
Source: BMRB Access

WHAT ABOUT SALES?

Aim

To achieve 25% market share of single beds bought at the £300 to £400 price point.

Result

Over 14,500 My First Beds sold to date – 50% market share.

CONCLUSION

We successfully launched My First Bed as a unique product into a traditional marketing environment and far exceeded the objectives that we had set out to achieve.

Our media was far from traditional:

- we used cinema when no other bed manufacturer was using it
- we put beds in cinema foyers for the first time ever and let kids *play* with them
- we timed the campaign carefully, so that each medium had a specific role to play in a specific order
- we established a future for the branded kids' bed market
- the media we chose engaged our audience in such a way that we managed to develop a relationship that provoked pester power, initiated intrigue and was, crucially, founded on trust.

'I certainly wouldn't buy a bed for my children if I didn't trust the manufacturer but, on this occasion, I probably wouldn't have bought a new bed at all if Simon hadn't got so excited about the Hippo. Now his little sister wants a flipping duck!'

Simon's mum, Lorraine

'now that Im goin to be 8 reely reely soon and ive been reely reely good for ages I am hoping that my mum an Dad mite get me a football bed, becoz i like football now and I can keep Harry in the cubord so we wont say goodbuy.'

Simon

---

1. Source: Silentnight.

22

UniBond Sealant Range

Sealing a successful future for UniBond

Principal author: Rob Gray, BDH\TBWA
Contributing authors: Paul Keen and Yoshio Tazaki, BDH\TBWA

EDITOR'S SUMMARY

In 2002 UniBond was the UK's biggest sealant brand, with a 40% market share. Henkel had big ambitions though, and wanted further growth.

Historically, sealants had been structured around the product formula, with the sales fixture divided into polymer, acrylic and silicone. But research revealed that consumers were shopping with a specific task in mind (e.g. sealing a window frame) and were struggling to find the right product, as they did not understand the benefits of each formula.

A fundamental change in approach ensued, affecting everything from product formulation and packaging, to category management and advertising. A restructured range of task-specific sealants made the benefits of premium silicone products more apparent. Meanwhile, as competitors struggled to catch up, advertising established UniBond as the most credible brand to deliver superior performance

Sales volume did increase slightly, but the big gain came from value growth. Through driving trade-up to premium products and advertising to reinforce the strength of the brand, UniBond was able to grow average price relative to the competition by 41%, which generated 21% extra revenue.

This case illustrates the principle that supporting a higher price is often much more profitable than chasing extra volume. It also shows how a good agency can do much more for a brand than simply making ads.

INTRODUCTION

In 2002 UniBond was the biggest brand in sealants, with a 40% share of the £45m market. It had a product portfolio of 43 SKUs, covering every task, formula, colour and price the consumer could desire. UniBond had distribution in all the major DIY multiples, which accounted for 80% of sales.

In 2002 there was no reason to change; it would have been easy for Henkel to sit back and enjoy its success. Fortunately, resting on laurels means nothing to this company.

This is the story of how Henkel's determination to grow uncovered a consumer insight and revealed just how much improvement there could be. This led to a complete overhaul of product, packaging, category management and advertising. Not just for UniBond, but for competitors too.

BACKGROUND

UniBond has a strong record of innovation and brand leadership. Historically, sealant had been available in only two formulas: acrylic and silicone. In 1995 UniBond introduced a new polymer formula, marketed as Super All Purpose. This delivered the versatility of an acrylic but with performance approaching that of a silicone.

In 1998 UniBond turned its attention to methods of application and launched the piston format, which could be applied without a separate sealant gun.

By 2002 these innovations had established UniBond as the market leader. Super All Purpose was delivering 30% of UniBond's total sealant sales, while the piston pack was achieving an average price of £5.81, adding significant value when compared with cartridges, which had an average price of £3.87.

WHY CHANGE?

As brand leader, UniBond was vulnerable and an easy target for competitors. Sealants are low-interest products with little brand loyalty, meaning any innovations by competitors can quickly win them market share. Vallance and Polycell are strong brands, and at the time Polycell had just introduced a new 'squeeze and seal' pack format. Furthermore, the rise of own-label was putting brands under increasing pressure to justify their price premium.

While the DIY market continued to increase in size, the rate of growth was slowing (Figure 1). Market indicators revealed that the slowdown in DIY expenditure would continue.

Henkel was not content with the anticipated growth rates. It wanted to seek further opportunities to grow its sealants business and protect it from competitors. However, with an already high market share, it could no longer rely on increasing volume sales to deliver this. *Growth would have to come through adding value to the UniBond offering.*

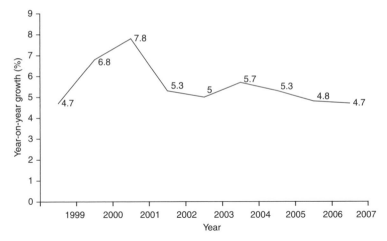

Figure 1: *Growth in DIY expenditure, 1999 to 2007 (est.)*
Source: Verdict

WHERE TO ADD VALUE?

Looking at the category in store started to reveal potential improvements. The 12-foot fixture (Figure 2) presented the consumer with a daunting selection of formulas, colours and pack formats. The basis for category structure was formula, with the fixture divided into polymer, acrylic and silicone sealants. However, did consumers understand the applications and benefits of each?

Figure 2: *Sealant sales fixture, 1996*

Exploratory research undertaken in February 2002 revealed that they didn't.

'If I read it, it says silicone sealant on this one, and this one says acrylic sealant, but the pictures are exactly the same. At this point I would probably have to go and ask someone.'

Fifth Dimension research

'I want one that spells it out so it's so bleeding obvious you can't go wrong.'

Fifth Dimension research

The complexity of sealants contradicted the trends that had driven growth over the previous five years. Home-improvement TV shows like *Changing Rooms* and the raft of spin-offs had given people the confidence, ideas and inspiration to undertake DIY themselves. Retailers and manufacturers exploited this by making DIY more accessible to amateurs. However, sealants were clearly not accessible and not in line with Henkel's vision of 'making DIY easier'.

The research helped uncover the opportunity for improvement by confirming that consumers were entering the store with a specific job or task in mind (e.g. sealing the shower). Their whole selection process was based around finding the most suitable sealant for this job.

'The first thing I would look for is the area of the house.'

Fifth Dimension research

This insight shed new light on the success of Super All Purpose. Unable to identify the most suitable sealant for their task, the consumer was defaulting to all-purpose. However, as this retailed at £4.99, UniBond was forfeiting additional revenue from consumers who would have traded up to more expensive silicone sealants.

This was the opportunity to add value. A task-based range of sealants would make product selection easier and highlight the task-specific benefits of premium products. This would require a change much more fundamental than a bit of category management: product formulation, packaging and advertising would all have to be based around task-specific products and benefits.

Product requirements of different tasks

To produce a strong range of task-specific sealants we needed to identify the key features required for different tasks. Most features could be delivered through currently available formulations, however the research revealed there was significant demand for a sealant with superior mould resistance for sealing baths and showers.

'It's one of those things that they get black mould and it makes the whole place look grubby.'

Fifth Dimension research

'You know 12 months down the line you'll get a line of mould down the bath. Your wife will be nagging at you to scrape the silicone out because you can't clean it.'

Fifth Dimension research

As well as revamping the current products to be task specific, BDH\TBWA recommended that UniBond develop a high-performance shower and bathroom sealant to deliver superior mould resistance. The premium commanded by this sealant would be a further opportunity to add value.

PRODUCT, PACKAGING AND CATEGORY MANAGEMENT

The marketing objectives were as follows:

- introduce a task-specific approach to the category;
- make it easier for consumers to select the most suitable product for their task;
- encourage consumers to trade up to premium products by making the performance benefits for a task clear.

A new range of UniBond products was developed to deliver the key benefits required for specific tasks. Two all-purpose products were still included in the range for consumers who had more than one task to do. These were called Super All Purpose Paintable and Super All Purpose Silicone (Waterproof) to make their applications clear.

BDH\TBWA designed new packaging, which was colour-coded to make identifying suitable sealants straightforward (Figure 3). The benefits the product offered for the task were clearly communicated (Figure 4).

ADVERTISING

It was very apparent that the UniBond relaunch would change the dimensions of the market and competitors would have to follow. UniBond needed to make sure that it benefited itself rather than its competitors.

Figure 3: *New UniBond range of piston pack sealants, 2003*

Area of use (task) ⟶

Colour ⟶

Product benefits
(4 maximum) ⟶

Figure 4: *New UniBond packaging design, 2003*

This is where advertising came in. We needed to convince consumers that, even if competitors claimed to deliver task-related benefits, UniBond was a more credible brand to deliver the required performance.

Our advertising strategy was to use the new High Performance Shower & Bathroom sealant as a 'hero product'. This would benefit the whole sealant range by demonstrating UniBond's credentials in innovation and superior performance.

The advertising objectives were as follows:

- raise awareness of the new product;
- build its mould-resistance credentials;
- use as a flagship product to build the image of UniBond as a high-quality, market-leading brand with task-specific products.

The proposition for creative was 'UniBond High Performance Shower & Bathroom Sealant has guaranteed mould resistance'. A television advertisement was developed by BDH\TBWA using UniBond's guarantee as support for the proposition (Figure 5).

THE CHALLENGE

The importance of the UniBond relaunch to Henkel should not be underestimated. In 2002 sealant sales accounted for 12% of Henkel's Consumer Adhesives business, with all-purpose products accounting for 49% of sealant sales. Super All Purpose was its most successful product, with sales of £5.4m a year.

MVO: Some things go mouldy in days

Some in weeks

Some take a couple of months

But UniBond Shower & Bathroom Sealant stays mould resistant for years

Figure 5: *Storyboard for UniBond sealant TV ad*

Most of the products in the current range would be replaced with products retailing at the same price. The key to success was encouraging consumers to trade up from Super All Purpose to task-specific products that retailed at a higher price (Figure 6).

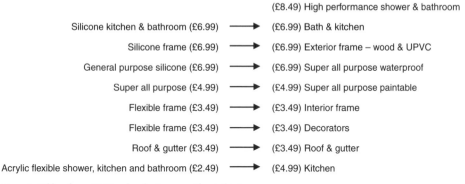

Figure 6: *Old and new UniBond sealant range with retail prices*

WHAT HAPPENED?

Henkel had set out to grow through adding value. By the end of 2003, less than 12 months since the relaunch, the average price of UniBond sealant had risen by 92p, from an average of £5.32 in 2002. By the end of 2004 the average price had increased even further, to £6.51 (Figure 7).

Over the same period, the average price in the rest of the market grew only 18p, from £3.41 to £3.59. As a result UniBond's price premium over competitors grew by 41% (Figure 8).

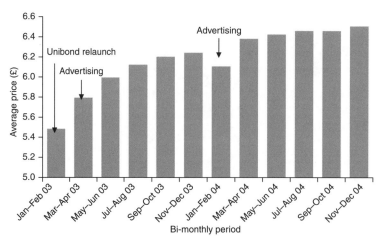

Figure 7: *Average price of UniBond, 2003 to 2004*
Source: GfK

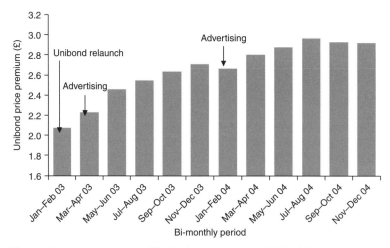

Figure 8: *Average price premium of UniBond over competitors, 2003 to 2004*
Source: GfK

The increases in average price produced value growth of 21.4% between 2002 and 2004. This was achieved during a period when, as expected, volume growth was low at only 1%.

TRADING UP

The average price had risen dramatically, but was this due to consumers trading up?

Immediately following the relaunch in mid-February 2003 sales began shifting to task-specific sealants. Sales of Super All Purpose fell by 61% as consumers switched to task-specific products. The contribution of all-purpose products to total volume sealant sales fell from 46% to 28% (Figure 9).

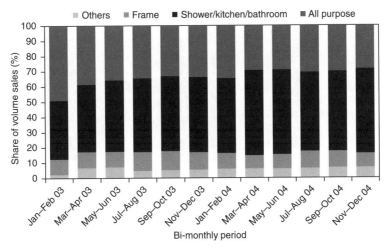

Figure 9: *UniBond volume sales by task, 2003 to 2004*
Source: GfK

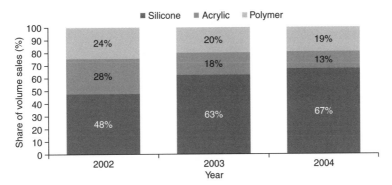

Figure 10: *UniBond volume sales by formula, 2002 to 2004*
Source: GfK

Crucially consumers were switching out of low-end acrylic and polymer products and into premium silicone sealants. The task-based range had given consumers the confidence to trade up (Figure 10).

Feedback from the trade supported what the sales figures were showing:

'The retailers have noticed a real decline in customers asking them about which sealant to buy. The choice is much easier now.'

Marshall Hollis, Henkel Senior Product Manager

As expected, competitors and own-label quickly converted their ranges to be task specific. They were now experiencing similar shifts towards silicone, but without the same increase in average price (Figure 11).

THE CONTRIBUTION OF ADVERTISING

With competitors quickly following UniBond's lead, advertising was crucial to positioning UniBond as the market-leading brand. UniBond needed to be credited

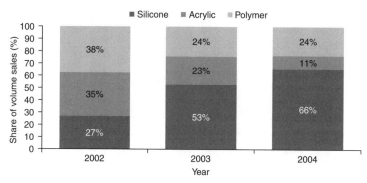

Figure 11: *Market volume sales by formula, 2002 to 2004*
Source: GfK

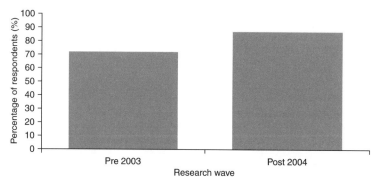

Figure 12: *UniBond prompted brand awareness, 2003 to 2004*

with the innovation and perceived as a more credible brand to deliver superior performance in order to justify a price premium over strong competitors.

The advertising campaign for UniBond was split into two waves in 2003 and 2004, each over the key Easter period. The creative proved very impactful and delivered a memorable message with photo prompt recall of 43% (2004 tracking).

This increased prompted brand awareness from 72% to 87% and cemented UniBond in consumers' minds (Figure 12).

Most importantly, the advertising built UniBond's credentials in sealants. High Performance Shower & Bathroom sealant was established as a premium product with clear benefits of mould resistance, staying white and having a good guarantee (Figure 13).

Perceptions of UniBond as a brand were significantly improved, with increases in attributes such as 'performs better', 'good quality' and 'worth paying more for'.

The position of UniBond as brand leader was reflected in purchase intentions picked up by the tracking (Figure 14).

RESULTS

Since launch, sales of High Performance sealant have rocketed, such that the product now accounts for 34% of UniBond's value sales (Figure 15).

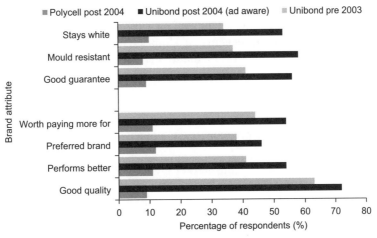

Figure 13: *Brand attributes associated with UniBond, 2003 to 2004*
Note: Polycell brand attributes were not tracked in 2003. However the low scores in 2004 suggest the increases seen by UniBond were not the result of increases across the market.

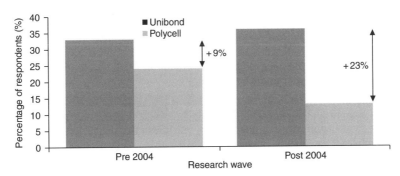

Figure 14: *Sealant brand most likely to purchase, 2004*
Note: this question was not included in the 2003 tracking questionnaire, so only 2004 data are shown.

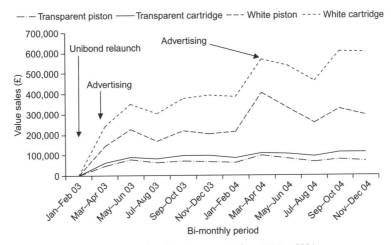

Figure 15: *Value sales of UniBond High Performance Sealant, 2003 to 2004*
Source: GfK

However, the role of the advertising was much broader than a single product. While consumers had been switching to task-specific sealants the advertising convinced consumers that the benefits of UniBond were worth paying more for. This meant that, while competitors made the same changes to their ranges, UniBond's average price rose £1.19 over two years while competitors experienced real-term price drops.

GROWING THE MARKET

Between 2002 and 2004 the sealant market grew by 26% in value. The drivers of this growth were UniBond and own-label.

UniBond grew through brand building and the switch to task-specific products, which increased its average price. Own-label followed UniBond's lead and introduced a task-based range but grew through increasing volume over the period by 25.7% (compared to UniBond's 1%). Its inability to justify the same premium prices as UniBond meant that, by the end of 2004, UniBond's price premium over own-label had risen to £2.41, up from £1.76 in 2002 (Figure 16).

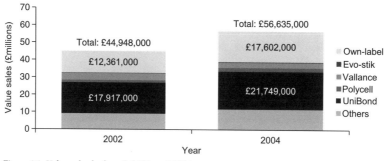

Figure 16: *Value sales by brand, 2002 and 2004*
Source: GfK

Own-label grew as a result of the change in market dynamics resulting from UniBond's relaunch. Due to the increased strength of the UniBond brand it was Vallance that really suffered from this growth.

COULD OTHER FACTORS HAVE CAUSED SUCH A CHANGE?

Distribution

Eighty per cent of sealant sales are through the DIY multiples of which B&Q, Homebase and Focus Wickes control 90% of the market. As such only these three retailers can have a significant impact on distribution. Stocking in these three retailers has remained constant since the relaunch.

---

1. Mintel, 2004.

Promotions

While UniBond has a comprehensive promotional calendar, these promotions work to produce temporary uplifts in volume sales. Promotions could not have delivered the consistent increases in average price that have been achieved and, in any case, volume sales showed little growth through the period.

Seasonality

The sealant market, like all sectors of the DIY and gardening market, experiences sales uplifts each year over the Easter and May bank holiday periods. However, like promotions, this produces a short-term increase in volume sales, not consistent growth in average price.

PAYBACK

In 2002 the average price of UniBond was £5.32. Assuming UniBond had not been relaunched this could (optimistically) have been expected to increase in line with inflation (2.9% in 2003 and 3% in 2004).

Using these price projections, combined with actual volume sales in 2003 and 2004, provides a projection of value sales in each of these years. This shows that incremental sales as a result of the relaunch were £1,515,340 in 2003 and £2,456,955 in 2004.

Factoring out retailer margin and subtracting all costs associated with the relaunch in both 2003 and 2004 (including advertising production, media spend and packaging redesign) confirms that, so far, the payback to Henkel has been nearly £1m in additional revenue.

Not only has the financial return been excellent but Henkel's innovation and drive for growth has demonstrated to DIY retailers that it is a company that can lead markets and build brands to complement own-label.

'The relaunch of sealants has significantly strengthened my relationship with retailers. It has really built our credibility as a company that can be category champion.'

Barry Jiggins, Henkel National Accounts Controller

CONCLUSION

This paper has demonstrated how a consumer insight led to a fundamental change in UniBond's approach to sealants. This change resulted in:

- an easier purchase decision for consumers;
- the benefits of premium silicone sealants becoming more apparent;
- consumers trading up and, as a result, sales of premium silicone sealants increased from 48% of total volume to 67%.

This changed the dynamics of the market such that own-label and branded competitors quickly followed suit. However, advertising to position UniBond as a market-leading brand with the credibility to deliver superior performance resulted in:

- an increase in average price of £1.19 while the rest of the market experienced real-term price reductions;
- an increase in price premium over competitors by 41%;
- value growth of 21.4% in under two years on volume growth of only 1%;
- a payback of nearly £1m in additional revenue.

It is brands like UniBond – brands that never sit back but continuously seek out new opportunities for growth – that truly lead their markets and enjoy long-term success.

23

West Midlands Hub of Museums

Bringing the wolves to the door ...
and across the threshold!

How the West Midlands Hub of Museums
attracted a new breed of visitor

Principal authors: Trevor Lorains and Ian Mitchell, BJL Group
and Richard Taylor, Consultant
Media agency: Mediaedge:cia, Manchester

EDITOR'S SUMMARY

Museums and art galleries have traditionally been the preserve of the educated middle-classes. This campaign shows that it is possible to broaden their appeal to a wider audience, if you approach them in the right way.

The key insight was that museums and galleries could be sold to parents desperate to find something for the kids to do during the school holidays. A test campaign in the Wolverhampton area used mailings, local press and a website to inform families of all the fun things to see at museums and galleries in their area.

The result was a significant increase in visitor numbers, and not only that, a broader social mix of visitors, in line with the Government policy of widening the appeal of cultural institutions. Despite having a tiny budget, this campaign achieved all its goals and set a template for future activity.

The judges were also impressed by the tightness of the proof here. Clients with much bigger budgets could learn a lot from this paper's rigorous approach to evaluation.

INTRODUCTION

Museums needn't be the worthy preserve of the middle classes. It is possible to attract a wider market. It doesn't rely on changing the product or investing in big-budget campaigning. The solution relies simply on dissolving resistance to the unknown and the uncomfortable: a big step forward in the field of arts marketing.

The resultant increase in visitor figures achieved by our new client hints at a trend that could revolutionise the relationship between the general public and its local and national institutions. Ultimately, we would venture that the initial success of this fully integrated pilot campaign could provide a template whose broader application could deliver a profound impact on the attitude of future generations to accessing their history and culture.

And we have the evidence to prove such a claim – achieved on the smallest of budgets with a media spend of under £10,000.

Like any good story, though, there has to be an insurmountable hurdle to the progress of our 'hero'. And in this case, the villain is prejudice.

'THE LAST PLACE I'D THINK ABOUT!'

The villain of the piece

Our story begins with a government initiative. Committed to lifelong learning and social inclusivity, museums have been tasked to attract more C2DEs through their doors. Test campaigns were encouraged to evaluate performance with the lure of funding related to success.

Current visitor statistics leave one in no doubt as to the scale of the problem. The visitor profile is staunchly ABC1. TGI indicates that as much as 70% of visitors are ABC1. So what exactly are we dealing with?

It's called 'socialisation'. Evidence suggests that attitudes to museums and art galleries are inherited at an early age, through family values and education. We're either comfortable with culture or we're not. And if we're not, then it's perceived as totally irrelevant to our lifestyle and decidedly not on our 'leisure agenda'.

It doesn't help, either, that many of the venues themselves look like traditional British institutions symbolising prejudices of a bygone era. Little wonder, then, that the C2DE consumer is not interested. It's like asking someone to put his hand through a hole in a wall.

The hero of our story

The West Midlands Hub of Museums was formed in 2004. It embraces five areas of the region:

1. Birmingham
2. Wolverhampton
3. Ironbridge Gorge
4. Stoke
5. Coventry.

These locations are home to over 30 stunning museums and galleries. The variety and importance is impressive. From a complete recreated Victorian town to amazing collections of Pop Art, from Jacobean architecture and medieval guildhalls to the world's finest collection of Staffordshire ceramics. There is literally something for everyone.

Because of limited funding for a test campaign, the agency recommended a focus on Wolverhampton. The catchment area demographically typified the West Midlands, the media costs were relatively low and the product was consistently good.

Our challenge was simple.

- We couldn't change the product.
- We had to work on a media and production budget of £30k.
- We had to generate a significant increase in C2DE visitors during summer 2004.
- If we delivered quantifiable results the Museums Libraries and Archives Council would fund a regional roll-out in 2005, benefiting the entire hub.

Our test campaign ran from late July through to the beginning of September, utilising advertising and PR across a range of locally targeted media. As a result, Wolverhampton Museums & Art Galleries (WMAG) saw a 25% year-on-year increase in visitors during the campaign period.

Not only that, but the visitor profile changed, too. Over the period, our analysis and independent research has confirmed a shift in the proportion of C2DEs crossing the threshold.

So how did we win reluctant converts to our cause?

UNDER THE SKIN

So much at stake. So little information. To be successful we had to understand why C2DEs weren't visiting. To do this we revisited the results from focus groups that had previously been undertaken by the client. And two key findings opened our eyes.

Are you talking to me?

C2DEs don't visit museums and galleries because they simply *don't understand what's inside*. Current museum advertising doesn't talk 'their language', either. They see it as elitist and, consequently, irrelevant.

Revelation

Yet when they *do* visit, far from feeling uncomfortable, most have a great time.

Get them to trial and it could be the start of a rich relationship. But what would get more C2DEs to cross the threshold?

A closer look

Through focus groups commissioned via Morris Hargreaves McIntyre (MHM), a cultural and visitor attraction specialist research agency, we next explored people's motivations and expectations. Thanks to MHM's analysis we can reveal a clear hierarchy of visitors' relationships with museums and galleries (Figure 1).

Immersion
I go to experience what it was actually like to live in the past

Self-improvement
I visit to improve my knowledge

Child education
I take children to encourage their interest in history and the world around them

Nostalgia
I visit museums to remind me of what the world was like when I was younger

Aesthetic pleasure
I go to see beautiful and fascinating things

A social activity
Museums are a good place to spend time with friends and family

Entertainment value
I like to see the major attractions in the area

Figure 1: *Hierarchy of visitors' relationships with museums and galleries*

At its most sophisticated we found that some visitors (a relatively small proportion) see the visit as almost spiritual – an opportunity to escape or recharge their batteries in a stimulating environment or through quiet contemplation. At the other extreme, a more basic level, the experience can simply provide the opportunity for enjoyable social activity in the secure company of friends and family.

Class act
A key finding from this research was that the hierarchy clearly reflects a social class split. Non-visiting C2DEs perceive a visit as fulfilling a purely 'social' function. Conversely, ABC1s, for many obvious reasons, start at a higher level of expectation for their first visit.

Safety first
To attract more C2DEs, we therefore had to present the visit as a 'social/seeing and doing' experience. But we first had to find a specific group of people that we could target and that might respond positively to our message. And change the habits of a lifetime.

By definition, this kind of 'social' visit involves a group – and, indeed, given our target audience's discomfort about the 'unknown', safety in numbers would offer much needed comfort to encourage trial. But what kind of group would be right for our summer campaign? The answer was obvious: C2DE families.

Here was a group who naturally go on trips out (although currently not to many museums), see leisure time as 'family bonding' and would be ideal for our previously identified 'social/seeing and doing' message.

Little people

The school summer holidays can exert major stress on parents. The children are at home for six weeks. Someone has to entertain them, and trips out can be a costly business. While teenagers are likely to pursue their own agendas, primary school children need entertaining and stimulating, whether by grandparents, mum or dad. So we decided to attract families with five- to nine-year-old children. But how?

Parents' priorities provided our next clue. In our qualitative research, ABC1s and C2DEs revealed exactly what prompted them to take their children to museums. There was a very simple, but significant, difference in emphasis (Figure 2).

ABC1s 'Learn something and have fun'
C2DEs 'Fun and maybe learn something too'

Figure 2: *What prompts ABC1s and C2DEs to take their children to museums?*

Consistent with our 'social visit' theory, this also gave real clarity to the creative work.

The next step was to tickle the interest of parents who drive the decision-making on days out. There would be very little 'pester power' from kids to visit a museum or a gallery! But we had ideas to break down their resistance along the way.

GETTING THROUGH

'That's amazing!'

You don't need research to know that kids thrive on excitement. So what better way to introduce something alien into their lives than to tease them with the prospect of discovery – particularly if you can demonstrate the fun they can experience in the process (Figures 3 and 4).

Featuring puzzles and games in the mailing leaflet, so it hooks kids in the minute they or their mum/dad picks it up off the doormat, proved a great way to encourage involvement (Figure 5).

As you can see in Figures 3–5, the bright and bouncy tone delivers the prospect of a high-energy adventure. Note how visual consistency maximises message integration and reinforces the opportunities for recall.

The post-campaign quantitative research confirmed the impact of the creative work, with 57% of respondents rating the work for 'its brightness and appeal to children and showing hands-on activities'.

You will see the other hub locations featured on the creative work – for funding reasons this was obligatory – although the marketing efforts and evaluation criteria were entirely focused on Wolverhampton.

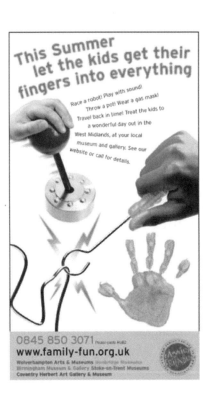

Figure 3: *Press ads*

Figure 4: *A3 poster*

Figure 5: *Mailing leaflet*

We think our campaign hit the mark. But don't just take our word for it ...

> 'My eyes went straight to that one!'
> *C2 mother, two children 5–8*

> 'My kids would love doing that!'
> *DE mother, three children 4–11*

These are typical comments from respondents in our post-campaign focus groups. We exposed them to a choice of 10 press advertisements for different visitor attractions and museums, including our own. The hub campaign was picked out as 'the best' by more mums than any other ads.

So how did we reach those parts that other museums fail to touch?

SHOESTRING CAMPAIGNING

Budget

Believe it or not, we saved our client money! We came in under the allocated £30k. And managed to s-t-r-e-t-c-h the budget to include a comprehensive range of media channels (Table 1).

TABLE 1: MEDIA SPEND (£)

Local press media	6,370
Door-to-door distribution	2,270
Production/print	12,800
Leaflets (150,000)	
A3 posters	
Press ads	
Website construction	
Research	7,300
Total	28,740

Press

Local press was a core element – it's where 58% of mums look first to find ideas on where to go.[1] Campaign impact relied on concentrating press activity into the critical school summer holidays, to take immediate advantage of our audience's freedom to visit.

We made frequent use of 'where to go' supplements in both paid and free Wolverhampton papers to target those actively looking for ideas; plus some run-of-paper positions to catch those not interested.

Leaflet distribution

Confidence in the impact of our leaflets allowed us to rely on the cheapest method of distribution: Newshare. We were able to cover most households in Wolverhampton and topped up with a street distribution of extra leaflets to target families before the August bank holiday weekend. Mosaic profiling, which identified types with a higher incidence of C2DEs, informed our targeting and helped reduce wastage.

Posters

Our client's influence within the locality gave our leaflets and posters a very public profile in such venues as bus depots, hospitals, libraries, leisure centres, council offices and park noticeboards. We believe this significantly helped frequency of exposure.

Website

Like everything else, this was fully integrated into the campaign and included kids' games to encourage stickiness. And we monitored it too. We received 851 'unique visits', of which 90% occurred in July and August, in line with ad activity. We initially had expected more usage, but our quantitative research confirmed that 54% of actual visitors had seen the leaflet that gave them all the details of individual museum activities.

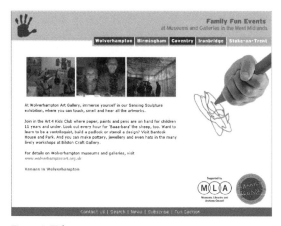

Figure 6: *Website*

---

1. Source: Newspaper Society.

Public relations

Although outside our budget, PR activity was an integral part of our campaign. Under the campaign umbrella, the client's PR company ISIS organised a series of high-profile activities, kicking off with a launch in the week before the school holidays. Analysis indicates that the majority of PR exposure occurred during the first two weeks of the campaign, helping to build a momentum of awareness.

One of the key reasons, we believe, for the success of this campaign is the joined-up thinking right from the start that resulted in this integrated campaign – from the teamwork involving client, BJL, research and PR agencies (which included blending of both existing and specifically commissioned research) to maximising every media opportunity to support each other, both in timings, cross-referencing and creative synergy. This is a real testimony to complete integration.

But now we need to prove that it worked.

THE RESULTS

In September, MHM conducted research with almost 300 family groups in Wolverhampton (96 inside the museum and 195 in street interviews) with the following results.

Awareness

A total of 27% of all Wolverhampton C2DE family respondents claimed to have seen the campaign.

Impact

A total of 66% of the target had learnt about previously unknown museums; 71% testified to being reminded of places they had long forgotten (Figure 7).

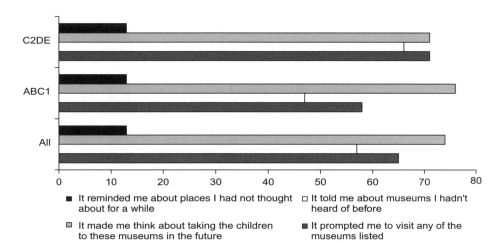

Figure 7: *Effectiveness of advertising by social grade*
Source: West Midlands Hub 'Family Friendly' Evaluation, September 2004 (Morris Hargreaves McIntyre)

Behaviour change

Motivated: 71% claimed they were 'likely' to visit with the family.
Converted: 13% of those who recalled seeing the campaign, had actually visited one of WMAG museums.

Visitor numbers

Comparing year-on-year figures across the same holiday period for 2003 and 2004, visitor numbers rose markedly: last two weeks July +26%, August +19%, September +32% (Figure 8).

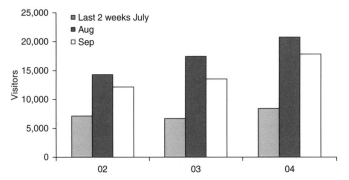

Figure 8: *Wolverhampton Arts and Museum Service Attendances, July–September*
Source: West Midlands Hub Visitor Analysis, 2003–04

Compared to 20 other museums and galleries across the West Midlands, this represented a real achievement (Figure 9).

Overall, across WMAG, this shift represented a year-on-year increase of 9327 people from the last two weeks of July until the end of September 2004. But, for those sceptical readers among you, how much was down to the campaign? And what other outside factors might have influenced success?

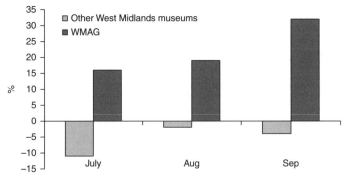

Figure 9: *Comparison of changes in visitor figures, 2004 vs 2003*
Source: West Midlands Hub Visitor Analysis, 2003–04

PLAYING DEVIL'S ADVOCATE

A quick glance at the figures should do the trick.

The increases correlate directly with the timing of our campaign and, by indexing visitor figures against 2003, we can demonstrate that these increases were over and above those associated with school holidays (Figure 10).

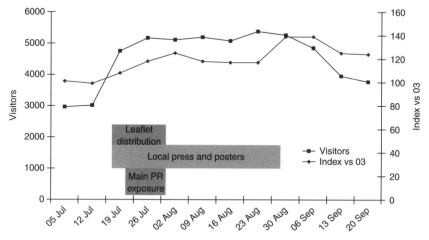

Figure 10: *Wolverhampton Museums and Art Galleries, weekly visitor figures*
Source: WMAG

Table 2 illustrates that this correlation was not a coincidence. Visitors to WMAG generally were not increasing compared with the previous year in the three months prior to the commencement of the campaign. And, as previously shown, visitor increases at WMAG were in contrast to museum performances elsewhere in the region.

TABLE 2: WOLVERHAMPTON VISITOR FIGURES APRIL TO JUNE 2003
VS 2004

	2003	2004	Index
April	11,218	10,995	98
May	11,511	9,947	86
June	11,458	10,576	92

Given that WMAG attracted over 9000 more visitors over the campaign period and research (e.g. TGI and MORI) consistently indicated that 27%+ would be C2DEs, we are confident that we attracted significantly more C2DEs.

However, Tables 3 and 4 also illustrate our success at increasing the proportion of C2DEs over the campaign period. We used Mosaic to profile postcodes from visitors to the WMAG for the July to September period for both 2003 and 2004 to demonstrate this. This demonstrates a significant increase in the proportion of C2DEs among visitors. This is confirmed, directionally, by MORI research conducted in

---

2. We accept that this is an indicative rather than a definitive measure, particularly given that this calculation may overstate the proportion of C2DEs.

TABLE 3: 2003 EXIT SURVEY, WOLVERHAMPTON MUSEUMS AND ART GALLERIES

MOSAIC groups	Wolverhampton Museums and Art Galleries	Proportion of C2DEs in Mosaic group	Est. total C2DE	C2DEs as % of visitors
A High Income Families	170	18%	31	
B Suburban Semis	70	32%	22	
C Blue Collar Owners	47	53%	25	
D Lo Rise Council	9	71%	6	
E Council Flats	12	69%	8	
F Victorian Low Status	16	49%	8	
G Town House & Flats	13	51%	7	
H Stylish Singles	28	26%	7	
I Independent Elders	11	48%	5	
J Mortgaged Families	95	42%	40	
K Country Dwellers	14	40%	6	
	485		165	34%

TABLE 4: 2004 EXIT SURVEY, WOLVERHAMPTON MUSEUMS AND ART GALLERIES

MOSAIC groups	Wolverhampton Museums and Art Galleries	Proportion of C2DEs in Mosaic group	Est. total C2DE	C2DEs as % of visitors
A Symbols of Success	104	14%	15	
B Happy Families	53	37%	20	
C Suburban Comfort	94	34%	32	
D Ties of Community	51	56%	29	
E Urban Intelligence	34	30%	10	
F Welfare Borderline	25	68%	17	
G Municipal Dependency	19	80%	15	
H Blue Collar Enterprise	29	69%	20	
I Twilight Subsistence	9	61%	5	
J Grey Perspectives	16	38%	6	
K Rural Isolation	14	38%	5	
	448		174	39%

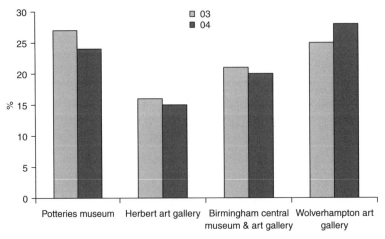

Figure 11: % of C2DE visitors to venues (data weighted to visitors September–August 2003 and 2004)
Sample: 2020
Source: MORI fieldwork, 23 October–14 November

October 2004, which shows a positive shift in the proportion of C2DEs from 2003, during a period when other museums in the area showed a decline (Figure 11).

Finally, other explanations can be ruled out.

Competitive activity

An analysis of NMR figures confirms that competitor museums and attractions in the region did not substantially alter their promotional spend during the vital campaign period:

- 2003 – £238,000
- 2004 – £231,000.

Admission charges

Entry to most of the hub museums is free and has always been. In 2001, many national museums became free entry. This is too long ago to affect this case study.

Increased levels of tourism

At the time of writing, tourism statistics for the Midlands in 2004 are not available. Our discussions with the Heart of England Tourist Board lead us to believe that there were no exceptional increases in tourism in general, or visits to visitor attractions in particular, that would account for the significant growth WMAG achieved in the summer of 2004.

Wolverhampton Museums and Art Galleries marketing activities

There was no difference in the amount of the client's own marketing expenditure between 2003 and 2004, nor was there any significant change in the type of temporary exhibitions between the two years.

The weather

True, August 2004 saw the heaviest rainfall. That may well have prompted families to consider an 'under cover' venue. But two-thirds of the year-on-year increases occurred during July and September (Figure 12).

School holidays

There were no changes in the timings of school holidays in the West Midlands between 2003 and 2004:

- 2003 – w/c 17/07–w/c 21/08
- 2004 – w/c 19/07–w/c 23/08.

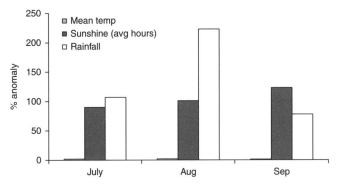

Figure 12: *Midlands – variances in weather 2004 vs regional norms*
Source: Met Office

CONCLUSION

This journey started with big prejudices and little money to tackle them, but we have proven that, with a sound product, insightful research, powerful creative work and a fully coordinated campaign, we can start to change the habits of a lifetime.

How to Access the
IPA dataBANK

The IPA Effectiveness dataBANK represents the most rigorous and comprehensive examination of marketing communications working in the marketplace, in the world. Over the 25 years of the IPA Effectiveness Awards competition, the IPA has collected over 1000 examples of best practice in advertising development and results across a wide spectrum of marketing sectors and expenditures. Each case history contains up to 4000 words of text and is illustrated in full by market, research, sales and profit data.

ACCESS

The dataBANK is held in the IPA Information Centre for access by IPA members only. Simply contact the Centre by emailing *info@ipa.co.uk*. Simple or more sophisticated searches can be run, free of charge, by qualified, professional knowledge executives across a range of parameters including brand, advertiser, agency, target market (by age, sex, class, and so on), medium and length of activity, which can be specified by the user and the results supplied by email or other means as required.

PURCHASING IPA CASE STUDIES

Member agencies are allowed a maximum number of 25 free case studies in any given calendar year, after which they will be charged at £17 each. Alternatively, members can sign up to warc.com (see overleaf) at a beneficial IPA rate and can then download case studies as part of that subscription.

FURTHER INFORMATION

For further information, please contact the Information Centre at the IPA, 44 Belgrave Square, London SWIX 8QS.
Telephone: +44 (0)20 7235 7020
Fax: 020 7245 9904
Website: *www.ipa.co.uk*
Email: *info@ipa.co.uk*.

www.WARC.com

The IPA case histories dataBANK can also be accessed through the World Advertising Research Center (WARC). Reached by logging on to *www.warc.com*, the world's most comprehensive advertising database enables readers to search all the IPA case histories, over 2000 case histories from similar award schemes around the world, including the Advertising Federation of Australia and the Institute of Communications and Advertising in Canada, plus thousands of 'how to' articles on all areas of communication activity. Sources include the Journal of Advertising Research, Canadian Congress of Advertising, *Admap*, and the American Association of Advertising Agencies, as well as the IPA.

IPA dataBANK Case Availability

* Denotes publication in the relevant *Advertising Works* volume.
** Denotes cases published in *Area Works* volumes 1–5.

NEW ENTRIES 2005

2005	Arriva Buses*
2005	ATS Euromaster*
2005	Bakers Complete*
2005	Bank of Ireland
2005	Baxters Soup
2005	Belfast City
2005	Blood Donation*
2005	bmi baby
2005	Broadband for Scotland*
2005	BT Broadband (Consumer)
2005	Children's Hearings System*
2005	Consensia/Police Service of Northern Ireland
2005	Deep River Rock – Win Big
2005	Fire Authority for Northern Ireland*
2005	First Choice*
2005	First Great Western and First Great Western Link
2005	Fox's Rocky*
2005	Fybogel
2005	Hidden Treasures of Cumbria*
2005	Highlands and Islands Broadband Registration Campaign
2005	Inland Revenue – Self Assessment*
2005	Kelso Racecourse
2005	Lancashire Short Breaks Campaign*
2005	Lay Magistrates
2005	Lift Off
2005	Metrication
2005	Northern Ireland Office Community Safety Unit*
2005	Nambarrie Tea
2005	Noise Awareness*
2005	onlineni.net
2005	Oral Cancer Awareness*
2005	Payment Modernisation Programme
2005	Progressive Building Society – Financial Services
2005	ResponsibleTravel.Com
2005	Roundup Weedkiller*
2005	Scotch Beef
2005	ScottishPower*
2005	Scruffs Hard Wear
2005	Senokot
2005	Silentnight My First Bed*

2005	Standard Life
2005	The Irish News
2005	Tizer*
2005	Travelocity*
2005	UniBond Sealant Range*
2005	University of Dundee*
2005	Waste Awareness
2005	West Midlands Hub of Museums*
2000	1001 Mousse*
2003	55 Degrees North**

A

2004	AA Loans*
1982	Abbey Crunch
1990	Abbey National Building Society
1990	Abbey National Building Society (plc)
1980	Abbey National Building Society Open Bondshares
1990	Aberlour Malt Whisky*
2004	Ackermans (SA)
1996	Adult Literacy *
2002	Aerogard Mosquito Repellent (Australia)
1999	Agri Plan Finance**
1986	AGS Home Improvements*
1988	AIDS
1994	AIDS*
1986	Air Call
1990	Alex Lawrie Factors
1980	All Clear Shampoo*
1992	Alliance & Leicester Building Society*
1990	Alliance & Leicester Building Society*
1988	Alliance & Leicester Building Society*
1984	Alliance Building Society
1990	Allied Dunbar
1984	Allinson's Bread
1984	Alpen
1990	Alton Towers
2003	Alton Towers 'Air'**
1999	Alton Towers 'Oblivion'**
1992	Amnesty International
1990	Amnesty International*
1990	Anchor Aerosol Cream
1994	Anchor Butter
1988	Anchor Butter
1992	Andrex

1992	Cadbury's Crunchie	1988	Clarks Desert Boots*
1984	Cadbury's Curly Wurly*	1996	Classic Combination Catalogue
1980	Cadbury's Dairy Box	1994	Clerical Medical
2004	Cadbury's Dream (SA)	1992	Clorets
1982	Cadbury's Flake	1988	Clover
1984	Cadbury's Fudge*	1984	Clover
1994	Cadbury's Highlights	1980	Cointreau
1999	Cadbury's Jestives**	1998	Colgate Toothpaste*
1990	Cadbury's Mini Eggs	1990	Colman's Wholegrain Mustard
1994	Cadbury's Roses*	2000	Confetti.co.uk*
1986	Cadbury's Wispa	2000	Co-op*
1988	Café Hag	2004	Co-op Food Retail
1996	Californian Raisins	1996	Cooperative Bank
1980	Campari*	1994	Cooperative Bank*
1992	Campbell's Condensed Soup	1990	Copperhead Cider
1988	Campbell's Meatballs*	1982	Country Manor (Alcoholic Drink)
1994	Campbell's Soup	1986	Country Manor (Cakes)
1996	Cancer Relief Macmillan Fund	1984	Cow & Gate Babymeals*
1984	Canderel	1982	Cracottes*
1992	Caramac	2004	Cravendale (Milk)*
1994	Car Crime Prevention	2000	Crime Prevention
2003	Carex**	2003	Crimestoppers Northern Ireland**
1998	Carex	1990	Croft Original*
1997	Carex**	1982	Croft Original
1996	Carling Black Label	1980	Croft Original
1994	Carling Black Label	2003	Crown Paint**
1984	Carousel	2002	Crown Paint
1998	Carrick Jewellery	1999	Crown Paint**
1986	Castlemaine XXXX*	2004	Crown Paints
1992	Cellnet Callback	2000	Crown Paints*
1988	Center-Parcs	1990	Crown Solo*
2004	Central London Congestion Charge*	1999	Crown Trade**
1992	Central Television Licence Renewal	1999	Crown Wallcoverings**
2000	Channel 5	1984	Cuprinol*
1990	Charlton Athletic Supporters Club*	1999	Cussons 1001 Mousse**
1980	Cheese Information Service	1986	Cyclamon*
1996	Cheltenham & Gloucester Building Society		
		D	
1988	Chessington World of Adventures	1996	Daewoo*
2003	Chicago Town Pizza, The**	1982	Daily Mail*
2002	Chicago Town Pizza	2002	Dairy Council (Milk)*
1998	Chicago Town Pizza	2000	Dairylea*
1994	Chicken Tonight	1992	Danish Bacon & Meat Council
2000	Chicken Tonight Sizzle and Stir*	1980	Danum Taps
1994	Child Road Safety	2003	Data Protection Act
1992	Childhood Diseases Immunisation	1990	Data Protection Registrar
2004	Children's Hearings (Scottish Executive)*	1980	Day Nurse
		1994	Daz
1990	Children's World	1996	De Beers Diamonds*
2001	Chiltern Railways (Clubman Service)**	2002	Debenhams
		1980	Deep Clean*
1984	Chip Pan Fires Prevention*	2000	Degree
1990	Choosy Catfood*	2003	Demand Broadband**
1998	Christian Aid*	1980	Dettol*
1992	Christian Aid	2002	DfES Higher Education
1994	CICA (Trainers)*	1984	DHL Worldwide Carrier
1992	Citroën Diesel Range	1998	Direct Debit
1988	Clairol Nice n' Easy	2004	Direct Line*

H

1990	H. Samuel
1992	Häagen-Dazs*
2002	Halifax Building Society*
1994	Halifax Building Society
1992	Halifax Building Society
1982	Halifax Building Society
1980	Halifax Building Society Convertible Term Shares
1994	Halls Soothers*
1982	Hansa Lager
1999	Hartley's Jam**
2002	Hastings Hotels (Golfing Breaks)*
2001	Hastings Hotels (Golfing Breaks in Northern Ireland)**
2000	Health Education Board for Scotland
1994	Heineken Export
1980	Heinz Coleslaw
1980	Heinz Curried Beans
1984	Hellman's Mayonnaise*
1982	Henri Winterman's Special Mild
1996	Hep30 (Building Products)
1992	Herta Frankfurters
1990	Herta Frankfurters
1980	Hoechst
1992	Hofels Garlic Pearles
1984	Hofmeister*
1984	Home Protection (Products)
1982	Home Protection (Products)
2004	Honda*
1990	Honda
1994	Horlicks
1986	Horlicks
1986	Hoverspeed
2002	Hovis*
1996	Hovis
1992	Hovis
1984	Hudson Payne & Iddiols
1996	Huggies Nappies
1994	Hush Puppies

I

1996	I Can't Believe It's Not Butter!*
1992	Iceland Frozen Foods
1980	ICI Chemicals
1984	ICI Dulux Natural Whites*
1992	IFAW*
1998	Imodium
2004	Imperial Leather*
2003	Imperial Leather**
2002	Imperial Leather
2001	Imperial Leather**
1990	Imperial War Museum
1998	Impulse
1988	Independent, The
1998	Inland Revenue Self Assessment
1988	Insignia
1982	International Business Show 1981

1990	International Wool Secretariat
1992	IPA Society
1992	Irn Bru
2003	Ironbridge Gorge Museums**
1994	Israel Tourist Board

J

1998	Jammie Dodgers
1994	Jeep Cherokee
2002	Jeyes Bloo
2001	Jeyes Bloo**
1992	Jif
1999	JJB Super League**
1988	Job Clubs
2002	John Smith's Ale
1994	John Smith's Bitter*
1982	John Smith's Bitter*
1998	Johnson's Clean & Clear*

K

1992	K Shoes*
1995	K Shoes (Springers)**
1996	Kaliber
1992	Kaliber
1990	Karvol
1980	Kays Catalogue
1992	Kellogg's All Bran*
1984	Kellogg's Bran Flakes*
2000	Kellogg's Coco Pops*
1994	Kellogg's Coco Pops
1984	Kellogg's Coco Pops*
1982	Kellogg's Cornflakes
1980	Kellogg's Frozen Waffles
2000	Kellogg's Nutri-Grain*
2002	Kellogg's Real Fruit Winders*
1980	Kellogg's Rice Crispies*
1982	Kellogg's Super Noodles*
1998	Kenco
1986	Kensington Palace*
1998	KFC
1984	KFC
2000	KFC USA
1988	Kia Ora*
2004	Kiwi (SA)
1984	Kleenex Velvet
1990	Knorr Stock Cubes*
1988	Kodak Colour Print Film
1994	Kraft Dairylea
1984	Kraft Dairylea*
1980	Krona Margarine*
1986	Kronenbourg 1664

L

1990	Lada
1992	Ladybird
2004	Lamb (Meat & Livestock Australia)*
1990	Lanson Champagne*
1992	Le Creuset

1990	Navy Recruitment
1988	Nefax
1982	Negas Cookers
1982	Nescafé
2000	Network Q
1992	Neutrogena
2003	Newcastle Gateshead Initiative
1982	New Man Clothes
1994	New Zealand Lamb
1980	New Zealand Meat Producers Board
2001	NHS Missed Appointments**
1996	Nike
1994	Nike
1994	Nissan Micra*
2000	No More Nails*
1986	No.7
1988	Norsk Data
2003	Northern Ireland Social Care Council
2003	Northern Ireland Tourist Board
1998	North West Water
1998	North West Water – Drought
1997	North West Water (Drought)**
2002	Norwich Union Pensions
1998	Norwich Union
2004	Northern Ireland Tourist Board
1990	Nouvelle Toilet Paper
2000	NSPCC*
1990	Nurofen
1986	Nursing Recruitment
1994	Nytol

O

2004	O$_2$*
1980	Observer, The – French Cookery School Campaign
2002	Ocean Spray*
1988	Oddbins*
1998	Olivio*
2002	Olivio/Bertolli*
1998	Olympus
1982	Omega Chewing Gum
1998	One2One*
1992	Optrex*
1998	Orange*
1996	Orange*
2000	Orange International
2000	Orange Just Talk*
1984	Oranjeboom
1990	Otrivine
2001	Our Dynamic Earth Visitor Attraction**
1992	Oxo*
1990	Oxo
1988	Oxo
1998	Oxo Lamb Cubes
1988	Oxy 10

P

1986	Paignton Zoo
2000	Pampers South Africa*
1988	Paracodol*
1984	Paul Masson California Carafes
1982	Pedal Cycle Casualties*
1998	Penguin
1994	Peperami*
1994	Pepsi Max
1990	Perrier
1986	Perrier
2000	Persil*
2000	PG Tips*
1990	PG Tips*
1996	Philadelphia*
1994	Philadelphia
1994	Phileas Fogg
1988	Phileas Fogg
1988	Phileas Fogg
1980	Philips Cooktronic
1980	Philips Video
2003	Phoenix Natural Gas
2003	Phones 4u**
1998	Physical Activity Campaign (HEB Scotland)
1990	Pilkington Glass
1992	Pilsner
1986	Pink Lady
1998	Pizza Hut*
1996	Pizza Hut
1994	Pizza Hut
1996	Pirelli
1990	Pirelli
1986	Pirelli
1984	Pirelli
1990	Plax
1980	Plessey Communications & Data Systems
1998	Polaroid*
1994	Police Federation of England and Wales
2004	Police Officer Recruitment (Hertfordshire Constabulary)*
2002	Police Recruitment*
2002	Police Recruitment (Could You?)
2002	Police Recruitment Northern Ireland
2001	Police Service of Northern Ireland**
1996	Polo Mints
1984	Polyfoam
1986	Portsmouth News
2004	Postbank (Post Office SA)
2002	Post Office*
1980	Post Office Mis-sorts
1986	Post Office Special Issue Stamps
1996	Potato Marketing Board
1998	Pot Noodle
1984	Presto
1980	Pretty Polly*

1996	So ...? (Fragrance)	2002	Tommy's: The Baby Charity*
1986	Soft & Gentle	1984	Torbay Tourist Board*
1996	Soldier Recruitment	1986	Toshiba*
1995	Solpadol**	1986	Touche Remnant Unit Trusts
1994	Solvent Abuse	1992	Tower of London
2000	Solvite*	2004	Toyota Corolla
1999	Solvite**	1996	Toyota RAV4
1996	Solvite	2003	Translink CityBus
1992	Sony	2003	Translink Smartlink
1988	Sony	1982	Trans World Airlines
1992	Sony Camcorders	1984	Tri-ac (Skincare)
2004	Sony Ericsson T610*	2004	Tritace
1996	Springers by K (Shoes)	1980	Triumph Dolomite
1984	St Ivel Gold*	1994	TSB
2004	Standard Bank (SA)	1988	TSB*
2000	Standard Life	1986	TSB*
2000	Star Alliance	2004	TUI (Germany)
2002	Stella Artois*	1982	Turkish Delight*
2000	Stella Artois*	1986	TV Licence Evasion*
1998	Stella Artois	2000	Twix Denmark
1996	Stella Artois*		
1992	Stella Artois*	**U**	
2002	Strathclyde Police	1984	UK Canned Salmon
1994	Strepsils*	1986	Umbongo Tropical Juice Drink
1990	Strongbow	2003	UniBond
1982	Summers the Plumbers	1999	Unibond No More Nails**
1980	Sunblest Sunbran	1998	UPS
1990	Supasnaps	2003	UTV Internet
2000	Surf*	2001	UTV Peak Soaps**
1980	Swan Vestas*	1990	Uvistat*
1984	SWEB Security Systems		
1992	Swinton Insurance	**V**	
1998	Switch	1988	Varilux lenses
1996	Switch	1994	Vauxhall Astra
2003	Syndol (painkillers)**	1996	Vauxhall Cavalier
		1990	Vauxhall Cavalier
T		1999	Vauxhall Network Q**
1992	Tandon Computers	1996	Vegetarian Society
1990	Tango	2004	Vehicle Crime Reduction (Home Office)
1986	TCP*		
2003	Teacher Training Agency**	2001	Vimto**
2001	Teacher Training Agency**	1986	Virgin Atlantic
1986	Teletext	2004	Virgin Mobile*
1986	Territorial Army Recruitment	2004	Virgin Mobile Australia*
2000	Terry's Chocolate Orange*	2004	Virgin Trains*
2002	Tesco*	1994	Visa
2000	Tesco*	1986	Vodafone
1980	Tesco	1998	Volkswagen*
1990	Tetley Tea Bags	2002	Volkswagen (Brand)*
2004	The Number 118 118*	2004	Volkswagen Diesel*
1984	Thomas Cook	2002	Volkswagen Passat*
1992	Tia Maria	1992	VW Golf*
1990	Tia Maria		
1990	Times, The	**W**	
1994	Tizer	1980	Waistline
1980	Tjaereborg Rejser*	2002	Waitrose*
2004	Tobacco Control (DH)*	2003	Wake Up To Waste (Northern Ireland)**
1980	Tolly's Original		

Index